Wilhelm Busch

Jesus our destiny

D1634927

Wilhelm Busch

Jesus

our destiny

BRUNNEN

VERLAG BASEL·GIESSEN

Original title: "Jesus, unser Schicksal"
Published by Neukirchner Verlagsgesellschaft
Neukirchen-Vluyn, Germany.

© of the English edition by:
          Brunnen Publishing
          Wallstrasse 6
          4002 Basel
          Switzerland

Eleventh edition 2015

Translation: Doris Orrett Huser

Cover: Gerd Meussen

Printed in Germany
by CPI – Ebner & Spiegel, Ulm

ISBN 978-0-86347-024-0

Who was Wilhelm Busch?

Almost unknown in English-speaking countries, Wilhelm Busch was one of the most well-known and popular evangelists in Germany in the years before and after the Second World War. His direct, frank, and personal way of preaching biblical truth attracted thousands of people who flocked to hear him.

Wilhelm Busch was convinced that the message of the Gospel is the most extraordinary message of all times. His sermons and writings, in which he forcefully but simply presents the biblical answer to modern man's most pertinent questions, can be appreciated by the young and old alike, the rich and the poor, the well-educated and the man in the street.

Born in Wuppertal-Elberfeld, Germany, in the year 1897, Wilhelm Busch spent his youth in Frankfurt-on-Main, where he pursued and finished his secondary school studies.

Busch served in the German army during the First World War. Though still young, he held the rank of lieutenant. There on the battle-field, he met the living Saviour and gave his life to God. This decisive step was to change the course of his own life and to influence the lives of many thousands in years to come.

When the war was over, Wilhelm Busch studied theology at Tübingen, after which he entered the ministry and served as pastor in the Lutheran Church first at Bielefeld, then in a mining area, and at last in the city of Essen. He was pastor and youth leader there until the time of his death. But throughout his entire ministry, he travelled extensively in all of Germany and other European countries, preaching God's Word everywhere.

Because he adopted the strong uncompromising position of the German Confessing Church against the intrigues of the Third Reich in the life of the Church, and dared to proclaim his faith openly, Busch was imprisoned several times by the Nazis.

At the end of the Second World War, Wilhelm Busch once again took up his travels as an itinerant evangelist. And in 1966, after several decades of incessant labours, the Lord called his servant to himself.

Table of contents

Why do I need Jesus?

God, yes; but why Jesus?

I am an old pastor. I have worked all my life in big cities. Year in and year out the same questions keep on coming up. There are heartfelt questions like, "How can God allow that?" And there are some old chestnuts like, "Who was Cain's wife?" But the question that people seem to throw at me the most readily is this one: "Pastor, you are always talking about Jesus. You are a fanatic! It doesn't matter what religion you have. What counts is to have respect for holy things."

That is as clear as daylight, isn't it? Goethe, who came from Frankfurt as I do, said something similar: "Feelings are everything; the name is only noise and smoke..." Whether we speak of Allah, of Buddha, of fate or of "the Supreme Being" is of no importance whatsoever. Believing in *something* is what counts. Wanting to specify your beliefs is fanaticism. Isn't that what most people think? I remember a middle-aged lady saying to me once, "Pastor, you bore us with your talk about Jesus. Didn't he say, 'In my Father's house are many rooms'? Everyone shall find a place!" My friends, that is a very serious mistake.

I was in Berlin one day, at the Tempelhofer Feld Airport. Before boarding the plane, we had to go through Passport Control. In front of me was a big man, massively built, with an enormous travelling-rug tucked under his arm. He thrust his passport at the customs officer. "One moment!" said the officer. "Your passport has expired!" "Come on! Don't be so fussy," the man retorted. "The main thing is to have a passport." "That's where you're wrong!" declared the officer. "The main thing is to have a passport that is valid."

The same holds true of faith. The fact of believing – of believing in any old thing – is not what matters in the end. Because everyone in his own way believes something. Someone said to me the other day, "I believe I can make a good stew out of two pounds of beef." Well, that is belief – of a kind! What matters is not to have just any kind of faith, but to have the true faith, a faith which enables you to live when all around becomes dark, which supports you when you risk falling into temptation, and which helps you face death. Death is a good test of the genuineness of your faith. Will yours stand the test?

Now there is only one true faith. One only which enables us to live and to die worthily. It is faith in the Lord Jesus Christ, the Son of God. It is true that Jesus said: "In my Father's house are many rooms." But he also said that there is only one door by which to enter: "I am the gate; whoever enters through me will be saved."

Jesus is the door. I know very well that people do not want to hear that. They are willing to discuss God for hours, to exchange bright ideas about what he might be like. But Jesus cannot be a subject for discussion.

I repeat: it is only faith in Jesus, the Son of God, which can save us and enable us to live and die in peace.

I realized just how ridiculous this seems to some people when I was walking through the city of Essen one day. I met two men, most likely miners, standing on the pavement. One of them greeted me, "Hello, Pastor!" When I was nearer, I asked him, "Do you know me?" He began to laugh and said to his companion, "This is Pastor Busch! A nice fellow!" I thanked him. "Yes, a nice fellow," he repeated, "but he's crazy!" I was indignant and shouted rather heatedly, "What? Crazy? How can you say such a thing?" But he said again, "Pastor Busch! A nice fellow! Only, he never stops talking about Jesus." I was delighted. "My friend, I'm not crazy!" I said. "A hundred years from now, you will be in eternity. The only thing that will matter then will be whether or not you have known Jesus. That is what determines whether you will be in heaven or hell. Tell me, do you know Jesus?" With a laugh, he turned to the other miner, "You see, there he goes again!"

And that is exactly what I want to do now. There is a verse in the Bible which will serve as a spring-board. It goes like this: "He who has the Son (of God) has life." You may have heard about Jesus in Sunday School, but that does not mean that you *have* him. "He who *has* the Son of God" – listen carefully! – "*has* life" – beginning now and for eternity! "He who does not have the Son of God does not have life." It is the Word of God which says so. You know the old proverb: "A bird in the hand is worth two in the bush!" Well – in your own interest – I would like to persuade you to accept Jesus Christ and to put your life into his hands. Because without him life can be really wretched.

But why does only Jesus count? Why is faith in him the only true faith? May I be more personal? I would like to tell you why *I* need Jesus and why *I* believe in him.

1. Jesus reveals God to us

When someone says to me, "I believe in God, but why do I need Jesus?" my reply is that that is nonsense! God is a hidden God. Without Jesus we can know absolutely nothing about him.

Men can invent their own god, to be sure; there's "the good Lord" who won't let a decent chap down as long as he doesn't drink more than five pints of beer a day! But that is not God! Allah, Buddha – these are only projections of our desires. But God? Without Jesus we would know nothing about him. Jesus reveals him. In the person of Jesus, God came to us.

Imagine a dense blanket of fog. Behind this is God. As men cannot live without him, they set about searching for him. They try to penetrate the fog. That is what the different religions do. Through them, men attempt to find God. But they all have this in common: they have all gone astray in the fog and have not been able to discover God.

God is a hidden God. The Jewish prophet Isaiah understood this. That is why he cried out, "We cannot reach you. Oh, that you would rend the heavens and come down." And the amazing thing is this: God heard that cry! He tore through the blanket of fog and came down to us – in the person of Jesus Christ. In the fields of Bethlehem, when the choir of angels sang, "A Saviour has been born to you. Glory to God in the highest!" – God had come to us. And now Jesus says to us, "He who has seen me has seen the Father." Without Jesus I would know nothing whatever about God. He is the only person from whom I can gain a sure knowledge of God. How can anyone even dare do say, "I can do without Jesus"?

2. Jesus is the liberating love of God

Some time ago I was interviewed by a journalist. When he asked me why I held meetings like the one we were at, I replied, "I do it because I fear that people will go to hell!" "Come off it," he said smiling. "There is no such place as hell!" Thereupon, I said to him, "We shall see. In a hundred years you'll know whether it is you or the Word of God which is right. Tell me," I asked, "have you ever been afraid of God?" "What!" he exclaimed, "no one needs to be afraid of the good Lord!" "My friend," I said, "you haven't got the slightest idea what it's all about. If you had the right concept of God, you'd know that nothing is more terrible than the holy and just God, the judge of our sins. Do you think he'll overlook your faults? You speak of 'the good Lord'. The Bible speaks of him differently: 'It is a dreadful thing to fall into the hands of the living God.'"

Have you ever been afraid of God? If not, then you haven't even begun to perceive the awful reality of the holiness of God and the terrible reality of your sin. But if you have, you won't be long in asking, "How can I stand before God?" I believe that the greatest folly of our age is that we no longer fear the wrath of God. When a nation ceases to take the living God and his wrath against sin seriously, this is a symptom of a dreadful hardening.

Professor Karl Heim once told me about a trip he made to China. In Peking, he was driven to the top of a mountain where there was an altar called "the altar of heaven". His guide told him that on "the night of reconciliation", hundreds of thousands of people used to walk up the mountain, each one bearing a lantern. Then the emperor would climb up to the top – this was before the revolution – and offer a sacrifice of reconciliation for his people. Professor Heim remarked, "These pagans knew what the wrath of God is, and understood that man needs to be reconciled to him."

And the cultivated Westerner thinks that he can casually talk of "the good Lord" and that God will be happy as long as people give their offering without grumbling! It is time we began to fear God again! For we have all sinned. Yes, all of us.

Once we have learned to fear God again, we shall be asking, "How can we escape the wrath of God? Who will deliver us?" It is then that our eyes will open and we shall understand that Jesus is the liberating love of God. "God wants all men to be saved." But he cannot save us at the expense of justice. God cannot turn a blind eye to sin. It is for this reason he gave his Son for the salvation and reconciliation of the world.

Come with me to Jerusalem. On the outskirts of the city is a hill. Thousands of people are gathered there. High above the heads of the crowd are three crosses. The man on the cross at the left is, like us, a sinner. So is the one on the right. But look at the man in the middle. He is none other than the Son of the living God.

> O sacred Head once wounded,
> With grief and pain weigh'd down,
> How scornfully surrounded
> With thorns, Thine only crown!
> How pale art Thou with anguish,
> With sore abuse and scorn!
> How does that visage languish,
> Which once was bright as morn.

Why is he nailed to a cross? Because this cross is the altar of God! And Jesus is the Lamb of God who bears the sin of the world and reconciles us to God.

Until you have found Jesus, the wrath of God rests upon you, even if you don't know it, even if you deny it. Only the person who comes to Jesus can enjoy the peace of God. "The punishment that brought us peace was upon him."

Allow me to use an illustration. During the First World War, I served as a gunner. Our guns had shields on each side. One day we found ourselves positioned in the front line without a single infantry batallion in sight. And it was on that particular day we were attacked by tanks! A hail of bullets from the enemy lines rained on our gun shields, but the armour-plating was so thick that we were sheltered behind them. And I thought at that moment, "If I simply stuck out my hand, it would be riddled with bullets – and I would bleed to death. But here, behind the shield, I am safe."

This portrays just what Jesus means to me. I know that without Jesus I would be destroyed by the judgement of God. Without Jesus, no matter what I did, I could never have peace of heart. Without Jesus, I could not die without terrible anguish. Without Jesus, I would be walking straight towards eternal damnation.

And eternal damnation does exist, without a shadow of a doubt. Wait a little while, and you will see that what the Bible says is true!

But if I find shelter behind the cross of Jesus, I am as safe as I was behind that armour-plating. I can know for certain that he is my redeemer, my Saviour. Yes, Jesus is the liberating love of God.

Listen to me carefully. God wants all men to be saved. For this reason, he gave his Son for your salvation, for your reconciliation with himself. Do not rest until you have obtained this peace from God, this salvation!

Why do I need Jesus?

3. Jesus is the only one who can solve life's greatest problem

Do you know what life's greatest problem is? For older people it might seem to be their bladder or kidney complaint! Or for young people, their girlfriend or boyfriend. Everyone has a problem. But, believe me, the greatest problem in life is our guilt before God.

For many years I worked among young people. And I was always on the lookout for new illustrations to help them understand this truth. I would like to use one of these pictures again. Imagine that from birth we carry a heavy iron collar around our necks. Suppose that each time I commit a sin a link is soldered on to it. I have an impure thought: a link is added. I am nasty to my mother: and another link is added. I speak evil of another person: and another link is added. I spend a day without praying, acting as if God did not exist: a new link is added. I am dishonest, I tell lies: and one more link is added.

Try to imagine the length of the chain we drag behind us – the chain of our guilt. Though this chain cannot be seen, our guilt is nonetheless very real.

In fact, it is enormous. And we drag it with us everywhere we go. I have often wondered why people are not more happy and satisfied. Things are not going too badly. It seems as though they have every reason to be happy. But they are not. And they cannot be because they are weighed down by the heavy chain of their guilt. Now no one can relieve them of it, not even a pastor, or a priest, or an angel. God himself cannot simply take it off, for he is just: "A man reaps what he sows."

But there is Jesus. He is the only one who can resolve life's greatest problem, because he died for our sins. By dying, he the just for us the unjust, Jesus has atoned for our sins. That is why he is able to free us from the chain of our guilt – and he alone is able to do so. I can say by experience that it is a real deliverance to know that our sins have been forgiven. It is the greatest liberation that one can experience. And it not only transforms our life, but also our death. You elderly people will understand this; it is one thing to die and to know that your sins are forgiven, and it is another thing to enter eternity with all the weight of your wrong-doing. It is a sobering and dreadful thing to think about.

I know many people who have claimed throughout their whole lives that they are good, that they do what is right. But one day they will die and will have to let go of the last friendly hand, only to discover that their life's boat is being swept along by the current of eternity to meet God. They can take nothing with them: not their little house, nor their bank account. Nothing, except their guilt. This is the way they will go to appear before God! How terrifying! But this is the lot of humanity. You may say, "That's how all men die. That's all there is to it." My friends, you need not die like this. Jesus offers forgiveness of sins. It is the greatest liberation that you could possibly experience. And it is possible right now.

I was eighteen when I learned from experience what forgiveness of sins means. My chain was broken and fell off.

Then, as the hymn says: "My heart was free. I rose, went forth, and followed thee!"

My wish is that you too might hearken to these words of life. Draw near to Jesus today. He is waiting for you. And say to him, "My life is a big mess. I've made so many mistakes. I've never wanted to admit it. On the contrary, I've always spoken highly of myself. Now I bring you all my mistakes. And I want to believe that your blood can take away my guilt."

In the seventeenth century, a man by the name of John Bunyan lived in England. He spent many long years in prison on account of his faith. Some things never change! After the Word of God, the next most stable thing in the world is prison! There in his prison cell, Bunyan wrote a marvellous book which is still relevant today – *The Pilgrim's Progress*. In it, he compared the life of a Christian to a journey full of adventures and snares. The book begins like this: A man living in the City of Destruction is suddenly overcome by anxiety. He says to himself, "What's wrong? I have no peace and I'm unhappy. I must get away from here!" He shares his concern with his wife, but she replies, "Your nerves are on edge. You need a good rest." But this does him little good. The anxiety persists. Then one day he says to himself, "It's no use! I must leave this city at all costs!" And he runs away. After his first few steps, he becomes conscious of a heavy burden upon his back. He wants to get rid of it, but he cannot. As he hurries on, his burden becomes heavier. Before starting on his journey, he had scarcely ever felt the weight of it. To him it only seemed normal. But as he hurries away from the City of Destruction, his burden becomes heavier and heavier. At last he can scarcely put one foot in front of the other. With great effort, he manages to climb up a mountain path. His burden is almost unbearable. Then suddenly, at a turning in the path, he sees a cross before him. Feeling faint, he collapses at the foot of the cross and clutching it, lifts up his eyes. At this precise moment, he feels the burden roll off his back and sees it disappear into the abyss with a loud crash.

This story is a beautiful illustration of what a man experiences when he draws near to the cross of Jesus Christ.

Upon that Cross of Jesus
Mine eye at times can see
The very dying form of One
Who suffered there for me;
And from my smitten heart, with tears,
Two wonders I confess –
The wonder of His glorious love,
and my own worthlessness.

I have forgiveness of sins because my Saviour suffered in my place. The chain of my guilt has been removed. My burden is gone. Truly, no one but Jesus is able to bestow such a gift: the forgiveness of our sins.

Why do I need Jesus? I must bring before you yet another reason why I believe in him.

4. Jesus is the Good Shepherd

At one time or another, everyone feels terribly alone and life seems terribly empty. Then we suddenly realize this: "Something is missing in my life. But what?" Let me tell you. You are lacking the living Saviour!

I have just told you that Jesus died on the cross to atone for our sins. Take note of this verse: "The punishment that brought us peace was upon him." After he had died, they laid him in a tomb which had been cut out of the rock. Then they rolled a heavy slab of stone before the entrance of the sepulchre. And to be absolutely sure, the Roman governor set his seal upon it and posted a squad of Roman soldiers to guard it. I imagine that there were some tough warriors among them who had fought in all the countries of the known world: Gaul, Germania, Asia, Africa. Their bodies were probably badly scarred. On the third day, at dawn, they were all standing about, their shields on their arms, their spears in their right hands and their helmets on their heads. A Roman soldier could be trusted when he was on guard. Now, the Bible says: "An angel of the Lord ... rolled back the stone." And Jesus came out of the tomb. It was such a terrifying sight that these tough soldiers fainted. A few hours later, Jesus encountered a poor girl. The Bible says that Jesus had previously cast seven demons out of her. That morning, the girl was in tears. Jesus approached her. But *she* did not faint! On the contrary, her tears turned to joy as she recognized the risen Lord and cried out, "Master!" She was comforted because she knew that Jesus, the Good Shepherd, was living and that he was near her.

You see, it is for that very reason that I, too, am so keen to have Jesus. I need someone who will take me by the hand. Life has dragged me into deep waters. I was thrown into prison by the Nazis because of my faith. There, at times, I thought, "One step further, and you will sink into the darkness of insanity – and you will never be able to escape them." But Jesus drew near to me. And everything came back to normal again. I can testify to that.

I spent one night in prison when it seemed that all of hell had broken loose. There had been an arrival of prisoners who were in transit to a concentration camp. The people had no hope left. Among them were both criminals and innocent people – Jews. On this particular night, it was a Saturday, their hearts were filled with deep despair. Suddenly they all started screaming at the top of their voices. You cannot imagine the scene. An entire building filled with desperate people yelling and banging against the walls and doors of their cells. The guards fired shots at the ceiling and then, running from one cell to another, started lashing out left and right. Sitting in my cell, I said to myself, "It must be like this in hell!" It is difficult to describe such a scene. But at that exact moment, the thought came to me, "Jesus! Surely he is here!" Believe me, I have lived all that I am telling you about. Inside my prison cell, I whispered softly, very softly, "Jesus! Jesus! Jesus!" And within three minutes, silence was restored.

Do you understand? I cried out to him. No one but Jesus heard it – and the demons had to withdraw. Then, although it was strictly forbidden, I sang in a loud voice:

> Jesus, Lover of my soul,
> Let me to Thy bosom fly,
> While the nearer waters roll,
> While the tempest still is high:
> Hide me, O my Saviour, hide,
> Till the storm of life is past;
> Safe into the haven guide,
> Oh, receive my soul at last!

All the prisoners heard this song. The guards did not breathe a word, not even when I began to sing the second stanza:

> Other refuge have I none
> Hangs my helpless soul on Thee;
> Leave, oh leave me not alone,
> Still support and comfort me:
> All my trust on Thee is stayed,
> All my help from Thee I bring;
> Cover my defenceless head
> With the shadow of Thy wing.

My friends, on that occasion, I was able to experience what it means to have a living Saviour.

I have already alluded to the fact that we must all one day pass through that momentous crisis, death. Someone once reproached me by saying, "You pastors, you are always frightening people by talking to them about death." "I have no need to prompt this kind of fear in anyone," I replied. "We all, by nature, are afraid to die." What a comfort, at the moment of death, to be able to hold the Good Shepherd's hand! But people say – and I believe it is true – "Today, man is less afraid to die than to live. Life is far worse for him than death." I can assure you, however, my friends, that Jesus will also help you to live.

There is another story which I must tell you. I have often used it as an illustration. It is an incredible account, and yet it is true. I got to know an industrialist in the city of Essen. He was one of those people who are always good-humoured. He used to say to me, "Pastor, you are right to encourage young people to live decently. Here is a gift of 100 marks for your work!" But when I would ask him where he stood with regard to the faith, he would quickly reply, "Don't trouble me, Pastor. I've come to my own conclusions about the world!" He was that kind of person: a good man, but as far from God as the east is from the west.

One day, I had to take a wedding, which is not always very pleasant in our big empty churches. The young couple arrived, accompanied by about ten other people. They were lost in that huge church. My cheerful industrialist friend was one of the couple's witnesses. I really felt sorry for the poor man. He was standing there in elegant morning dress, with his top-hat in his hand, totally ignorant about how to behave in church. One could read on his face what he was thinking: "Do I have to kneel? Or cross myself? I just don't know!" I tried to make him feel at ease by taking his hat from him and putting it at the side. We then began to sing a hymn. He hadn't the faintest idea how it went, but at least he pretended to join in with the others! Just picture him. And yet he was perfectly at ease in any fashionable circle.

Then, a very extraordinary thing happened. The bride was a Sunday School teacher, so during the ceremony about thirty young girls, high up in the gallery, began to sing a hymn for her. With their sweet, childish voices, they began the first verse:

> Saviour, like a shepherd lead us,
> Much we need Thy tend'rest care;
> In Thy pleasant pastures feed us...

I glanced at my friend and all of a sudden thought, "What is wrong with him? Is he going to be ill?" He had broken down. His hands were covering his face, and he was shaking. My first thought was, "Something has happened to him! I must call a doctor quickly." But just then I noticed that he was weeping his heart out. The children continued to sing:

> In Thy pleasant pastures feed us,
> For our use Thy folds prepare.
> We are Thine: do Thou befriend us,
> Be the Guardian of our way;
> Keep Thy flock, from sin defend us,
> Seek us when we go astray.

And there was this man, this great business man, seated in the pew, weeping.

Suddenly I understood what had happened. He must have said to himself, "These children have something that I don't have: a Good Shepherd. I am a poor lonely man, a lost man!"

And you too, whoever you may be, man or woman, you will not get very far if you cannot say with these children: "I am happy to belong to the Lord Jesus' flock, to have him as Saviour and as Shepherd." No, you will not get very far. So why not take that vital decision which will enable you to make these words your own?

Why have I believed in Jesus Christ? Because he is the Good Shepherd, the best Friend, my living Saviour.

Why do I need Jesus? I would like to point out one last reason:

5. Jesus is the Prince of Life

Many years ago, I organized a camp in the forest of Bohemia. After the young people had left, I had to wait a whole day for someone to come and pick me up by car. I spent the night in an old hunting lodge which, in days gone by, had belonged to a king. At the time, its only inhabitant was a forest-ranger. The building was half in ruins. There was no electricity. But there was an immense living room, with a fireplace in which a small fire had been lit. The ranger put an oil lamp on the table and bade me good night. Outside the storm was howling. The rain came pouring down through the fir trees around the house. It was an ideal place for a good mystery story.

Now, just on that particular evening, I had nothing with me to read. And then I discovered a little book on the edge of the fireplace. I began to glance through it by the glimmer of the oil lamp. Never had I read anything so terrifying. In its pages, a doctor was pouring out his anger against death. Page after page, there were passages like this: "O Death, the worst enemy of the human race! I struggled a whole week to snatch one human life out of your claws and just when I thought I had pulled him through, you stood up at his bedside and seized him with a sneer – and it was all of no use. Heal men as I might, I know that when you arrive with your skeleton hand, the struggle is in vain. O Death, you are a deceiver, an enemy!" He gave vent like this to his implacable hatred of death on every single page.

Then came the worst passage: "O Death, full stop, exclamation mark!" I quote him precisely: "Curse! If only you were just an exclamation mark! But when I gaze at you, you turn into a question mark. And I wonder whether or not you are a full stop! If not, then what? O Death, abominable question mark!"

That's where you can get to! But I can assure you that all is not finished with death. Jesus, who knew all about it, said, "Broad is the road that leads to destruction . . . and narrow the road that leads to life." Our lot is decided here on earth. That is why I am glad to have a Saviour who gives life here and now – who is life and who leads to life. For this reason I love to preach this message to others.

During the First World War, we fought for weeks near Verdun at the time when one of the worst battles was raging. There were heaps of dead bodies between the two enemy lines. And I have never in all my life been able to drive the sickly smell of those bodies out of my nostrils. Every time I stand at a war memorial, I can smell that stench of Verdun, that reek of dead bodies. And every time I say to myself, "In a hundred years' time, none of us shall be here any longer," that same horrible smell of death makes me gasp. Can't you smell it, too?

But in this mortal world, there is one who rose from the dead! And he says to us, "I live, and you shall live also! Believe in me! Come to me! Turn to me! Enter into my kingdom! And I will lead you to life."

Isn't that marvellous? How can you live in this mortal world without this Saviour who is life and who leads to eternal life?

A few days ago, I read an old letter which Professor Karl Heim had had printed. It was written by a Christian soldier who fell in Russia during the Second World War. The letter reads something like this: "What is happening around us is atrocious. When the Russians fire their rockets, we are panic-stricken. And such cold! And all this snow! It is terrible. But I have no fear! If I were to die, it would be wonderful. In one leap, I would enter into glory. The turmoil would be over – I would see my Lord face to face and be enshrouded in his brightness. No, I would not mind dying here on the battle-field." And that is exactly what happened to him a short time later. I could not help but think, when I read this letter, what an amazing thing it was that a young man hadn't the least fear of dying simply because he knew Jesus.

Yes, Jesus is the Prince of Life. And he gives to his own the assurance of eternal life.

On the annual Church Day in Leipzig one year, there was a reception at the Town Hall. All the important people of the city and the dignitaries of the Church were gathered there together. The speeches were as non-commital as possible to avoid stepping on one another's toes. Heinrich Giesen, who was at the time general-secretary of the Church Day, was to bring the ceremony to a close. I can still see him standing up and saying, "You ask us, gentlemen, what kind of people we are? I shall tell you in one short sentence. We are people who pray: 'My Lord, make me holy so that I may go to heaven!'" Then he sat down. It was startling indeed to see how such a simple declaration had deeply upset those who were present.

Years ago, a Christian poet wrote this prayer:

> Oh, let me see Thy footmarks,
> And in them plant mine own;
> My hope to follow duly
> Is in Thy strength alone.
> Oh, guide me, call me, draw me,
> Uphold me to the end;
> And then in heaven receive me,
> My Saviour and my Friend!

My desire is that you, too, may in this way continue your journey through this world.

Why do you need Jesus? Because everything, absolutely everything, depends on your relationship with him!

What is life all about?

Everything revolves around this question: What is life all about? What is the meaning of my life?

I received a phone call one day from a industrial tycoon of the city of Essen. He was very upset. "Pastor, please come right away!" In a flash I was on my way and when I arrived was greeted with these words, "My son has killed himself!"

I knew this young man. He was a student. He had everything one could wish for in life: he was young, rich and handsome, in perfect health, had his own car, and had never been mixed up in any shady business. And it was this young man who had just put a bullet through his head! He left these few lines to explain his act: "I have no reason to continue living any longer. So I am putting an end to my life. It has no meaning whatsoever." Isn't this a staggering declaration?

The question as to what life is all about is of great importance. It is all the more important because we have only one life to live. Have you ever thought of the personal consequences of this fact? Only *one* life to live!

When I was a school boy, I was not very good in arithmetic. My teacher couldn't understand my way of finding the solution to problems. When I had finished my homework, he would mark my exercise-book with red ink to show how little he appreciated my talent for finding wrong answers. When an exercise-book was completely covered in red, I would throw it away, sometimes even before it was full. Then I would buy another one. This one would be nice and new... and clean! So I could begin afresh.

Wouldn't it be wonderful if we could do this with our lives? Believe me, millions of human beings at death's door have had to confess, "If only I could start all over again! I would do things altogether differently." We can buy a new exercise-book and start all over again, but we cannot do so with our lives. *We have only one life to live*. How terrible to spoil it by using it in the wrong way. We have only one life to live. If we have lost it, we have lost it for eternity. What I have to say must be taken seriously. It is a matter of life and death!

This morning a large herd of cows passed by the hotel where I am staying. I thought, "Those cows are lucky. They don't have to ask why they're in this world. For them it's clear: they're here to give milk and when they can't give any more, they provide meat." Do you understand what I mean? An animal does not have to question what life is all about. That is the difference between man and animal. Unfortunately, large numbers of people live – and die – without having ever asked themselves, "What is the real purpose of my life?" There is no difference between them and animals. A man will never be a real man until he has asked himself, "What is life all about? Why am I a man? What is the purpose of my life?"

1. Superficial and thoughtless answers

What is the purpose of my life? A whole series of superficial and thoughtless answers can be given to this question. Many years ago, I heard them all at the same time. It was in 1936 during the Third Reich. Some students from Münster, in Westphalia, had asked me to come and hold a discussion group with them on the theme: *What is the purpose of my life?* They made it clear to me from the start that they did not want a sermon but an open discussion on the subject. "All right," I said to them, "I'll let you begin. What is the purpose of our life? Why are we on earth?"

As the Nazis were in power at the time of this meeting, it was natural that one young man should stand up and declare, "I live for my people. It's a bit like the leaf and the tree. The leaf is nothing, the tree is everything. I live for my people."

"That may be so," I answered him, "but tell me: why is the tree there, for what purpose does *it* exist? And the people, why do *they* exist?" Silence. He didn't have the answer to that! Instead of solving the problem, he had only put it off. So I said to them, "My friends, you are dodging the question with answers like that!"

"What is the meaning of life? Why are we here on earth?" I asked again. Another student declared, "I live to do my duty." To this I replied, "That's the root of the problem. Just what is my duty? I, myself, am convinced that my duty is to preach the Word of God to you. Mathilda Ludendorff thinks that her duty is to deny the very existence of God. So, what is duty?"

A high government official said to me one day, "Pastor, just between you and me, I do nothing but sign papers from morning till night. But I know that if all these papers should happen to burn one day, the world would carry on. It really bothers me to have to devote my time and energy to such a senseless job."

Just what is duty? Under the Third Reich, thousands of SS men assassinated hundreds of thousands of human beings. And when they were put on trial, they all said, "We only did our duty. We had received orders." Do you think it is a man's duty to assassinate his fellow-beings? I cannot accept this myself.

I then said to these students, "That is the root of the matter. What is duty? Who can tell me? Here we are at a dead-end again!"

The young people looked thoughtful. Then one of them got up and proudly boasted, "I am a member of an old aristocratic family. I can trace my genealogy back to the sixteenth century. My ancestors were nobles of the purest stock. Isn't trying to perpetuate such a noble ancestry enough to fill a whole life?" I could not help but reply, "I'm sorry! But if you don't know what the past generations lived for, then it's not worthwhile producing another one!"

Numerous superficial and thoughtless answers to our question obviously can be found.

Some death announcements in our newspapers begin like this:

> So hard through all your life you worked,
> Your duty never dreamed to shirk.
> Yourself you totally forgot
> And 'twas of others that you thought.

These lines always drive me up the wall! I can't help thinking, "Why, that's a horse's obituary!" Am I wrong? A horse can't do anything but work. It seems to me that a human being is not on earth just to slave all his life. That would be very sad indeed. If that is all life is about, then it would be better to commit suicide at the age of ten. "So hard through all your life you worked..." It gives me the shudders! No, that isn't what life is all about either!

Another student said to me in the course of the discussion, "Look, I'm going to be a doctor. And if I can save human lives, isn't that a good reason for living?" I flashed back, "What you say is fine, but if you don't know for what purpose a man is alive, then it's senseless to want to save his life. It would be far better to give him a needle so that he could die right away." Now, don't misinterpret what I have just said! What I mean is that the answer the student doctor gave was not really a solution to our problem – the problem of what life is all about.

Surrounded by all these students, it gave me quite a shock to realize that even well-educated young people today let themselves drift along without knowing just why they are in the world.

You see, when you have gone through what we went through in

Germany – I just want to mention this in passing – it is tempting to reply, as certain students did back in Münster, "Life has no deep meaning at any rate. It was through mere chance that I was born. So why bother looking for a reason? Let's enjoy life to the full; that's the best thing to do."

This attitude is tempting to the man who suddenly begins to think, "My life is absurd, it is senseless. If my parents hadn't married, I wouldn't have been conceived and I wouldn't have been born. It's by mere chance I exist. In reality, my life is completely absurd." And if this man encounters difficulties in his life, he is just one step away from suicide. The argument goes: Why carry on living? If life is nothing but mere chance and absurdity, then I might as well put an end to it.

Did you know that in West Germany the rate of suicides is higher than the rate of fatal road accidents? Did you know that about 50 % of the victims are young people under thirty? This is the most staggering evidence that our generation has not found out what life is all about.

I have often spoken to people who say, "Life is so senseless. So I'll either spend it enjoying myself or I'll put an end to it by committing suicide." "But," I have asked them, "supposing life does have a meaning after all? Just suppose it *does* have a purpose and you have spent your life as if it didn't have one? What will become of you at the end of your life?"

There is a verse in the Bible which should fill us with fear: "Man is destined to die once, and after that to face judgement." No person can honestly consider his life if he is not acquainted with this biblical truth.

What *is* the purpose of my life? How can I die and face God's judgement if I have failed to see the very meaning of my life?

That is what is at stake.

2. Who can give us an answer?

What is life all about? Who can answer this question? My church? No. My priest or my pastor? No. He is in the same predicament as I am. Scientists? Philosophers? They, too, are incapable of answering our question. Only one can tell us. We owe our very existence to him. He is the one who created us: *God*.

I'm going to use a rather silly illustration. Suppose one day I go into an apartment and find a boy sitting there, tinkering with some wire and light bulbs. "Tell me," I say, "what kind of infernal machine are you making? What will it turn out to be in the end?" He tries to explain it all to me, but I have to admit I don't understand a thing. And inwardly I think, "No one can guess what it will be. Only the inventor can know what it's for and how it should be used."

It is the same with our lives. Only the one who created us can tell why he created us. In other words, it is only by revelation that we receive an answer to our question: What is life all about? God must give it to us.

If I were not already a diligent reader of the Bible, this question in itself would force me to read it. Personally, I would find it unbearable not to know why I am in this cursed world. Does the expression "cursed world" seem too strong to you? It is found in the Bible. On the other hand, you only have to spend six months with a pastor in one of our big cities to understand what I mean when I claim that the world is under a terrible curse. I couldn't endure living if I didn't know the answer given through God's revelation.

Yes, God does answer our question as to what life is all about. He does so in the Bible. And that's why the Bible is so important. I know people who take on an air of superiority and say, "But we don't read the Bible!" To them I can only say, "Then as far as I can see, you've never really given serious thought to the question of what life is all about." Stupidity is a widespread disease and if it were painful, the whole world would resound with shrieks of pain.

I shall sum up the Bible's answer in one sentence: God created us so that we might become his children. As a father likes to see himself in his son, so God made man "in his image". God wants us to become his children, children who will speak with him and with whom he will speak; children who will love him and whom he will love. Do you ever pray? It is a terrible thing for a father if his son hasn't spoken to him for years. And if a man does not pray, then he does not speak with his heavenly Father. Yes, God would like us to be his children: children who speak with him, who love him and whom he can love. That is the meaning of our existence. I am not talking about the Church, about doctrine, or about religion. I am talking about the living God!

God created you so that you might become his child. Are you his child?

I must go one step further. We have to *become* God's children. We are not born God's children. Right at the very beginning of the Bible, it says: "God created man in his own image." It then goes on to give an account of a great disaster: God had created man a free being, with the power to choose between good and evil. But man chose to be against God. He ate the forbidden fruit. That was his way of saying to God, "I want to be independent. I can get along without you." Adam didn't doubt the existence of God. He only wanted to escape from his authority. "I want to do my own thing!"

The other day a man stopped me in the street. "You talk about God all the time," he said to me. "But I can't see God. Tell me how to find him." I replied, "Listen very carefully to what I am going to say. Just suppose there's a machine which could take me back in time. Suppose that I went right back to the beginning of human history and that one evening I am strolling in the garden of God. (You probably know the story of the Fall.) Well, there I meet Adam, the first man. 'Good evening, Adam,' I say. 'Good evening, Pastor Busch,' he replies. Then I explain how I got to the Garden of Eden. 'You seem thoughtful,' says Adam. 'What are you thinking about?' I answer, 'Oh, I was just thinking about a question a man asked me recently: How can I find God?' Adam burst out laughing. 'How to *find* God is not the real problem. He is here. Be honest. What is really preoccupying you all is how you can get *rid* of him! But you can't get rid of him. That's the big problem!'"

Could Adam be right? God is here. We can find him. But we cannot get rid of him.

When I think of the evolution of human thought through the past three centuries, I can see that we have tried everything to free ourselves from God. But we have not succeeded. In reality we all believe that God exists, but we simply don't want to have to bother with him. We just copy everyone else: we leave the question of God unanswered. We do not deny the existence of God, but we do not want to be bothered with him. We would not describe ourselves as his enemies, but neither are we his friends.

The biggest problem in life still remains to be resolved.

A Swiss doctor claims in one of his books that if a man does not resolve the important question of life, he will suffer deep mental and emotional disturbance. He goes on to say, "We Westerners, we are suffering from a lack of God. We do not deny his existence, but we have no relationship with him. We don't want to have anything to do with him and that is why we are suffering from a lack of God." I share his opinion.

Almost everywhere I hear people say, "Modern man is not interested in God." I can only reply, "Modern man's condition is very serious. I, too, am a modern man but I am interested in God. I don't believe I'm old-fashioned because of that! It's a very alarming fact that people today don't take the matter of salvation a bit seriously."

I shall use a rather simple illustration once again. Try to picture an apprentice-cook. One day I hear the head cook say, "That boy is not at all interested in cooking!" So I ask, "Well, what is he interested in then?" He answers, "In pop music and girls!" "You should bring yourself down to his level," I say, "and from now on talk to him only about pop music and girls!" "Not on your life!" retorts the chef. "If that boy isn't interested in cooking, then he has missed his vocation."

Can you see the point I want to make? Our vocation is to become children of God. When modern man shows no interest in this, then he has missed his vocation as a man. Under these circumstances it is useless to discuss all kinds of possible or impossible things with him, even if the subject interests him. He must be told over and over again: "You will begin to be a real man only when you have become a child of the living God."

3. God's answer

I want to repeat that we are not born children of God, but that the purpose of life is to *become* children of God. Something, then, has to happen to us.

Think seriously about all this.

We must face it: we are not children of God, we do not love God, we break his commandments, we do not care a bit about him, we do not pray – though in emergencies we may ring the alarm bell! So it is vital for us to know the answer to the biggest question of all: How can I become a child of the living God?

Some people would say, "By being good." Others, "By believing in God." But all that is not enough!

Our question has not been answered.

How do I become a child of the living God?

The answer to this supremely important question can be received only by revelation. That means that God himself must tell me how I can become his child. No man – not even a pastor – can make it up. Now the Bible gives a very clear answer. Here it is: only through Jesus! Yes, to become a child of God, I must approach God through Jesus.

There is a verse in the Bible which, when translated word for word, reads like this: "Jesus came from the world of God into this world." Nowadays we repeatedly hear that the Bible is based on an outdated view of the world. What a mistake! It tells us vital things about God and about ourselves. It tells us that God is present everywhere. Even if I were to hide in the depths of the earth, God would be there. The Bible holds what we call in modern language a multi-dimensional view of the world. We live in a three-dimensional world. There is length, height and depth. But other dimensions exist. And God is in another dimension. He is very near, within hand reach. He accompanies us. He sees us when we wander astray. But it is impossible for us to tear down the barrier separating us from this other dimension. Only God is able to do this. And he tore it down by coming to us in the person of Jesus.

Another verse in the New Testament, when translated literally, says this of Jesus: "He came to that which was his own," – and indeed the world does belong to him – "but his own did not receive him." Here we have the whole history of the Gospel right up to our day. Jesus comes and man refuses to let him in. "He came to that which was his own, but his own did not receive him." From a human standpoint, this is a dead end and should put an end to God's relations with man. But – how astonishing – the story does not stop there! "Yet to all who received him . . . he gave the right to become the children of God." It is by receiving Jesus, then, that we become children of God.

Have you as yet opened the door of your life to him? "To all who received him . . . he gave the right to become the children of God."

During the First World War I was a young officer and was living far from God. Yet it was at that particular period of my life that I opened my heart to Jesus and let him in. This experience completely changed my existence. I have never had the least regret since. Though, to follow Jesus I have had to tread many difficult paths. I have been in prison. And on numerous occasions I have been in distress. But even if I had a hundred lives to live, as soon as I had the faculties to think straight, I would each time cling to this verse: "To all who received him . . . he gave the right to become the children of God." Why? Because from the instant I become a child of God, my life takes on meaning. It makes no difference who I am: whether I be a pastor or street cleaner, manager or locksmith, housewife or school teacher, my life takes on meaning only from the moment I become a child of God.

Yes, you ought to let Jesus into your life. Only then will it have true purpose.

It is interesting to study the characters of the New Testament in this light. Take Mary Magdalene. Her life had absolutely no meaning at all. It is said of her – the only allusion to her past – that she was possessed by seven evil spirits. (I personally know some people who are possessed by a good many more than seven evil spirits.) It must have been terrible: a life dominated by the senses, a life of slavery. The poor woman must have suffered a lot leading such a senseless existence. And then one day, Jesus, the Saviour, the Son of God, entered into her life and drove the evil spirits away. He can do it and he did it! From that hour, Mary belonged to Jesus. At last her life had purpose. But the day came when Mary Magdalene witnessed the crucifixion and death of Jesus. On that day a sudden fear came over her – a fear that her past life would begin all over again. On the morning of the third day after the crucifixion, she was on her knees, weeping, in the garden where Jesus had been buried in a rock tomb. She had come to the tomb and had found it empty. The stone had been rolled away and there was no trace of Jesus' body. That is why she was weeping.

I can understand her perfectly. For if I lost Jesus, it would lead me also to the depths of a meaningless existence. Yes, I can understand her. "The Lord is gone! My life has no meaning any longer."

But then she suddenly heard a voice behind her, "Mary!" She turned around and saw the risen Jesus there before her. The tears of despair flowing down her cheeks were changed into tears of joy. And a cry sprung up from the depths of her soul, "Rabboni! Master!"

This woman's story is confirmation that we do not need the great theories of philosophy to find the answer to the problem of what life is all about. Even the least educated man knows for a fact that his life has no meaning. And he too wonders, "What is the purpose of my life?" Does he want an answer to that question? He has only to accept Jesus. Then, like her, he will become a child of God. And his life, like Mary's, will be lived from then on in the light of a deep, exciting plan, God's plan.

My friend, I urge you to accept Jesus too. He is waiting for you. Talk to him. He is very near to you. All you have to say is, "Lord Jesus, my life has no meaning. Come to me."

When I accept Jesus, a real revolution begins in my life. I reap all the benefits of the death of Jesus: his death deals a finishing blow to my past life; I am also raised up with him and live a new life, the life of a child of God; he gives me his Spirit who changes my desires and even my way of thinking. Accept Jesus, and you will know about these things by experience.

Yes, it's true; the man who accepts Jesus begins a completely new life. Becoming a child of God means that not only our way of thinking changes, but also our entire way of living.

In the last century, a shoemaker by the name of Rahlenbeck lived in Westphalia. People had nicknamed him the "Pietistic Preacher" because of his eagerness to follow Jesus. He was a man of great spiritual insight, a man blessed by God. A young pastor came to visit him one day. "Pastor," Rahlenbeck said to him, "your theological studies don't guarantee salvation. You must accept Jesus!" The young pastor replied, "I do have Jesus. His picture is hanging on the wall in my study." Old Rahlenbeck answered back, "Jesus is very still and peaceful on your study wall. But if you let him into your life, then there'll be lots of noise!"

I hope there will be lots of noise in your life. I hope you will be able to put a cross on your past and praise your heavenly Father for making you his child, for giving purpose to your life, and for enabling you from now on to honour him in word, thought, and deed.

Have you understood that this is not a religious craze I am talking about or the personal opinion of a pastor, but a question of life and death, of eternal life and eternal damnation?

The Lord Jesus says, "Here I am! I stand at the door and knock. If anyone hears my voice and opens the door, I will come in." He says this to you too.

One day an old miner came to find me, and he said, "Pastor, I must talk to you." He was well over seventy. "I attended an evangelistic meeting when I was seventeen. There I felt that Jesus was knocking at the door. But I thought, 'I bet all my friends will make fun of me if I take these things seriously and accept Jesus! No, I just can't do it!' And I ran out." He concluded, "Here I am at the end of my life. I'm old and I realize that my life is a failure. It's a failure because on that particular occasion I didn't open the door to Jesus."

We have only one life to live! For this very reason our question – What is life all about? – is of prime importance. God has given a clear, plain answer to it. The answer is in Jesus, the Crucified and Risen One.

This Jesus is standing now at your door. He is knocking. Open up your life to him.

You will never regret it!

I don't have time!

"You should come and hear Pastor Busch speak!" How often an invitation like that meets with the reply: "Sorry, but I don't have time!"

I once had to stay for a while in a convalescent home. An elderly gentleman sat opposite me at meal-times. We got along very well together. "Now there's someone who enjoys life!" I would always think when I saw how much this imposing old man enjoyed his food, or when I watched him dozing peacefully in the sun. As time went on, however, the superficiality of our conversations began to weigh on me.

You might ask, "What's wrong with that?" Well, it's like this: for me, God is the greatest reality in life. My life changed totally when I understood the great work he had accomplished: "For God so loved the world that he gave his one and only Son, that whoever believes in him shall not perish but have eternal life." It's difficult to watch someone neglect such a salvation day after day. This was obviously the case with my elderly friend. I wondered how he would feel when his turn would come to stand before Almighty God.

One day at the dinner table, I handed him a small booklet I had written and said, "I'd like you to read this little book. It's a collection of stories about some people's experiences of God. It should give you something to think about." Do you know what his reaction was? He thanked me warmly, then said, "I'm here to convalesce. But perhaps when I'm back home I'll find a moment to read your booklet." And he laid it aside.

I was very sad, for I knew that never again would this man have as much spare time as he had then. The truth of the matter was that he simply did not want to take time for God.

1. A strange situation

Why is it that we never have time? First of all I want to draw your attention to a strange situation which has always puzzled me and which no one has ever been able to explain to me.

A hundred years ago when a merchant living in Stuttgart had

some business to do in Essen, it took him five days by stage-coach to get there and five days to come back. That made ten days of travelling in all, and, let's say, two more days of negotiating to conclude his business. So almost a fortnight was spent on this one piece of business. Nowadays, a businessman has only to make a telephone call and he has saved twelve days. And yet, I get the impression that not a single one of the many businessmen I know has twelve days to spare! They all tell me rather, "I haven't the time!" Why is that?

When I was young, I used to visit my grandparents. They lived in the Swabian Jura. It was a real expedition in those days to go by train from Elberfeld to Urach. Today, with the Trans-European Express, the same trip can be made in five hours.

Surely people today ought to have a lot more spare time! Years ago we used to have a sixty-hour working week. Nowadays we have a forty-hour week (and sometimes even less). Yet, no one has time! Why is that?

Everything has been done in our days to make life easier. My mother used to read four chapters of the Bible every day and she also took time each day to pray for her family. There were no washing machines or electrical appliances then, either. She had to care for eight children. Their clothes were not drip-dry. She had to darn all their socks, too! And yet she had the time to read her four chapters of the Bible each day.

Do you have the time to do this? Probably not!

Why is that?

Great efforts are made today to help us save time – and yet no one has time to spare! Can you explain that? I have thought about this problem time and time again, but I simply cannot see through it.

The only explanation I can come up with – I know people will not want to hear it, but I can suggest no other – is that behind the scenes there is Someone who harasses us. This Someone arranges circumstances in such a way that we never have time. This Someone, like a lion-tamer at the circus, never stops cracking his whip to keep us "on the go".

The Bible says exactly the same thing. This Someone *does* exist . . . he is called the Devil! Regardless of what your opinion may be about it, the "powers of darkness" do exist.

A man recently told me that he had given up on Christianity. I said to him, "You're making a big mistake. The Devil has you under his control. He'll make an end of you!" Smiling at me, he answered, "But the Devil doesn't even exist!"

The Bible tells us that Jesus was led by the Devil up to the top of a very high mountain. Spread out before them was a view of the entire region. The Devil "drew back the curtains" and Jesus was able to see, in spirit, all the kingdoms of the world and their glory. The Devil then said to Jesus, "I will give you all their authority and splendour, for it has been given to me, and I can give it to anyone I want to. So if you worship me, it will all be yours." This passage of the Bible moves me deeply. The Lord Jesus did not contradict the Devil. He admitted that the Devil holds sway over this world.

Let me give you two or three examples to illustrate this. I think of the great number of men and women who are slaves to their own vices. Once there was a knock on my door in the middle of the night. Standing there was the manager of a local factory. It was obvious that he had been drinking heavily, but his mind was still clear enough to be able to cry, "Please, help me! I *have* to drink, I can't help it! My father was an alcoholic. I inherited it from him. I just can't help it!"

We shall never know how many people are sighing deep down in their hearts, "I can't help it!" Who rules over them with a rod of iron? Observe a little more closely all the misery in the world today and you will conclude that what the Bible says is true: the powers of darkness do exist!

Think for a moment of all the sexual disorder there is in our days. I knew a man who had a delightful family and a lovely wife. He fell one day under the charm of one of his female employees. I went to visit him. "My friend," I said to him, "you are in the process of ruining your own life and your family's and of losing your children's respect." I can still see this industrial manager sitting before me, and hear his pitiful answer, "Pastor, I can't give up this girl. Really, I can't!" In situations like this, can we not feel the hold of the powers of darkness?

The well-known English author, Somerset Maugham, wrote an important book entitled: *Of Human Bondage*. How easily men let themselves live in a state of subjection. You older people can remember how you submitted to Hitler. "I believed that two multiplied by two made twenty," many have since admitted. "I believed it because the Führer had said so!"

You cannot deny the existence of the powers of darkness. You cannot deny the existence of the Devil.

Goethe, the great German poet, wrote a heart-gripping drama called *Faust*. A young girl, Gretchen, is one of the leading characters in the play. She was a pure young girl. Then someone seduced her. Her brother, wanting to avenge her honour, was killed in a fight with his sister's seducer. Later, so that her lover could come and join her, Gretchen gave her mother a sedative to drink. But the drink provoked her death. And when the child she was expecting was born, Gretchen killed it.

(Women in our days, by the way, do exactly the same thing when they abort. They are guilty of a very serious offence.)

At the end of the play, the young girl is standing there – she has been responsible for three deaths: her brother's, her mother's, and her child's – and she says a startling thing, "Yet, what pushed me to do it, my God, was so beautiful, so pure!"

Goethe was no fool. He made it quite clear in *Faust* that the Devil had manipulated the whole affair.

As a pastor working in a big city, I am constantly confronted with this kind of problem. When someone says to me, "There is no Devil," I can't help but ask, "What remote corner of the country do you come from?" And I know, of course, that the Devil is certainly active even there.

Unfortunately, I am forced to admit the reality of the Devil when I observe how blind real Christians can be when it comes to seeing their own faults. I think of one Christian lady in particular. She was extremely self-centred. She tormented her daughter-in-law until the poor girl almost went out of her mind. The mother-in-law wasn't the least aware of the harm she was doing. And yet she was a pious woman! You pious people, never forget to ask God to protect you from the powers of darkness.

It is totally impossible to understand the present state of the world if we have not accepted the fact that behind the scenes are the Devil and the powers of darkness. The powers of darkness work with a very precise goal in view. They keep us running – and that is why we never have time. Every imaginable device is used by the Devil to hinder us from finding time to think – for if we did we would discover that we can be delivered from his hold.

2. A wonderful reality

Yes, there is a way for us to be liberated!

In Germany, during the Carnival festivities, some comedian always puts on a show. I have often wondered what he thinks of his own jokes when he is in his room at the end of the day and has finished taking off his make-up. If he is honest with himself, he would most likely admit, "I earn my living by saying stupid things, by telling dirty jokes that pollute people's minds." He may even end up being disgusted with himself!

How glad I am to be able to tell you about a grand and wonderful reality: there is a chance of deliverance for those who want to escape the hold of the powers of darkness.

The Apostle Paul described the Christian in these terms: "God has rescued us from the dominion of darkness and brought us into the kingdom of the Son he loves, in whom we have redemption, the forgiveness of sins." A Christian is not someone who has been baptized and confirmed, or who gives his tithes and offerings. No! A Christian is someone whose whole life has been transformed. He has been pulled out of the clutches of the powers of darkness and has begun a totally new life under the leadership of a new Master.

To illustrate this point, I want to tell you a story that one of the workers of the Berlin City Mission told me. For some time he had been trying to help a man who was an alcoholic. Such bonds are hard to break. One day the Christian worker learned that during a bout of heavy drinking his friend had smashed the furniture in his house and beaten his wife. So he went to visit him. It was five o'clock in the afternoon. He found the poor man sitting in the kitchen, drinking a cup of coffee. His five-year-old little boy was sitting beside him. The missionary greeted the drunkard kindly. Then he asked, "Things have gone wrong again?" Gritting his teeth, the man stood up like a shot. Without saying a word, he went into the next room and came back with a clothes line in his hands. Still not uttering a word, he began tying his little boy to his chair. The missionary thought, "What is he doing now? Is he still drunk?" He let him go on. When he had finished tying up his son, the man made a knot, then shouted, "Get up!"

The little fellow began to cry. "But I can't get up!" he sobbed. Then the drunkard turned to the missionary and with a painful expression on his face, he said, "You have heard: 'But I can't!' Well, it's the same with me. I can't either!"

Isn't that heart-breaking?

After a moment, the missionary stuck his hand in his pocket and pulled out a pen-knife. Then, paying no attention to the damage he was doing, he cut the brand new clothes line. Quietly he said to the lad, "Get up!" And the boy got up! Turning to the drunkard, the missionary said, "There, you see!" "Of course," he snapped back, "you cut the cord." The missionary replied, "Someone came to cut all the bonds of sin that hold us. Jesus!"

Thousands upon thousands of people throughout the vast world can testify to this.

What a wonderful reality! We can be delivered from the powers of darkness.

3. The core of the matter

The moment has come to speak to you about Jesus. And in talking about him, I come to the very heart of my subject.

I remember having been invited once to a Coloured People's Club in New York. You are all aware of the racial tensions existing in America. In the lounge of the Club stood a marble statue placed on a pedestal. The statue was obviously not that of a coloured person. I was astonished that coloured people should have erected a monument to a white man in this particular place. So I questioned a black gentleman. "My friend," I asked, "who is this man?" I shall never forget what followed. The man stood still a moment before the statue, then solemnly declared, "This man is Abraham Lincoln, my liberator!" And I remembered how, at the price of years of civil war, President Lincoln had won freedom for the slaves.

The man I spoke to was not even born then; yet he was a free man that day because of the rights Abraham Lincoln had won for him on bloody battle-fields.

As I went upstairs, I could see him still standing before the monument and could hear him murmuring, "Abraham Lincoln, my liberator!"

In the same way, I can stand before the cross of Jesus Christ and say, "Jesus, my liberator!"

There is a rather strange verse in the Bible: "Through Christ Jesus the law of the Spirit of life set me free from the law of sin and death." There are laws of nature. When I hold up a handkerchief, then drop it, it will inevitably fall to the ground because of the law of gravity. No one can change this. But if I catch the handkerchief, it will stop falling. This means that if a greater force intervenes, the law of gravity is overcome. By nature we are subjected to the law of sin and death. All of us are falling, all of us are tumbling down the hill that leads to eternal damnation. And we know it only too well.

If our fall is to be stopped, then a greater force must intervene. This is the only way it can be stopped. God has given us this greater force in the person of Jesus. He gave Jesus for our salvation and liberation. Jesus took away the Devil's power. And with the strength of the Holy Spirit which Jesus bestows upon us, we can live a new life of freedom.

Isn't it strange that the world cannot get rid of Jesus? Do you know why? Someone once said that Jesus was like a foreign body in this world. Yes, that is exactly what he is – a foreign body straight from heaven!

Just who is he, this Jesus?

Don't look for information about Jesus in the first magazine you come across. Don't let yourself be led astray by people who don't even know him. Only the New Testament can give us the exact facts about Jesus. From what he had discovered in the Bible, Martin Luther, the great Reformer, defined Jesus like this: "Jesus is true God, begotten of the Father from all eternity; and true man, born of the Virgin Mary." Both God and man! In Jesus, heaven and earth came together.

Jesus is *"true man"*.

He wept near Lazarus' tomb. I can picture him laughing on another occasion as he said to his disciples, "Look at the birds of the air; they do not sow or reap or store away in barns, and yet your heavenly Father feeds them." Oh yes, I can almost hear Jesus chuckling, "Those cheeky little sparrows! They don't worry about a thing, and yet they eat their fill and become big and fat!" What an extraordinary man Jesus was!

The Bible records that right after preaching a sermon one day, Jesus fed 5 000 men – not counting the women and children. What a crowd! And he didn't have a public address system either! He must have had an extraordinary voice.

Jesus was a fantastic person indeed!

And now we come to one of the most impressive scenes of the New Testament. Pontius Pilate, the Roman governor ruling at the time of Jesus' ministry, had just had Jesus whipped. They had placed a crown of thorns on his head; his face was all bloody; his back was bruised; there were still traces of spit on his face. He was a human wreck. It was in this pitiful condition that Jesus was led outside before the crowd.

Pilate gazed at Jesus a moment. Then, turning to the people, he pointed his finger at Jesus and said in a moving tone, "Here is the man!" What did Pilate mean? "I have seen many of these two-legged creatures, but they were famished wolves, blood-thirsty tigers, cunning foxes, conceited peacocks, monkeys. But Jesus, he is *a man!*"

Jesus was also *"true God*, begotten of the Father from all eternity."* This point alone could be discussed for hours on end.

To illustrate it, let me describe a scene which took place on the Lake of Galilee. A storm took the disciples by surprise in their boat. In a matter of minutes the deck was covered with water. Then the mast broke. "That's nothing to frighten a fisherman!" they probably said to each other with a touch of pride. (There were several experienced fishermen among them.) But fright finally took hold of them all. They even became panic-stricken. And they cried out,

"Where is Jesus? Oh yes, he's sleeping in the cabin!" And away they went scurrying into the cabin – with the water rushing in after them – and started shaking Jesus to wake him up! "Master, we are sinking!" they shouted.

I can picture Jesus going up on deck, right into the heart of the storm. We like to keep Jesus locked up in our cosy church buildings. But here he went right into the heart of the storm! It almost looked as though he would be washed over-board. But he stretched out his hand and with a loud, majestic voice said to the angry sea, "Peace, be still!" Instantly the sea was calm and the clouds broke. And the sun began shining again. Awe-stricken, the disciples threw themselves down on their knees crying, "Who is this man? He is not like any one of us!"

Later they did find the answer to their question: Jesus is God in the flesh. The disciples did not fully understand this until Easter morning when Jesus came out of the tomb alive!

I am not telling you fairy-tales. I would never dare to proclaim these things if I were not absolutely sure that in all truth the living God came down to us in the person of Jesus, the Risen One.

But it is the vision of Jesus hanging on the cross which moves me most. There he was truly "*God and man*". How can I even attempt to describe him? This One who was crowned, but with a crown of thorns – an object of derision! His hands, once so powerful, were pierced by nails. And after much suffering, so touchingly set down by the hymnwriter, he hung his head and died.

> O sacred Head once wounded,
> With grief and pain weigh'd down,
> How scornfully surrounded
> With thorns, Thine only crown!
> How art Thou pale with anguish,
> With sore abuse and scorn!
> How does that visage languish –
> Which once was bright as morn.
>
> O sacred Head, what glory,
> What bliss till now was Thine!
> Yet, though despised and gory,
> I joy to call Thee mine:
> Thy grief and Thy compassion
> Were all for sinners' gain;
> Mine, mine was the transgression,
> But Thine the deadly pain.

Look at him, this Jesus! Stand before him and ask, "Why is he hanging there?" Keep on asking yourself this question until you find an answer.

This is the answer: by his sacrifice on the cross Jesus delivers us from the powers of darkness. He tears us away from the Devil's grip. By identifying yourself with Jesus on the cross through faith in him, you can understand and be certain of the truth that there on the cross you have been delivered from the powers of darkness and have become a child of God, a liberated man. You need no longer let yourself be tormented by the Devil. Because of the cross, you can have full assurance that the Devil's hold is gone; that Jesus is the winner; and that he has liberated you forever and made you a child of God!

Forget about all the senseless theories of our times. You must face the facts: we *can* be liberated from the powers of darkness and we *can* become children of God. God himself fulfilled all the necessary conditions so that this could be achieved. He gave Jesus. And Jesus was crucified and rose again from the dead for us.

I know that people usually feel uneasy when we begin speaking about "God". Why is that?

It's because we are all in the same position as the prodigal son in the Bible story. He had left home. And away from home he had become very unhappy. He was longing to go back to his family, but he was afraid and didn't dare to. Why? Because too many things had come between him and his father. That's how it is with many people. They daren't approach God. They think, "Too many things have come between God and me. We have nothing in common any more." They are absolutely right. In fact, they are under the domination of the powers of darkness and this hinders them from having communion with God.

But if Jesus came to save us from the powers of darkness and to make us children of God, don't you think he can also brush aside the obstacles that are separating us from God? That is exactly what he did when he died on the cross. In him we can find forgiveness of sins. Yes, it is true: the crucified Saviour forgives *all* our sins.

Paul understood this great truth when he wrote: "For he has rescued us from the dominion of darkness and brought us into the kingdom of the Son he loves."

We are by nature the Devil's playthings. But Jesus, the Son of God, delivers us from him by offering forgiveness of sins.

And God grants us the time to accept this salvation.

4. Someone who didn't have time

In the New Testament we read of a man who didn't have time. He was an influential man, a Roman Governor. His name was Felix. He had a wife whose name was Drusilla, and there was a prisoner in his care called Paul.

Having some spare time one day, he said to his wife, "Come, let's go and question this Paul a little." So together they walked to the court-room and settled down in great pomp and ceremony. On their right and on their left stood Roman soldiers on guard. The prisoner was brought in and the Governor indicated that he could speak in his defence. So Paul began one of his powerful discourses. As he went on talking, the tone of his discourse became more and more serious, and the presence of God Almighty could be felt in the room. Paul spoke of the justice which ought to characterize the functions of a judge. This went right to Felix's heart. He couldn't help but think of all the times he had accepted bribes. Then Paul talked of purity. It was Drusilla's turn to almost fall off her chair! "Well," she thought, "here is someone who is obviously behind the times!" Both Felix and Drusilla had to blush when Paul said, "God wants us to be just and self-controlled."

Paul then went on to talk about the judgement of God and of the eternal destruction which can follow it. Frightened, Felix suddenly jumped up from his seat and said to Paul, "Stop! That's enough for now! What you say is interesting and probably has its importance. When I find it convenient, I will send for you again. You may leave now. I don't have any more time to listen to you." And Felix had Paul taken back to his cell.

He never again had time...

I am afraid that if we don't take time to let God speak to us of justice, purity and the coming judgement things will be the same for us as they were for Felix. We feel ill at ease when we find ourselves face to face with the reality of God, don't we? So what do we do? We run to the cinema or turn on the TV. In other words, we choose to stay in a more cheerful atmosphere which does not disturb our peace – and we leave things as they are.

Isn't it terrible to have to say of someone that all his life he let things stand? The Son of God comes and says to us, "Behold, I make all things new! I forgive your past. By my death I redeem you and allow you to enter into the Kingdom of God. I give you the gift of the Holy Spirit so that you may become new men." What do we say then? "Bah!" And we let things stand as they are!

Oh, my friends, I hope this is not the case with you.

5. Someone who has time

As long as Satan rules over us, we will be pressurized and short of time. There are women who are always complaining: "My husband never has time for me." Men, too, can be heard to wail: "My wife never has time for me." And as for young people, many loudly protest that their parents never have time for them.

But Jesus has time – and he has time for YOU!

I discovered this truth in an altogether new way one day. I was experiencing great difficulties. I was so discouraged that my wife couldn't help but remark, "You look wretched! But I do understand, you know!" I blushed and ran into the forest. There, in the silence of the woods, I spoke with my Saviour. "Lord Jesus, let me explain all this sad business to you . . ." And I poured out my heart to him. He took the time to listen to me – and I was able to tell him every little detail. Two hours slipped by as in a moment. Then I opened my New Testament. As I read it I felt that every word was God's answer addressed personally to me.

How happy I was when I went home. I had just made a wonderful new discovery – Jesus had time for *me*!

In the New Testament there is a very touching story. A blind man was sitting by the side of the road, begging. A wooden bowl was in his hand and each time someone passed by, he would stretch out his hand and shout, "Charity, please!" Suddenly he heard in the distance the sound of a large crowd approaching. "What's happening?" he thought. "Is there a procession or is it a military parade?" Finally he yelled at the top of his voice, "Hey, what's up?" And someone close by hollered back, "Jesus has just come to town." A bell rang . . . Jesus! He had already heard about him. He believed that this Jesus was the Son of God! No doubt about that! So he began to shriek, "Jesus, Son of God, have mercy on me! Jesus, Son of God, help me!"

The noise began to get on people's nerves, so they told the blind man, "Oh shut up! We want to hear what Jesus is saying." But the blind man took no notice and continued to call, "Jesus, Son of God, have mercy on me!" He shouted louder than ever. The crowd began to get angry and menacing. "If you don't keep quiet, we're going to beat you up!" An angry mob can be very dangerous, you know. But the blind man wasn't the least bit troubled and went on, "Jesus, Son of God, have mercy on me!"

If I had been there and the blind man had talked to me, I would probably have said this, "Listen to me! There is something you must understand. Jesus is on his way to Calvary! There he intends to die for mankind. The world is on its way to destruction because of its sins, but Jesus wants to resolve the problem of sin by bearing in his own body the transgressions of the whole world. That's how he'll make peace with God for us. Then he is going to rise from the dead and triumph over death. Can't you see that this is a critical moment? It's no time to be bothering him!"

But the blind man continued to shout with all his might, "Jesus, Son of God, have mercy on me!" Then follows one of the most beautiful sentences in the New Testament: "Jesus stopped."

How often I am tempted to pray when I have to go to some important meeting, "Oh, Lord Jesus! Please, I don't want to be bothered by anyone just now."

But Jesus stopped! Then he said, "Call him!" Jesus was on the verge of battling with the world's most serious problem – and yet he had time to deal with a poor blind man. That's how much he values one single person.

And you, too, have great value in Jesus' sight. Do you know of any other person in the world who values you so much? But you don't have time for him! The Devil certainly has succeeded in twisting you around his little finger!

I was told an incredible story. A boat was about to sink. One of the stewards was running along the halls shouting, "Everybody up on deck! The boat is sinking!" He also went down to the kitchens. The chef, oblivious to everything, was busily roasting his chickens. "I've got to get the dinner cooked first," was the answer. He went back to his chickens, and, incidentally, went down with them!

I get the impression that people today are just like that man. "Jesus," they say, "he's not for our generation. He doesn't interest me. In any case, I don't have time!" This is the way the world rushes on its way – without Jesus – straight to hell!

I believe priorities should be respected. If God offers salvation to us, then it is an absolute priority to accept it. Why not bow down right now before the cross of Jesus and as you do claim these words of the hymn as your own?

> I lay my sins on Jesus,
> The spotless Lamb of God;
> He bears them all, and frees us
> From the accursèd load.
> I bring my guilt to Jesus,
> To wash my crimson stains,
> White in His blood most precious,
> Till not a spot remains.

I lay my wants on Jesus;
All fullness dwells in Him;
He heals all my diseases,
He doth my soul redeem.
I lay my griefs on Jesus,
My burdens, and my cares;
He from them all releases,
He all my sorrows shares.

I long to be like Jesus,
Meek, loving, lowly, mild;
I long to be, like Jesus,
The Father's holy child.
I long to be with Jesus,
Amid the heavenly throng,
To sing with saints His praises,
To learn the angels' song.

Beware – Danger ahead!

As I was driving along the motorway at high speed a few hours ago, the theme of my talk kept running through my mind: Beware – Danger ahead!

You know as well as I do that in our generation people don't usually die in their beds at a ripe old age. Nowadays we die in accidents or from a heart-attack. In the old days, people would live to the ripe age of ninety, then they would lie down and die. But today things are different. An airplane crashes; there are many victims. A bus misses a curve in the road and goes crashing down the hill-side; there are at least forty killed. An explosion occurs in a factory; there are more deaths. In the depths of the coal mines there are always men losing their lives. And two world wars have broken out in the space of thirty years. The First World War claimed two million victims. The Second World War claimed five million in Germany alone. We are literally surrounded by danger. When I turn these things over coolly in my mind, I often think, "The chances of my dying peacefully in bed are really slim."

Try to imagine for a moment that you are going to have a fatal accident tonight at ten o'clock. It could happen. Where would you be at eleven o'clock? What would happen to you? Have you ever thought about that?

1. A serious situation

My grandfather, who was an excellent story-teller, used to tell me an interesting tale. A young man went one day to visit his elderly uncle. He said, "Uncle, you can congratulate me. I just passed my 'A' levels." "That's great!" answered his uncle. "Here's some money. Go and buy yourself something you'd like. But now, tell me, what are your plans for the future?" "To start with," answered the young man, "I'm going to continue my studies. I want to go to Law School." "Fine," said his uncle, "and after that?" "Well, after that, I'd like to get some experience at the County Court." "Fine," said his uncle, "and after that?" "After that, I shall be Assessor at the Court of Appeal." "Fine," said his uncle, "and after that?" "Well, after that, Uncle, I'll get married and raise a family." "Fine," said his uncle, "and after that?" "I hope to become influential – a judge at the Court of Appeal, perhaps, or a Public Prosecutor." "That's fine," said his uncle, "and after that?" The young man was beginning to get annoyed, but he answered, "I guess by then old age will be creeping on and I'll have to retire." "Fine," said his uncle, "and after that?" "When I retire, I'll settle down in some beautiful part of the country, build myself a house and grow strawberries!" "Fine," said his uncle, "and after that?" By then, the nephew was fuming. "After that, some day I'll die!" "Is that so?" asked his uncle, "and what then?" The young man wasn't laughing any more. He was panic-stricken. The old uncle insisted, "And after that?" "Uncle, I've never really thought about it." "What," exclaimed the old man, "you've just passed your 'A' levels and yet you're not intelligent enough to see further than the tip of your nose? Shouldn't a boy to whom God has given a sound mind have a little more foresight than that? *What will happen after that?*" The young man replied hastily, "But, Uncle, nobody knows what happens after death!" "You're wrong, my lad," said the old man. "There's one person who knows exactly what happens after death. It is Jesus. And Jesus said: 'Wide is the gate and broad is the road that leads to destruction, and many enter through it. But small is the gate and narrow the road that leads to life.' After death comes the judgement of God. People are either lost or they are saved."

Making plans for your life up to the grave is not enough. You have to plan for what happens beyond the grave as well.

When I was in youth work, I often said to my young friends, "If I had a pair of shoes that needed mending, I wouldn't go to a service station. Mechanics are nice people, but they don't know anything about repairing shoes. I would take my shoes to the shoe-repairer. If, on the other hand, I had car trouble, I wouldn't get if fixed by a shoe-repairer but by a car mechanic. If I wanted to buy some buns, I wouldn't go to the butcher or to the grocer. They are all very nice people, but they don't know anything about baking buns. If I had a longing for buns, I would go to the baker's. If my water-pipe was leaking, then I'd go and get the plumber. In other words, I'd look up someone in the right trade.

"But when it comes to finding out what happens after death, we listen to every Tom, Dick and Harry; or we rely on our own vague mixed-up ideas. Shouldn't we for this matter, more than for any other, ask a specialist? Where can we find a specialist? There is only one. He is the Son of God who came from heaven and who went to the realm of the dead. He died on the cross, but he came back to life. He knows all the facts about the hereafter. And he tells us: 'You can go to hell or you can go to heaven.'

"Even if twenty-five professors were to prove to me by logic that there is nothing after death, I would say to them, 'I'm sorry, but in spite of your university degrees, you are not experts on the subject; for the simple reason that you have never been to the other world. But I know someone who has been there: Jesus. And *he* has a totally different opinion from yours.'"

People today act as though death were final. They also seem to think that we will automatically go to heaven if we have been baptized and buried by a priest. If only I could convince you that you are in great danger! Hell will be crowded with people who were baptized and buried by the clergy. Sooner or later each one of us must appear before the tribunal of God.

I have to admit that it was the thought of the coming judgement that compelled me to become a Christian. During the First World War, I was a young officer in the German army. Our regiment had suffered heavy losses. I was just like any other officer, neither better nor worse. If someone had told me then, "You'll be a preacher one day", I would have burst out laughing. At the time I was living far away from God. One day my father asked me, "Don't you believe in God?" "I'm not silly enough to deny the existence of God," I answered. "You have to have a good dose of stupidity to be an atheist. But," I added, "so far I haven't met God personally, so he simply doesn't interest me."

A short time after this conversation with my father – it was during the German offensive in France – I was sitting beside a friend of mine, a young lieutenant like myself, in a trench near Verdun. We were waiting for orders to attack. To kill time, we started telling some dirty stories. (Everyone who has been in the army will know exactly what I mean.) I had just finished telling one of my barrack-room jokes when, to my amazement, I realized that my buddy hadn't laughed. "Kutscher," I said, "hey, Kutscher, didn't you find that one funny?" Just then he fell heavily on his side. He was dead! A tiny piece of shrapnel had hit him and lodged deeply in his heart. And there was I, a young boy in my eighteenth year, standing over the dead body of my friend.

It didn't really affect me at first. Jokingly I said, "Look here, old boy, what's the big idea of beating it like this before I've even finished telling my joke?" But a second later I was wondering: "Where is he now?" I can still see myself in that trench at the instant this truth dawned on me like a blinding light, more brilliant than the flash of a nuclear explosion: "He is standing before the holy God."

Then another idea seized me· "If I'd been sitting where he was, it would have been me who was hit – and right now I would be standing before Almighty God."

Not standing before just any old God, but before the God who has revealed his will and given laws which I had broken, every one! I knew then that I had broken all of God's laws and that if I were shot I would immediately appear in the presence of God. And there wasn't the shadow of a doubt in my mind that I was bound for hell.

The arrival of our boys with the horses put a stop to my meditations. "Quick march!" came the order. I mounted. But before leaving my dead friend, I did a thing I hadn't done in years: *I prayed.* "Oh God," I cried, "please don't let me die on the battle-field before I'm sure that I won't go to hell!"

A little later I went to see the chaplain. I asked him, "Chaplain, what must I do so that I don't go to hell?" His answer was: "Lieutenant, what counts right now is to win, to win, to win!" I exclaimed, "You don't even know yourself!"

Isn't it staggering to think that thousands of young men were going to die within the next few weeks without anyone being able to tell them how to be saved? And yet we lived in a supposedly Christian country!

I probably would have become very desperate if one day a New Testament hadn't come into my possession. I can still see the place where I was staying that day: it was at a farm in France behind the front. "A New Testament!" I thought. "If I read it, I could probably find out what to do not to be damned." But as the New Testament was not familiar to me, I started reading it at random: a little here, a little there. Then my eyes fell on this verse: "Christ Jesus came into the world to save sinners." It struck me like lightning. *A sinner.* That's exactly what I was! No one had to convince me of that. *I was a sinner!* This was very clear to me. And I wanted badly to be "saved". But I didn't understand exactly what this meant. I had at least understood that to be "saved" meant getting out of the state I was in and making peace with God. "Christ Jesus came into the world to save sinners." If Jesus could really do that, then I had to find him at all costs!

This went on for weeks. I looked for someone who could help me find Jesus; but I found no one.

Then I did something I wish all of you would do. Although a new offensive was on, I went off by myself one day and hid in an old French farm-house. It was largely in ruins and had been evacuated. One room, however, was still undamaged. The key was in the door. So I went in and locked the door from the inside. Then I fell on my knees and prayed: "Lord Jesus! In the Bible it is written that you were sent by God 'to save sinners'. I am one of those sinners. I can't make you any promises for the future, because I have such a bad character. But I don't want to go to hell if I get shot. That's why, Lord Jesus, I want to commit my whole life to you. Do what you want with me!"

There was no magic click. Nothing special happened. But when I came out of that room, I had found a master, a master to whom I have belonged ever since.

As the days went by, I began to understand that the world is living under a great threat. People are in danger of death. Men and women go through life without ever seeking forgiveness for their sins. What about your sins? Are you certain that they have been forgiven? No? Then how can you ever hope to stand when you come to trial in God's tribunal?

People go through life without ever knowing the peace of God. People go through life without ever putting their lives straight with God. They wear a thin varnish of Christianity, but underneath is a miserable heart without peace, because it has never been changed a scrap.

God doesn't want anyone to go to hell. The Bible says: "God wants all men to be saved and to come to the knowledge of the truth." That is why he sent his Son. But in order to be saved we have to take a step towards Jesus. We have to *belong* to him.

Beware – Danger ahead! We are heading towards the judgement of God.

There used to be a very nice boy in my youth group. For a time he came to our Bible study regularly. This was under Hitler's regime. And then one day the authorities forced him to follow a Nazi indoctrination course. He broke with the youth group then. I lost touch with him for a long time; then suddenly one day I bumped into him. "Hello there, Gunther!" I said. "Heil Hitler," was the reply. "Gunther," I said, "how are you? We haven't seen you for a long time!" He straightened up and answered, "My motto is: 'Do your duty, come what may!' And if sometimes I do happen to fall short of my duty, and if there really is a God, then I'll be honest enough to admit my faults to him. But I don't need a scape-goat, like Jesus, to die in my stead."

In my mind's eye I can see the millions of men and women who think like that. They boast, "My motto is: 'Do your duty, come what may', and as for the rest, I'll manage to explain things to God!" Not for anything would I want to come before God's judgement with only the words "I have done my duty". I know that I am heading for a sure condemnation if I stand on that ground. You can count on this: the day will come when every one of us must give account of himself to God.

The great sculptor Ernst Barlach also wrote a play entitled, *Boll the Drunkard*. The leading character, Boll, was a landowner. He was always a bit tipsy. One day, after a good meal and a good drink, he walked to the village square at an hour when the sun was at its highest. And there he suddenly found himself standing in front of the village church. On the church doors were sculptures representing four cherubim blowing their trumpets. As Boll looked at them, he had the curious impression that they had suddenly come to life and were announcing the Last Judgement: "The hour has come for all humans to appear before the tribunal of God." Barlach wrote these words: "You dead, come out of your graves! Don't try to invoke the decomposition of your bodies as an excuse! No! Come out!" Boll the drunkard had begun to understand. "I can't escape God. I'll have to appear before him in all my misery some day."

Deep inside we all know that we can't get very far with our self-righteousness. God's judgement is close at hand. On that day all our good works will melt like snow under the rays of the sun.

I know that people don't want to hear this sort of thing nowadays. When I declare that if we don't turn to Jesus we will go to hell, people just smile and say, "What? To hell? That's a medieval idea. Hell doesn't even exist!"

That kind of statement always reminds me of an experience I had during the last war. I had to make a call, so I started out; but on the way I was surprised by an air-raid. I ran into the nearest air-raid shelter and stayed there until the alert was over. Then I continued on my way until I finally got to the district where I had to make my call. None of the homes were damaged. And yet I had the impression that the area was totally abandoned. There wasn't a cat in sight! "You must be dreaming," I thought. "It isn't possible! The houses are undamaged and yet everyone has gone." A few minutes later I happened to meet the head of the area's civil defence. So I asked him, "Why has everyone gone?" By way of explanation, he took me by the arm and led me inside one of the houses. He took me up to one of the windows which looked out on the back. From there I could see that the houses encircled a lawn. And right in the middle of the lawn was a huge bomb, about the size of a steam locomotive's boiler! "It hasn't blown up yet?" I asked. "No," he answered, "it's a delayed-action bomb." These were the most treacherous bombs. They did not explode when they hit the ground, but five or even as many as twenty hours later. Usually these bombs would explode when the people had come out of the shelters. "Everybody here has run away," explained the man. "Can you hear it ticking?" We could easily detect the noise of the detonator's timer. The bomb could explode at any moment! "Come," said the civil defence man, "we had better not stay here any longer." We went back a few steps where we would at least be sheltered if the bomb exploded. Just then I saw a very unusual sight. A flock of sparrows flew down and landed softly on the bomb! One of them flew to the head of the bomb and sat right on the detonator. I shouted, "Look out, you sparrows, you are flirting with death!" But it seemed as though the whole flock was chirping in reply to my warning, "Ha, ha, we know what it's all about! Who in our day still believes in bombs? There isn't the slightest danger!"

People today show just as much stupidity when they laugh at the peril that is threatening them. God has already spoken very seriously to all nations by his Word and by the judgements which have fallen upon them.

The Son of God came, he was crucified and rose again from the dead. Everyone, then, should understand that God is real and that he is holy. But when a man stands up and says to people, "Beware – Danger ahead! Think about saving your souls," they just laugh and say, "Ha, ha, who believes in that nonsense nowadays?"

Even God makes some ironical remarks at times. The Bible refers only once to atheism, in this single sentence: "*The fool* has said in his heart, There is no God!" With the Bible's outlook on life, what else could be said?

2. To the rescue

God struck the world once before with a terrible judgement. Only one man and his family were saved that time. His name was Noah. God gave him instructions to build an ark before the disaster began. Just before the terrible cataclysm broke out, he ordered Noah to board the ark with his entire family. And when every member of the family was inside, God himself shut the door behind them.

The world is going on its way to meet God's just judgement. But there is an ark to rescue us: it is the grace which is offered to us in Jesus Christ. He came from God's world into our world of misery. He died for us on the cross. If God allowed his Son to die such a horrible death, the salvation which he acquired for us through his death must be great enough to save even the worst of sinners. Jesus rose from the dead and he calls us to him by the Holy Spirit. *Jesus is the ark of salvation.*

As God said of old to Noah, "Enter into the ark, you and your house!" he is now urging you by my words to get under the shelter of the grace of Jesus Christ. Take that step towards making peace with God. Let go of everything that is holding you back. Say to your Saviour, "A very great sinner is coming to you." Lay down your sins at the foot of the cross. Believe that Jesus' blood was shed for you personally and tell him, "Lord, I put my whole life into your hands." That is what it means to enter into the ark.

Beware – Danger ahead!

So many of us are heading towards God's judgement without salvation, without protection. Yet God's grace is so great we can take hold of it at any time. *Believing* means to step out of the sphere of God's judgement into the sphere of the grace of Jesus Christ. Taking this step is not child's play. But it saves us from danger, from the danger of death.

Albert Hoffmann, the well-known pioneer of missionary work in New Guinea, told me a story that I have never forgotten. I had said to him, "Brother Hoffmann, I find it a real struggle to live the Christian life. It's no joke, even for a pastor, to belong to Jesus Christ in a world like ours."

"I'd like to tell you about an experience I had," he said. "It was our custom in New Guinea to give some instruction in the Christian faith to the Papous who wanted to become Christians. This helped them to get to know Jesus better. Then on a chosen Sunday they would be baptized. It was always an occasion for a great feast. Many pagans attended each time. A great bonfire would be lit. The candidates for baptism would approach, carrying in their arms all their paraphernalia for fetish worship: objects of magic, statuettes, and amulets. When they came up to the bonfire they would throw all these relics of their former life into the flames.

"One evening, I watched a young native woman approaching the fire, her arms burdened with statuettes and amulets. But when the decisive moment came for her to throw them away, she couldn't do it. She must have thought, 'All this is part and parcel of my ancestors' way of life. My entire past is rooted in them. I can't possibly deny my heritage.' She took a step back. But at the same time another idea must have taken hold of her: 'In that case, I can't belong to Jesus.' So she took three steps forward, but a second later, feeling absolutely incapable of being separated from these objects, she went back three steps again. I went up to her," said the missionary, "and I said to her, 'It's too difficult for you! Perhaps you should think the matter over a little longer. You can be baptized at the next baptismal service.' The woman thought a moment, then moving forward quickly, she threw her fetishes into the fire and fainted."

I shall never forget what this missionary said, his face all wrinkled as though sculptured in wood, as he finished his tale, "I am sure that only those who have experienced an authentic conversion can understand this woman's struggle."

My friends, there is just one step between you and the ark. Escape from the danger of death and judgement by throwing yourself into Jesus' arms. This step is not an easy one to take. It demands a total rupture with the past. Nothing less!

Have I been clear enough?

I am always upset to see how many people continue on their way to everlasting damnation in spite of the warnings they have received. God does not want this. He wants you to be saved. And that is why he sent his Son to pay the penalty for your sins. All you have to do now is to recognize your guilt and to accept by faith the work of salvation that Jesus has accomplished for you.

I was summoned many times by the Gestapo under the Third Reich. On one occasion, they made me wait in a room where there was nothing but rows of pigeon-holes filled with all kinds of records. A tab was sticking out of each file and on each tab there was a name, such as: "Karl Meier" or "Friedrich Schultze". During that unending wait, surrounded by all those records, I thanked God that I wouldn't have to spend my whole life in their company. But as I was getting bored I started to read the names on the tabs. "Karl Meier" on one; "Friedrich Schultze" on another. Suddenly I read: "Wilhelm Busch". So I had a record of my own! As if by magic, the files didn't seem the least boring any more. My personal record was there on one of those shelves! Burning with curiosity, I was tempted to take it down and have a look at what those people had written about me. But I didn't dare take such a risk. Still, I literally trembled at the thought: "My record is up there!"

There was a period in my life when nothing bored me more than Christianity. I was a lot more interested in having my beer-mug filled up. Then one day, for the first time, I saw the cross of Jesus for what it really was: it had something to do with my record. It had something to do with my guilt and my salvation. Since that day the cross of Jesus is of the greatest interest to me.

Jesus is indeed the great Rescuer.

3. From death to life

Let's look at this from another angle. When this subject was trotting through my mind (Beware! You are in mortal danger! Stop! Turn around and go back! Search for your Saviour!), this thought suddenly came to me: only a person who is alive can be in danger of death.

Do you see what I am trying to get at?

You are in danger of never really finding life. You are in danger of going through life as a dead man and finally of being rejected as a dead man. The danger facing you is that you may totally miss out on life. The Bible states very clearly: "He who has the Son has life; he who does not have the Son of God does not have life."

Not too long ago I met a single lady from Berlin who teaches languages. "Excuse me, Miss," I said to her, "maybe a pastor has the right to be rude now and then! Tell me, how old are you?" As a rule, asking a lady her age is not the thing to do; but an old pastor can take this liberty occasionally. Without hesitation she answered, "Eight years old ... !" "Wait a minute," I said, surprised, "eight years old? You teach three languages, and yet you are only eight years old?" She started to laugh, then explained, "Eight years ago I came to know Jesus Christ." I was amazed. "That's a funny way to put it!" I said. She quoted the verse: "He who has the Son has life; he who does not have the Son of God does not have life." She went on, "In the past, I didn't have a Saviour; I wasn't really living. I was satisfied with making a lot of money and having a good time, but that was not living!"

Isn't that a courageous declaration? Truly, the person who has not surrendered his life to Jesus by a deliberate act of the will cannot say he is living. Without Jesus, we do not even know what life is all about. Only a person who has the Son has life.

Many years ago, a young man came to see me. "What brings you here?" I asked. "I really don't know myself!" he replied. "Only I have the feeling that the life I'm leading is no life at all." Astonished, I asked, "What? You have a good job as a locksmith and you are making good money." "But it's no life," he answered back. "No, it's no life at all. On Monday, it's the locksmith's; Tuesday, it's the locksmith's; Wednesday, it's the locksmith's; Thursday, it's the locksmith's; Friday, it's the locksmith's; Saturday, it's football; and Sunday, it's the cinema and girls. It really is no life at all!" "My friend," I said, "you're absolutely right. If you have understood that, you've already come a long way. It *is* no life! Let me tell you, my friend, what it means to live. In my own life, a complete change came about when Jesus made himself known to me. He became my Saviour; he reconciled me to God. When I understood this, I gave my heart to him. And ever since I have had life."

The young man finally found life too. I saw him again recently in Freiburg. "Well," I said, "how are things now? Are you really living at last?" His face shining with joy, he answered, "Yes, now I am really living!" As a matter of fact, he is a very outgoing Christian. He leads a young people's group and shows other people the way to the one in whom he himself found life – Jesus Christ.

One of my friends owns a business. He was invited recently to the home of a leading industrialist. The man had a beautiful home situated in a magnificent park. There were at least a hundred guests invited. Pressed by the crowd, my friend found himself at one point next to his host, so he said, "Aren't you lucky! You live like a king: you have a beautiful estate, a prosperous factory, a lovely wife and charming children." The man answered, "Yes, that is true, I am very lucky." Then suddenly becoming very serious, he said, "But all the same, don't ask me how things are in here," and with that he pointed to his heart.

When I walk down the street, I often think, "If people were really sincere, they would all stop and shout, 'Don't ask me how things are in here, in my heart!'" They have no peace. Their consciences are accusing them. They feel guilty.

And there is only one person who can heal us. Remember, God sees our misery. We cannot of ourselves go to him. But in his love he came to us in the person of Jesus Christ. That is the amazing message I have to announce to you. "God so loved the world . . ." I could not have loved the world. I would have beaten everybody with a club; this old world so full of defilement, wickedness and stupidity. Yet God loved it. I am dumb-founded! "God so loved the world that he gave his one and only Son, that whoever believes in him shall not perish but have eternal life."

Tell me, could God do anything more than that – deliver up his own Son to death – so that we could have life?

One more story. One evening after a church service, a young man went up to the great English preacher, Charles Haddon Spurgeon, and said, "Pastor, you are right. I, too, need to meet the man of Calvary and to become a child of God. I'll get converted some day." "Some day?" Spurgeon asked. "Yes, but later." "Later? Why not today?" An embarrassed look crossed the young man's face, but he replied, "I certainly do want to be saved and that's why I intend to get converted at some time, but before that I want to enjoy life a little." Spurgeon burst out laughing, then said,

"Young man, you don't have much ambition in life. I wouldn't be satisfied simply with enjoying life *a little*. I want a whole lot more out of life. I want life *in abundance*. In the Bible it says (he showed him the passage): 'Jesus said, I came that they may have life, and may have it abundantly.'"

God allowed Jesus to die on the cross for poor, lost sinners like you and me, so that here and now we might have life. When I wake up in the morning, I can sing for joy because I am a child of God and because I have found life in him. Yes, Jesus came to give us life down here on earth; he came to preserve us from God's judgement and to grant us eternal life. When we have accepted these things, we can walk along life's way with joy.

Just one last illustration. It is a November evening. Wet snow is falling. Two men are walking along a road. The first one has no raincoat, but his jacket collar is turned up. He doesn't seem to care about being soaked through. It matters little to him where he goes. He could go here, he could go there – it's of no importance – he is homeless. This is the way most people trudge through life. They have no goal in life.

What about you? Where are you going?

The German atheist and philosopher Nietzsche wrote these words in one of his poems: "Woe to the man who has no home!" Do you have an eternal home?

Now for the second man walking along the road. He has to face the same storm, the same mud, the same rain, the same snow. But he is whistling a tune and his step is lively. Why? Because shining in the distance he sees the lights of his home. There he will find warmth. There he will laugh at the hardships of the road. This, my friends, is the way people who have committed their lives to Jesus Christ and have found life in him go through the world.

God said to Noah: "Go into the ark." I urge you to look for some quiet spot. Jesus will be there. Have a little talk with him and tell him everything that is on your mind. Someone asked me once, "May I have a talk with you, please?" But I answered, "What's the use? It's not with me, but directly with Jesus that people should be talking!"

And that is exactly what you, too, should do!

What should you do?

In one of the many letters sent to me, I was asked the following question: "Do you proclaim your own views in your sermons or simply the doctrines of your church?" In my reply I wrote: "I preach the message of the Bible." And for my readers I add: You will be quickly frustrated if you only listen to the opinions of Pastor Busch. They will not be much use to you. What you need is to listen to the voice of Jesus, the voice of the Good Shepherd. My role is to help others, with the feeble means I have, to hear the voice of the Shepherd of our souls.

What should you do?

1. Put an end to your unbelief

Over many years of ministry in large cities, I have heard all sorts of arguments against the Bible's message. I have seen so much unbelief that I must urge you at the outset – because the salvation of your soul is at stake – to put an end to your attitude of unbelief.

For part of the last war, besides my work among young people, I was in charge of the chaplaincy in a big hospital. One day as I was about to knock on the door of a private patient's room, I saw a young nurse rushing towards me from the other end of the hall. All out of breath, she said, "Please, Mr. Busch, don't go into that room." "Why not?" I asked. "The man in that room," she explained, "totally refuses any pastoral calls. If you go in, he'll throw you out!" She pointed to the inscription on the door and I recognized the name of a well-known businessman. "Nurse," I answered, "don't worry. I've got nerves of iron." So I knocked on the door. "Come in!" said a loud masculine voice. I entered. A grey-haired old man was lying on the bed. "Hello!" I said. "My name is Busch, Pastor Busch." "Ah," he said, "I've heard a lot about you. You may come in for a short visit." "That's very kind of you," I exlaimed overjoyed. Quickly he added, "But don't start pestering me with your Christianity!" Laughingly I replied, "Bad luck! that's exactly what I came to talk to you about!" "No way!" he replied emphatically waving me away with his hand. "I've finished with religion. When I was a child, my parents stuffed me with psalms and when I couldn't recite them properly, I got a smack. I threw all that overboard when I grew up. I've formed my own philosophy of life. It's thinkers like Darwin, Häckel and Nietzsche who have inspired me."

At that I flared up. Unfortunately I lose my temper easily. "Listen to me, my friend," I said. "When a sixteen-year-old adolescent tells me that Nietzsche is his 'guru', I just chuckle to myself and think, 'Well, you're going through a period of transition. You'll end up discovering that modern philosophers themselves no longer believe in those who were their models.' But when an old man like yourself who already has one foot in the grave says things like that, it's very serious. You are critically ill. Do you think you will be able to talk such rubbish when you appear in the presence of God? I ask you!"

He looked at me, stunned. Obviously he was not used to being spoken to like that. "Careful," I said to myself, "don't get worked up! This is a hospital and we don't have the right to explode." Then a deep compassion for this poor man took hold of me. I changed my tone and, in spite of his initial refusal, began to explain how Jesus wanted to be his Shepherd too. The sick man sighed deeply and said, "Yes, it would be very nice. But what should I do with my philosophy of life? Do I have to throw overboard everything I have believed up until now?" "That's right, Sir," I said, my heart filled with joy. "Throw away everything that is useless to you in the light of eternity. Do it right now. Don't wait for tomorrow. You can neither live nor die in peace with unbelief like yours. When you have let everything go, throw yourself into the open arms of the Son of God who died to redeem you. He wants to become your Saviour too."

Just then the nurse came into the room and was very surprised to find us talking together like old friends. She motioned with her hand and I understood it was time to leave. I held the old man's hand for a long time, then left the room in silence. I shall never know whether he followed my advice. That night he died.

I was dismayed to see that day how even cultivated people allow themselves to be led by the nose by such men as Darwin, Häckel and Nietzsche. Their unbelief based on erroneous reasoning puts them in danger of missing out on eternal salvation. That is why first and foremost I urge you to throw away all the superficial thinking on which you base your unbelief. Get rid of it! Your unbelief is not worth a penny. The Bible says: "There is one God and one mediator between God and men, the man Christ Jesus."

I was sitting one day opposite a man whom I had nick-named "the striped man" because of the striped-design on his pullover. He was a great strapping man, built like a battle-ship. His wife had perished in an air-raid and his two sons had been killed on the front. Poor fellow! I had come that day to pay him a call. But no sooner had I sat down than he began railing at me. "Pastor Busch, shut up right away about your religion! I've seen plenty in my life-time and now I don't believe a thing."

I laughed and said, "That's impossible. You take the train sometimes, don't you?" "Yes." "I suppose," I continued, "that each time you do, you go and find the driver and ask him to show you his diploma?" "Of course not!" was the answer. "The railways can be trusted to employ drivers who..." "What," I interrupted, "do you mean to say that you get on a train without making sure beforehand that the driver has the qualifications to drive it? Do you put your life into his hands, without the least guarantee? Well, well! Did you know that putting your life into someone's hands is a form of believing? So you'd better not say any more that you don't believe in anything. You should say, 'I don't believe in anything – except in the railways!'" "Ah...!"

I went on questioning him. "Do you ever go to the chemist's?" "Yes," he replied, "I have quite a few headaches and I have to go to the pharmacist for some pills." "You probably know," I said, "that certain pharmacists have given poison to their customers by mistake. So I suppose you have the pills analysed before taking them?" He answered, "No, Pastor Busch. A certified pharmacist knows his profession. He wouldn't play a trick like that on me." "What?" I said astonished. "You take your pills without having them checked first? You entrust your life to a pharmacist? You take his pills without the slightest hint of suspicion? Well, I would call that faith! My friend, stop saying that you don't believe in anything; but rather say, 'I don't believe in anything – except in the railways and the pharmacist.'"

I continued to add to the examples. Finally I shared my own experience with him. "One day I met Jesus, the one God sent to us. Yes, Jesus, who rose from the dead and who still bears the nail prints on his hands. Those marks prove in an eloquent way that his love for me was so great that he even gave his life for me. No one in the world ever did as much for me as Jesus! No one is more worthy of my confidence than he is. Do you think Jesus ever told a lie, even one single time?" "No," was the reply. "I can't say as much for anybody else. But that day, many years ago, I said to myself, 'You can trust your life to Jesus. He is worthy of your confidence.' And that is what I did!"

"Is it as simple as that?" the man asked. "Yes," I said, "it's as simple as that. You trust all kinds of people around you – except Jesus. And he is the only one who is totally trustworthy. So get rid of the false reasoning your unbelief is built on. Then surrender your life to the Lord Jesus."

At a meeting once, I challenged a crowd of young people in this way: "I will give a one million mark reward to anyone who can bring me a single man or woman who regrets having let Jesus Christ into his or her life!" Obviously I didn't have such a large sum of money. But I could make the offer without hesitation – for no such person can be found. I have known, though, many people who regretted *not* having received Christ.

So I urge you once again to get rid of your unbelief. Trust Jesus who has done so much for you. This is a personal matter between you and him. Steal away into a quiet corner and say to him, "Lord Jesus, from now on I want to belong to you!"

2. Your good opinion about yourself must go!

The Bible says: "Christ Jesus came into the world to save sinners – of whom I am the worst." Many people reading this verse get annoyed and declare: "*I'm* no sinner. *I* haven't committed any crime." It is to these people that I will now direct my remarks.

What you have just claimed is totally and absolutely wrong. Can you imagine yourself on the Judgement Day saying to God's face, "*I'm* not a sinner. I have observed all your commandments." Would you dare say this to God?

Come on now! You have to give up that good opinion you have of yourself. Stop thinking – or pretending – that your life is in order. Nothing is in order, absolutely nothing!

I had a talk many years ago with a young man of twenty. I shall never forget him. Bumping into him one day, I said, "My dear Heinz, I haven't seen you for quite a while at our Bible studies or young people's meetings." "That's true," he replied. "Pastor Busch, I've been thinking it over. You are always talking about Jesus dying for sinners. As far as I'm concerned, I feel no need for a scapegoat to bear my sins. If I have done something wrong and if God does exist, then I shall answer him for myself. The idea of a Saviour dying in my place seems so ridiculous." "All right!" I answered. "When you are summoned before the holy God, you intend to appeal to justice. This is your right. You have the liberty to reject Jesus and to say, 'I appeal to justice.' But you must realize one thing: in England, people are judged by English law; in

Germany, they are judged by German law; and before God, we shall be judged by divine law. I hope you have never broken a single one of those laws – otherwise there's no hope for you. Goodbye!" "Wait a minute!" the young man exclaimed. "God is not that finicky!"

"Ha! What do you think the holy God is like?" I asked. "Let's suppose for a moment that after living honestly for fifty years, one day I commit a petty theft which takes three minutes at the most. The thing is eventually discovered and my case is brought to trial. During the hearing, I say to the judge, 'Your honour, don't be so strict. Three minutes of theft are greatly outweighed by half a century of honesty. Who could be so scrupulous as to penalize me for so little?' Do you know what would happen? The judge would reply, 'Just a minute! What concerns me right now are not your fifty years of honesty, but the three minutes it took to commit that theft. The law is judging you for that particular offence.' If an earthly judge would react in this way, why shouldn't God go just as far?"

Why not plead guilty before God? Why not recognize your need for pardon? Why not admit that you are a sinner? Get rid of your self-righteous attitude and look for the Saviour. He died for your sins and paid your debt. Receive him as your Saviour, confess your sins to him and say, "I throw myself at your feet with all my imperfections. Have mercy upon me and purify me by your blood."

3. Take the decisive step

Another illustration will help you to understand what I am trying to convey.

It was at the beginning of the Hitler regime. I had to contact a top Nazi official. I did so with fear and trembling, because the regime was not well disposed towards pastors. To my astonishment, instead of throwing me out the door, the official listened to me attentively. I said to him at the end of the interview, "I have seldom been treated with so much benevolence by any of your colleagues. I would like to thank you. And as you have been so kind to me, may I leave with you, as a gift, the message which has been entrusted to me: 'For God so loved the world that he gave his one and only Son, that whoever believes in him shall not perish but have eternal life.'"

He looked at me for a moment, then replied, "You need say no more. My parents are believers and they taught me those things from the cradle. But . . ." He put a large sheet of white paper on the table, took a pencil and drew a line across it. Then he continued,

"You see, Pastor, I know all about it. But in order to gain salvation, I would have to cross a line like the one I just traced on the paper. I am very near – and with his finger he pointed to a spot just below the line – but the decisive step over the line has yet to be taken." Then he added, a little embarrassed, "My social position, however, hinders me from taking that step."

I left him, sad at heart. This man died a long time ago. But his social position was of no help to him when he stepped into eternity. He had understood, nonetheless, that he had to take a decisive step, that he had to cross over the line, in order to enter into the Kingdom of God.

Do you have the courage to do this? It is well worth it. Jesus is waiting for you, his arms are wide open. Take the decisive step; cross over the line and you will find yourself in Jesus' arms!

4. Stop all deliberate wrong-doing

I know a man who has a mistress. One day I cornered him and said, "You are living in adultery. You are making your wife unhappy. You are on your way to hell." He answered, "What you say is absurd. Let me explain my situation to you. My wife doesn't understand me . . . " Then he told me a long story. Yet, deep down he knew only too well that his behaviour was wrong.

We often hear people who have fallen out with someone say, "He (she) started it all." Whatever the quarrel may be about, it is always the other person's fault. You never start the trouble, do you? No! The other person is always to blame!

Let me remind you that in God's sight a quarrel is just as serious as a murder. So why not settle that argument? "How should I go about it?" you may ask. Let me tell you how: stop all deliberate wrong-doing right now.

If only you would pause for just a moment and ask yourself this question: "What's wrong in my life? What needs to be put right?" Actually you know only too well what is wrong! Do you think Jesus will forgive you if you continue to sin deliberately? The Bible says: "Right about turn!" The prodigal son, whose story is told in the Bible, turned his back on his former life.

You too can come to Jesus just as you are: unbelieving and weighed down with your sins. But you must go a step further and do away with everything which is dragging you down to your ruin and which you consciously know to be evil.

In the many letters I receive daily, people sometimes get angry and write: "You are too severe in what you say. Such-and-such a thing is not sin." Then they list things I have never talked about! On such occasions, I become particularly aware how rebellious we are against having Jesus Christ rule in our lives. You will never be able to become a Christian or to live as a Christian if you do not have the courage to surrender your life to Jesus Christ and to give up once and for all those things in your life which must disappear.

5. Talk to God

Do you know how to pray? Perhaps you are able to recite some kind of formula, but do you really know how to pray? Some people's ideas about prayer are so strange that they could make my hair stand on end... if I had any left!

The other day I was visiting a family. The mother said, "We're good Christians too. Claire, come here." When her little four-year-old had come up to her, she continued. "Show the pastor how nicely you already know how to pray." The child began to recite a prayer. I interrupted her immediately. "Stop, sweetheart. You musn't show me how you can pray. Please don't!"

Real prayer is something totally different. Prayer is talking to the living God to whom we draw near through Jesus Christ. Prayer is pouring out our hearts to him. Have you ever prayed like that?

An Anglican bishop by the name of Robinson wrote a controversial book called *Honest to God*. In it he writes, among other things, that modern man no longer knows how to pray. I agree with him on this point. The fault is not with prayer, but with modern man. Robinson's theory is that the Christian faith should be completely revised because people today no longer know how to pray. It seems to me rather that people need to be taught how to pray again.

Why not have a try at praying? Even if you can only say: "Lord, let yourself be found!" Or: "Lord, please save me too!" Or: "Lord, help me find the true faith!" Or: "Lord, forgive me my sins!" Take the plunge! Your prayers at first may not be as nice as those pastors and priests recite with prayer-book in hand and glasses perched on the end of the nose! But it isn't necessary to pray nice prayers. What counts is that you learn to speak to the living God with an open and honest heart. Simply begin praying and the rest will follow naturally.

Faith is a living relationship between God and man. Dialogue is indispensable to that relationship. I talk to God; he talks to me.

6. Read the Bible

How does God speak to people? He speaks to them through the Bible. So it is absolutely essential that you begin to read it. You may be thinking that hardly anybody reads the Bible any more. This, unfortunately, is only too true.

Often, during my calls, people say to me, "Oh, Pastor, we have an old Bible dating from 1722. It's a family heirloom handed down from our great-grandmother." Then they show me a huge museum-piece which obviously nobody ever reads. I have lots of respect for old Bibles, but you go and buy yourself a nice little New Testament! Some of them are smaller than my hand. Certain editions are very attractive. Get yourself one of those modern New Testaments. And then put aside a moment of each day to read it. Simply listen to what Jesus is saying to you through its pages.

Undoubtedly you will come across some passages that you will not understand. Just go on reading. This is how I explain things to my young people: A Brazilian farmer told me that when he settled in Brazil he was given some land. Once on the site, he discovered it was just a patch of jungle. So he started to clear the trees, dig up the rocks, and uproot the stumps. The day came when he was ready to hitch a pair of oxen to a plough and begin ploughing. He had scarcely taken three steps when the ploughshare got blocked by a rock. So what did he do? Run home to get some dynamite to blow up the rock, plough and oxen? Of course not! He unhooked the ploughshare from the plough, passed around the obstacle, then went on ploughing. When he had finished, the result was not quite up to the mark. He sowed the land all the same and a few months later gathered in a small harvest. The next year it was a little better. He was able to dig up more rocks and uproot more stumps, which made it much easier for the plough to get through. The third year, the situation had greatly improved.

That is how you should read the Bible. The main thing is *to begin* reading. If there is something you do not understand, go around the difficulty and keep on reading.

In the very first chapter of the New Testament, after a long list of names which you will probably find dry and boring, you will suddenly come to this verse: "You are to give him the name Jesus, because he will save his people from their sins." You will probably respond to this verse by saying: "I can understand that! That's just for me!" Let God speak to you through the Bible in this way. Take the time to read it daily. And offer this prayer to God: "Lord, enlighten me! Give me intelligence to understand your Word."

One thing more: allow no one to denigrate the Bible. It is a unique book. No other book is as relevant or as fascinating.

As a young soldier in the First World War, I was sent one day on a special reconnaissance mission. It was evening, at dusk. I was sitting at the edge of a ravine. And then, suddenly, just before nightfall, I saw an enemy mobile kitchen bumping its way across a small clearing in the forest. It had probably left a little too early. We would never have guessed that they could pass by there! But that mobile kitchen, which had not waited until nightfall, had revealed to us one of the ways leading to the enemy positions. If a mobile kitchen could find its way through the forest, then enemy troop reinforcements and ammunitions could also find their way to their camp. Here was a strategic route and we had no intention of sparing it. On the contrary. We shelled it all night.

The Bible is the main line that God uses to send food and ammunition to Christians. And the Devil is smart enough to make it the object of his attacks. That is why the Bible is under persistent attack. The most stupid youngster says, "Bah, you have to be completely crazy to read a book like that!" The well-educated university professor tries to prove that the Bible is just another book. On this one point they all agree: heavy fire at the Bible. But if you want to become God's child, you must not let this stop you. Allow no one to denigrate the Bible. The Bible declares itself to have been written by men who were filled and enlightened by the Holy Spirit. And when you have begun to read it yourself, you will not be long in discerning that a different spirit, a divine spirit, breathes throughout its pages.

Somebody made this complaint to me: "The Bible is a closed book to me. I would like to be saved, but I get nothing out of Bible-reading." I replied, "Ask God to give you his Spirit. Pray, for months if it is necessary: 'Lord, grant me the gift of your Spirit so that I may understand your Word and come to have a living faith.' Believe me, God will answer your prayer."

7. Listen to the preaching of God's Word

Go and listen to God's Word where it is clearly preached. I must warn you that a diluted gospel message is being announced in many pulpits today. I wouldn't attend one of those churches if I were you. For myself, I don't want lemonade, but the pure wine of the Gospel. It will not take you long to recognize whether or not the pure Gospel is being preached. Fortunately, there are preachers almost everywhere who faithfully teach the truth. Go where they are and remain under the sound of the Gospel. Associate with other people who are intent on hearing God's Word.

A man recently said to me, "You know, I am an individualist." I couldn't help but answer, "You will never be able to keep your faith alive if you are not in contact with other Christians and if you don't attend a church where the Word of God is announced."

Before I finish, I would like to tell you a story about an old woman I knew. She played an important role in my own life and was the means of bringing three engineers I was acquainted with to the Lord. It seemed to me that a great spiritual force must flow from her, so on this particular occasion I went to visit her. She was a miner's widow. She was glad to see me and told me how she had come to the faith.

At the time, she was living in one of the former suburbs of Essen. It has since been incorporated into the city. The name of the suburb was Stoppenberg. She had read in the local newspaper that two new pastors were going to be consecrated at St. Paul's Church. So she said to her friends, "Let's go and see. Things like this are always quite an event in Essen." It was a long walk to St. Paul's, though they did take a short-cut across the fields. When they arrived, the vast building was already full to bursting point. So they had to stand at the back of the auditorium. One of the pastors who was consecrated that day, Julius Dammann, later had a great influence on the city.

This is the story the old lady told me: "When Julius Dammann occupied the pulpit for the first time, he read from the third chapter of John's Gospel: 'For God so loved the world that he gave his one and only Son, that whoever believes in him shall not perish but have eternal life.' Then he leaned forward and said, 'Of all the words in the Bible, there is not a single one I fear as much as the word "lost". You can be eternally lost, to the point that even God himself withdraws from you. That is hell!'" The lady continued: "There was I, a small young girl, standing at the back of that big church. I didn't hear one more word of the sermon. It was as if I had been struck by lightning. I kept repeating to myself, 'You too are lost. You are not at peace with God. Your sins have not been forgiven. You are not a child of God. You are lost!' Somehow I managed to return home, but it was as if in a dream. Three days later my father asked me if I were ill."

She tried in vain to explain to her parents what had happened. All they could say was that she had gone out of her mind, that she was having a nervous break-down. No one seemed to understand the deep anguish she was experiencing at the thought of being eternally lost.

"For four weeks," the old lady continued, "I just went round in circles, completely bewildered. Then I read in the newspaper that Pastor Dammann was going to preach again. So once again I walked all the way from Stoppenberg to Essen. I prayed the whole way. The same prayer – it was a verse of a hymn – kept running through my mind."

In this mood she arrived at the church. The building was packed. No seats were free, so she had to remain standing as before. She prayed again. Then she opened her hymn-book to the number indicated on the panel and discovered, to her great astonishment, that it was the hymn she had been reciting along the way. "If everyone would sing this hymn prayerfully," she thought, "something would very probably happen."

Pastor Dammann got up and read another text from John's Gospel: "Jesus said: I am the gate; whoever enters through me will be saved."

"It was the second time I had been in this church," she told me. "And once again I heard nothing but that one verse. 'I am the gate; whoever enters through me will be saved.' In an instant everything had become clear to me. The Risen Jesus was the door to life. And I walked through that door! I heard nothing more of the sermon; but what I heard was enough. I had taken hold of life."

I sometimes tell this story to people who say, "Oh, I never go to church. I can't stand the atmosphere in churches. I'd rather go for a walk in the woods where you can hear the birds singing and the breeze rustling through the trees." "Well," I answer, "that woman would never have come to believe if she had not gone somewhere where the Word of God was preached!"

So, what should you do?

1. Put an end to your unbelief.
2. Your good opinion about yourself must go!
3. Take the decisive step.
4. Stop all deliberate wrong-doing.
5. Talk to God.
6. Read the Bible.
7. Listen to the preaching of God's Word.

Each one of these points is important. But I want to sum up with a truth which is even more important.

The important thing is not what *we* do. It is rather what *God* has done for us in Jesus Christ. This is the good news which I am happy to announce to you: Jesus has done *everything* for each one of us. He came to us, he died for us, he rose again for us, he is seated at the right hand of God for us.

Jesus is the Good Shepherd who has done *everything* for his sheep. The author of the twenty-third psalm bears witness to this. He says: "The Lord is my Shepherd. I shall lack nothing." And he goes on to name all the things the Good Shepherd has done for him . . .

My greatest desire is that you too will come to say: "The Lord is *my* Shepherd."

How can God allow such things?

"64 persons die in air crash."

"Another earthquake: 1 200 dead and 6 000 wounded."

"7 killed in mine accident."

"Insane man attacks school children with flame thrower: 10 children killed; others seriously injured."

Whenever news like this is announced in the press or on television, we hear these questions asked all around us, "And what about God? Where is he? Why does he allow all this without doing something about it? Isn't he all-powerful? Is he there at all?"

Atrocities are being committed all over the world. Endless trials have revealed the horrors of the death camps at Treblinka and Auschwitz. And, most shocking of all, children are being tortured, murdered and abused everywhere.

How can God allow such things?

Well, it's quite a question!

To those who ask it in a thoughtless way simply in an attempt to clear their conscience of their indifference towards God, we have nothing to say. We shall answer only those for whom this question constitutes a real problem.

God in the dock?

How can God allow such things? If we intend to bring an accusation against God, we are being fools. Just imagine the following scene: It takes place in a courtroom. There am I, the man who is so offended and saddened by all the suffering in the world. And I am sitting on the magistrate's bench. Seated in the dock is ... God!

And then from the height of my magistrate's bench, I begin prosecuting God. "Accused, stand up! How could you have allowed such things to happen?"

There's no way that could happen! There's no way that God could go into the dock and be judged by us. It would make him a pitiful, ridiculous, weak figure. He would not be God at all.

The point is this: if God is God, then he is holy. He is the living God. It is he who is the judge and we who are the accused.

I remember once going to a turbulent meeting in the troubled period between the two wars. When the speaker spotted me in the audience, he cried out, "Well, well, there's the preacher! Come on up here!" When I went up, he said, "You think there is a God, don't you? Well, if he does exist, I suppose I shall meet him after my death . . . " I nodded assent.

He continued: "I'm glad of that, because when I meet him I'm going to say this to him, 'You knew that children were dying of hunger while others were stuffing themselves – and you did nothing about it! You allowed wars to happen – and innocent people suffered while those who were responsible for these killings made a fortune! You said nothing about all this distress – nothing against all this injustice, oppression and exploitation!' Yes, I'll throw all that in your God's face. And do you know what I'll do then? I'll say to him, 'Get out! Come down off your throne and beat it!'"

He had succeeded in making me angry and I interrupted him. "Fine! Me too! I'll yell with you, 'Come down from your throne and beat it!'"

A deathly silence fell on the meeting. The speaker looked at me, stupefied. He looked as though he thought he had made a mistake and that perhaps I was not the pastor after all.

When I saw the expression on the people's faces, I felt like laughing. And the atmosphere was no longer the same. It was the moment to speak and I must not miss it.

"Look here, a God who would allow himself to be insulted by you in such a way would be completely ridiculous. Let me tell you that such a God does not exist, except in your imagination. A God who could be called to account, a God who would stand before you as an accused before his judge – oh no! such a God could exist only in a sick mind. And I can only say this, 'Let's get rid of such a God. Let's put an end to him once and for all!'"

"But you are a minister, aren't you?" he stammered in surprise. "Certainly! And that's why I would like to say this." I raised my voice so that everyone could hear me. "I would like to testify before you all that there is another God, the true God. You will not be able to call *him* to account. On the contrary, it's he who will summon *you* to appear before his court of justice. When that time comes, you will keep your mouths shut. There isn't a God you can say 'Beat it' to.

But there *is* a holy, living, true God. And this God may very well say to you one day, 'Get behind me! Get out!'"

How can God allow such things? If we ask this question in an attempt to call the living God to account, our reasoning is completely wrong. We shall certainly not receive any answer. We only show how silly we are.

God a children's nursemaid?

"How can God allow such things?" many ask, frightened and revolted at the thought of all the terrible things that happen in the world. It is a question which Christians are often asked. "Give us an answer. It is your God we are accusing. What do you have to say in his defence?" Can Christians help to excuse or defend God? Again it is an absurd view of God which imagines that his creatures can defend him.

It is like thinking of God as a children's nursemaid, a nanny who has been employed to keep order in the nursery. If one of the children happens to fall out of the window, everybody is horrified. "Where was the nursemaid? How could she have let such a thing happen?" That is much the way some people think of God. It is his duty to keep an eye on the world so that things go smoothly. Nobody bothers much about him until something goes wrong. Then everyone is immediately shocked and wonders where the heavenly nursemaid could have got to. And the question is naturally directed to God's friends: "How can your God allow such things?"

Christians would be very foolish to try to come to God's defence!

We must not mistake God for a children's nursemaid! Where is it written that it is his duty to see that order reigns in this world of infamy and stupidity?

God is under obligation to no one. *He is the Lord!*

Can we flatly deny the existence of God?

Catastrophes happen. And God keeps silent!

For many the conclusion seems obvious: there is no God. There cannot be any God who is in control of the world. There can be no God who sees and hears everything. And so God gets pushed right out of our life. "We'll leave it to the theologians to sort out the problem." However, what happens if, after all, there actually is a

God? What if we have been too hasty in denying his existence?

Let me state in the strongest possible terms: God *is* alive! He *does* exist!

If you are wondering how I can be so certain, I can only reply, "God has made himself known. He has come to men in the person of his Son, Jesus Christ. Since Jesus came into the world, no one can deny the existence of God. To deny it is to admit either one's ignorance or ill will."

The Christian view of the world

If we want to understand what is happening in the world, we must know the Christian view of the world. Otherwise we shall never solve our problem. The Bible tells us that God, the Creator, made the world in harmony and complete goodness. Man was the masterpiece of his creative work. God placed him in a position of honour: he wanted to make him his partner. So man had to be totally free.

But catastrophe is recorded on the first page of human history: what Christians describe as "the Fall". Man abused his liberty. He turned against God. He wanted to be his own god. And this is what he still wants today.

From its very first chapters, the Bible states that man has separated himself from God. And at the Fall, he dragged all of creation with him. It is as though a lock-gate had been opened. Suffering, death, tears, distress, and injustice all flooded the world.

The Bible affirms clearly that the world we live in is not the way God wanted it. We live in a fallen world where sin reigns and where the devil, the "murderer" and "father of lies", holds such power that he is called "the god of this world".

The Bible's view of the world is very realistic and it corresponds precisely with what we see about us. It goes on to teach that God does not impose order in this rebellious world. The world must follow its course right to the very end. All that is horrible, frightening and evil must come to full fruition. When that time comes, God will put an end to it all and create "a new heaven and a new earth".

That is not to say that God has simply abandoned the world. No! He sent Jesus into it, to die on the cross for sinners and to rise from the dead. Wherever men believe in Jesus and accept him, God's new creation has already begun. All those who belong to the Lord Jesus bear this testimony: "God has rescued us from the dominion of darkness and brought us into the kingdom of the Son he loves."

Through the disciples of Jesus, God wants to bring consolation, peace, love, and help to this fallen world.

Christians do not always wonder why God allows suffering. They know it can't be otherwise in a fallen world. And, knowing this, they commit themselves to helping others. But most of all, they "look forward to a new heaven and a new earth, the home of righteousness."

But what about the question: How *can* God allow such horrors? Even if we agree that such things are inevitable in a fallen world, the problem still tortures those who have been personally touched by tragedy. I think of a young couple who had a little boy they loved very dearly. One day his dead body was brought back to them: he had been killed by a drunken driver. When that sort of thing happens, the question burns on our lips, "How *could* God have allowed such a thing to happen?"

Are we able to understand God's ways?

It seems to me that a God I could understand with my intelligence would not be God at all. He would be only a man like myself. A child does not understand what sort of man his father is. Is it conceivable that we should always be able to understand the ways of God?

There is an old story which I used to hear when I was a child. It makes the point clearly.

Once upon a time there lived an old hermit who was always grumbling about God's ways. But one day he had a dream.

A messenger from God appeared and told the hermit to follow him. They came to a house where they were given a warm welcome. The master of the house said to them, "Today is a great day for me. My enemy has made up with me, and as a sign of friendship he has sent me this golden cup." When they left the next day, the hermit noticed that the messenger was carrying the cup. He was about to speak angrily when the messenger said, "Hold your tongue! These are the ways of God." Soon they reached another house. The host, an old miser, cursed the unwelcome visitors and told them to go to the devil. "Let's get away from here!" said the messenger and as he did, he presented the golden cup to the miser. Again the hermit was about to protest and again the messenger stopped him. "Hold your tongue! These are the ways of God." Towards the evening they arrived at the home of a man who was very sad, because in spite of all his efforts he had always encountered misfortune. "God will come to your help," said the messenger, and as he took his leave, he set fire to the house. "Stop!" the hermit cried out. "Hold your tongue! These are the ways of God."

On the third day, they went to the home of a melancholic, sullen man. He was good to no one except to his young son whom he loved very much. When they left the following morning, the man said to them, "I can't accompany you, but my little boy will go as far as the bridge with you. Take good care of him." "God will protect him," replied the messenger of God. When they reached the bridge, he suddenly pushed the child into the river! "You hypocritical demon," screamed the hermit, "these were certainly not the ways of God..."

At that very instant, the messenger was transformed into an angel shining with celestial glory. "Listen to me carefully! That cup was poisoned. So I saved the life of the friendly man, whereas the old miser found his death by drinking from it. The poor man found a treasure hoard when rebuilding his house and was free from want for the rest of his days. As for the man whose child I threw into the river, he was a wicked sinner and left with him, the child would have become a criminal. The loss of his son led the father to repentance. And the child is well off where he is! So, you have been able to see something of the wisdom and the justice of God. From now on, you should bow down before the mystery of his providence!"

As I said, this story was well-known when I was young. People who have read stories like it in their childhood are not so hasty in prescribing what God can or cannot do. They know that we cannot understand God's ways.

We shall probably never meet an angel on our pathway to explain things to us as the hermit did. We can only continue to grope in the dark and to accept the fact that we cannot understand the ways of God.

God has said through the mouth of the prophet Isaiah: "My thoughts are not your thoughts, neither are your ways my ways. As the heavens are higher than the earth, so are my ways higher than your ways and my thoughts than your thoughts."

The great prophet himself solemnly declared: "His understanding no one can fathom."

A Christian poet also wrote:

> God moves in a mysterious way
> His wonders to perform;
> He plants His footsteps in the sea,
> And rides upon the storm.

Deep in unfathomable mines
Of never-failing skill
He treasures up His bright designs,
And works His sovereign will.

Judge not the Lord by feeble sense,
But trust Him for His grace;
Behind a frowning providence
He hides a smiling face.

Blind unbelief is sure to err,
And scan His work in vain;
God is His own interpreter,
And He will make it plain.

Christians learn to wait

The truth of the matter is that most of our difficult questions cannot be answered here on earth. We must accept that "his thoughts are not our thoughts". But we Christians are confident that we will not always grope in the dark. No, for in eternity all these disturbing questions will be answered. This picture helps to explain it: if you examine the wrong side of a persian rug, all you can see is an apparently haphazard tangle of threads. But when the rug is turned over, a magnificent design appears. Then you discover that perfect order exists in that apparent muddle.

In this old world we can see only the wrong side of life's rug. Everything seems so confused and senseless. But in heaven, we shall be able to admire the right side and then we shall be amazed at how wisely and how methodically God has patterned our life.

In our present state, we are like someone driving a car at night. He would be able to enjoy the countryside he is passing through, except that darkness is hiding it from his view. He cannot make out any of the scenery he would like to see. Still, he does have enough light to drive, thanks to his headlights.

There are many things we Christians would like to know and understand. We would like to understand God's ways, to be able to explain why God does this or that. Here on earth we are in the dark. Most things are hidden from us. But God has given us sufficient light to find the right way. His Word – the Law in the Old Testament and the Gospel of Jesus in the New Testament – shows us enough of the road to lead us to the eternal goal.

When we have reached heaven, the sun will rise for us. Then we shall be able to see clearly what was on the right and left of our way. We shall discover what was hidden from us on earth. And we shall understand why "God allowed all that".

Can't we get any answers now?

We have asked a huge question: How can God allow such things?

First of all, we have had to show clearly that we have no right to speak to the holy God as we would to a man. A person can be called to account, but God cannot. A person can act unjustly. But God never commits any injustice. A person can be analysed and understood. God is above that.

These things have had to be stated as clearly and simply as possible. But having cleared the ground, we are going to ask the question again, even more seriously than before: Why does God allow such things?

And there is an answer in the Bible. The problem is, man doesn't want to hear it because his reason for asking the question in the first place was to accuse God of injustice. The Bible's answer, however, reverses the roles and puts *us* into the dock.

Each disaster is a warning and an appeal

Luke, the gospel writer, records an episode which touches the very core of the matter. A group of people, upset and incensed by an act of political repression that had just taken place, came to find Jesus to inform him about it. One of the traditional festivals was being celebrated in Jerusalem. Sacrifices were being offered in the temple. As usual on such occasions, when thousands of Jews gathered in the capital, the Roman garrison was on the alert. On this particular occasion, a serious quarrel had taken place. It is not clear what had caused it. But it seems that some men who had come from the proudly independent area of Galilee had drawn the attention of some Roman soldiers. There had been a fight. And a large number of Galileans had been savagely massacred.

"How could God allow such a thing?" The question was terribly real for the people as they reported the incident to Jesus. Just a few days earlier, another disaster had upset the inhabitants of Jerusalem. A high tower with thick walls had suddenly collapsed, burying eighteen people under its ruins.

The question was there in many hearts. "And God?" Some theological know-all, of course, had the answer: "Those who perished were wicked sinners and this was God's way of punishing them."

But Jesus rejected this explanation. He showed very clearly that we cannot fathom the secrets of God. Then he said something which made a cold shiver to run down everyone's spine. What he said sealed the mouths of some and revolted the others: "Unless you repent, you too will all perish."

Every misfortune, he was saying, though it be wrapped up in mystery, is an appeal from God, and a warning to a world living in opposition to him.

These alarm signals are vitally necessary.

"I am the Lord your God... you shall have no other gods before me." That is God's prescription for our lives. But what have we done about it? Our money, our cars, our work, our health, our children: all have become our idols. These are the gods we serve.

"Remember the Sabbath day by keeping it holy." Think of all the weeks, months and years when we have had no time for God at all!

"Honour your father and your mother." Do we understand the first thing about "honouring" our parents today?

"You shall not murder." What value does our generation attach to human life? And no one can claim to be innocent in this respect. For the Bible says that "anyone who hates his brother is a murderer". If that is true, then how many homicides have been committed in secret in our homes and in our businesses!

"You shall not commit adultery." How many marriages have been broken, dissolved, destroyed! We joke about purity as if it were old-fashioned. Instead of taking God's commandments seriously, we talk of "sexual difficulties", of "not wanting to repress ourselves".

"You shall not steal." Stealing begins by not giving back books you have borrowed. If all our unjustly acquired possessions could cry out, what an uproar we would have in our homes!

"You shall not give false testimony against your neighbour." What have we done with this commandment? Public and private life are poisoned by slander. One person drags another through the mire. And envy? Has it not become one of the chief incentives of political life?

What did Jesus say? "Unless you repent, you too will all perish."

God rent the heavens and gave his Son so that we might have forgiveness of sins, life and salvation through him. And what is man doing today with this gift of God? He rejects it. He pretends he doesn't know what to do with it because of the problems he has to cope with.

We should stop asking why God allows these misfortunes. We would be wise to listen to his warnings and to repent.

A hard God?

"I grasp that," someone may say. "But if all tragedies are warnings from God, it follows logically that it is God who sends them and therefore he is responsible for them."

And I agree. In the Bible there is a terrifying sentence which says this: "When disaster comes to a city, has not the Lord caused it?"

I shall always remember that dreadful night when Essen was bombed for the first time. I was trapped in my house which was on fire. All around me was a world in flames! There was no way to put out the fire – all the water pipes had burst. Just when I was going to give in to despair, I remembered this word of the prophet Amos: "When disaster comes to a city, has not the Lord caused it?"

A great peace came over me. I had not been delivered into the hands of men or of chance: I was in the hands of the Father of our Lord Jesus Christ.

I felt then that our conception of God is so very often wrong. We need to get rid of the ideas about him we have invented for ourselves and to hold on to what God himself has revealed to us!

Our conceptions about God are vague, childish, foolish and superficial. God is not the "nice old grandfather" that we imagine. And when our pre-conceived idea of God does not correspond to reality, our first reaction is to throw God overboard! However, while it *is* possible to get rid of our false conceptions about God, it is *not* possible to get rid of God himself. (Though he could get rid of us!)

Where is it written in the Bible – God's own testimony of himself – that he is "the good Lord"? Doesn't it rather say that he is a "terrible God", a "jealous God", a "hidden God"? The Bible compares him to a roaring lion: "The Lord roars from Zion." And in the New Testament: "It is a dreadful thing to fall into the hands of the living God." Jesus, who is better informed than any of our teachers, said the same thing: "Do not be afraid of those who kill the body but cannot kill the soul. Rather, be afraid of the one who can destroy both soul and body in hell."

The Bible states, too, that the fear of God is the beginning of wisdom. And when we read the last book of the Bible, where future events are described, all desire to compare God to a "nice old grandfather" completely leaves us. For we discover that God can be terribly severe; and that is because he is just. He does not turn a blind eye to our sins. God is justice itself. He watches jealously over his own commandments.

Does that seem too hard to us?

Well, that's the way it is! God does not conform to our conception of him. Rather, it is up to us to adjust ourselves to the reality of God. At the Last Judgement, the man who has no fear of God will discover at his own expense how terrible God can be.

Of course, some people will say that they don't believe in the Last Judgement. To them we have to say this makes little difference! We have lots of time to wait and see who is right: the unbelieving mocker or the eternal Word of God. This Word certifies that there will be a judgement. All the disasters of this world are but a foretaste of it.

We find this sentence in the Bible: "Your wickedness will punish you; your backsliding will rebuke you. Consider then and realize how evil and bitter it is for you when you forsake the Lord your God and have no awe of me, declares the Lord, the Lord Almighty." This will be the experience of the world as a whole and of each individual in particular.

How can God allow such things? The question is based on a false conception of God.

That is why he sent his Son into the world. That is why the Son of God died on the cross for us. That is why God raised Jesus from the dead. That is why we can say today: "He who has the Son has life." It is up to us to accept this salvation which is offered to us and to become the children of Almighty God; children who need no longer fear him, because their sins have been forgiven.

God wants our salvation. That is why he warns us by his Word and by life's overwhelming events. "Turn to me and be saved, all you ends of the earth; for I am God, and there is no other."

The Bible dares to declare that "God is love" for this very reason. But it is altogether different to speak of him as some inoffensive "good Lord".

This great truth impressed itself upon me when I was in a particularly terrible situation. It was evening, and I was in a dismal courtyard. The day before, our city of Essen had been heavily bombed. They had just managed to clear an air-raid shelter from under the debris and to pull out the dead. There, stretched out around me were the bodies of seventy people, many of whom I knew. There were elderly people, young mothers, and children – all had been stricken by the war. Ah, those dear little children! They were lying there, suffocated, strangled, dead.

In my imagination, I could see the children playing in the sun in a flower-covered meadow. "That's how children ought to grow!" my heart cried. "They shouldn't be lying there dead!"

Then the old cry sprang up in my heart. "God, where were you then? Where are you now? How can you allow such a thing?"

There was no reply. Only a half-torn beam creaked eerily in the evening wind.

Suddenly a scene flashed into my mind. I saw Jesus on the cross. "For God so loved the world that he gave his one and only Son, that whoever believes in him shall not perish but have eternal life." That cross appeared to me as a sort of light, a lantern of God's love, placed in this world of misery.

I do not understand the ways of God. I am even terror-stricken when I see how God is able to "forsake" the world. But from the cross of Jesus beams a ray of light. There, I see into the heart of God. There, he shows his love for me and his longing to draw me, by his love, to himself.

What is the purpose of it all?

When we hear about disasters in the news, the question keeps coming back: Why does God allow such things?

But the question becomes all the more disturbing when we are involved ourselves. When we lose a child. Or when a staggering blow shatters our entire life. Then the question is no longer purely theoretical. It burns inside us like a fire: "Why did this happen to me? How can God do such a thing to me?"

And until we get an answer, we cannot feel any peace. One person who was an enormous help to me in understanding this was a miner by the name of Merle.

He had been a big, strong man, fearing neither God nor the devil. But one day he was trapped in a collapsing mine. His legs were left paralysed. So I set out to visit him. I found him at home, in a wheelchair, surrounded by several of his friends. When he saw me at the door, he started to make a big row, "Well, church-goer, where was your good God when the stones were falling over me? Oh, go to hell with all your nonsense." He was so terrible that I couldn't say a word and had to leave without opening my mouth.

But some miners – real Christians – began to feel concerned about him. They showed him the path to Jesus, the way of salvation. A great change took place in him. His sins were forgiven and he made peace with God.

I visited him one day after this. I found him on the street in front of his house sitting in his wheel-chair. By this time, we had become good friends.

I sat down near him on one of the steps of the veranda. For I could see from the expression on his face that he had something important to say to me. It was not long in coming. "You see," he said, "I feel as if I won't be living much longer. But I know now where I'll be going when I close my eyes. When I come into the presence of God, I'll fall on my knees and thank him for having broken my spine."

"Merle," I said, "what do you mean?"

He smiled, and explained, "If my accident hadn't happened, I would have carried on in my evil ways, far from God, until I ended up in hell. God had to take extreme measures to lead me to his Son, my Saviour. Yes, it was hard! But it was for my good, for my eternal salvation."

He paused. Then he said slowly, "Better to enter heaven crippled than to jump into hell with both legs."

I took his hand. "Merle, you've been through a hard school. But it wasn't in vain. You've learned your lesson." And we thought with sadness of all those people who are hit so hard, but who do not hear God calling them in the midst of their trials.

When a disaster comes upon us, we should not think, "Why does God allow such a thing?" but rather, "What is the purpose of it? What does he want to teach me through it?" Then we can understand what the hymn writer wrote:

> When through the deep waters I call thee to go,
> The rivers of woe shall not thee overflow;
> For I will be with thee, thy troubles to bless,
> And sanctify to thee thy deepest distress.
>
> When through fiery trials thy pathway shall lie,
> My grace, all-sufficient, shall be thy supply:
> The flames shall not hurt thee; I only design
> Thy dross to consume, and thy gold to refine.

One day a man came to visit an old and experienced Christian. He complained about the various trials which he had to bear. Then he said, "Why does God do this to me? How can he allow such things?" The elderly man replied, "Have you ever seen a flock of sheep? Well, some sheep want to be independent, so they wander away from the shepherd. The shepherd then sends his dog after them. The dog barks, the sheep are scared and they run back to find protection at the shepherd's side. Well, you see, suffering plays much the same role as the sheepdog. At first, it scares us. But its only purpose is to bring us back to the Good Shepherd, the Lord Jesus. So, instead of complaining, go right now to your Saviour. He comforts all those who are weary and heavy-laden!"

How can we cope?

In actual fact, I don't know how an unbeliever is able to cope with life's difficulties. He simply cannot face up to them. Everything in his life has to go smoothly. If some tragedy does fall upon him, he becomes bitter and takes both God and man to task.

Instead of wondering, "Why does God allow such a thing?", instead of accusing God, we should recognize that we are weak, defeated, incapable of finding our way out on our own.

I really don't know how a man can manage to get along without Jesus. And as the horizon darkens and becomes more and more threatening in this world, the disciple of Jesus learns to turn his eyes to the eternal goal, to the heavenly kingdom to which he has been called.

Let me tell you a true story: Many years ago, I was pastor in an important mining district. One day when I was out visiting, I went to the home of some people who were celebrating an anniversary. Bottles of liquor were being passed around and yelling and brawling could be heard from every corner. But when I appeared in the doorway, there was a lull. Then a man shouted, "Hey, the preacher! What's he doing here? Preacher, we don't care a damn about your nonsense. We'll gladly give up heaven to you . . . to you and the birds!"

"How kind of you," I replied, "but there is something I just can't grasp. How can you give up something that doesn't belong to you? Somehow I feel that you have no heaven to give me! It seems to me that your path leads to hell rather than to heaven. So what are you going to leave to me and the birds?"

The man looked embarrassed. Then he carried on, shouting, "Come on! Preachers always end up comforting people by promising heaven to them. And I'll bet you were about to do just that!"

"You're wrong!" I replied. "I don't have the slightest intention of giving people hope of a heaven to which they have no right. I can only urge you not to stay on the road that leads to hell and invite you to come to Jesus, the Saviour. He offers heaven to all those who accept him."

Don't fool yourself...

The hope of eternal life is a privilege which Jesus offers, out of pure grace, only to those who "receive" him.

Believers are not always wondering how God can allow such and such a trial. They suffer just like everyone else. They try to relieve this suffering world as much as they can. But as they continue along their way, in suffering as in joy, they sing in their hearts the words of the hymn:

> God holds the key of all unknown,
> And I am glad;
> If other hands should hold the key,
> Or if he trusted it to me,
> I might be sad.
>
> What if to-morrow's cares were here
> Without its rest!
> I'd rather he unlocked the day;
> And, as the hours swing open, say,
> "My will is best."
>
> The very dimness of my sight
> Makes me feel secure;
> For, groping in my misty way,
> I feel His hand; I hear him say,
> "My help is sure."
>
> I cannot read his future plans;
> But this I know:
> I have the smiling of his face,
> And all the refuge of his grace,
> While here below.
>
> Enough! this covers all my wants,
> And so I rest!
> For what I cannot, he can see,
> And in his care I saved shall be,
> For ever blest.

Nietzsche said in a poem: "Woe to the man who has no home!" Such is the affliction of this generation: men have to face life's ordeals with no resting place and no security. "Woe to the man who has no home!" This is the special tragedy of our age.

Let us earnestly set out in search of the Lord Jesus. It was he who said, "In my Father's house are many rooms."

Wouldn't you like to have one reserved for you?

Our right to love

1. An overwhelming distress

What a paradoxical era we live in! Never before have people lived so closely together – crowded and jammed as we are – yet never before have we suffered so much from loneliness.

A sixteen-year-old lad said to me one day, "I've no one in the world!" "Come now! Don't be silly!" I said. "What about your father?" "When my old man comes home from work, he grumbles a bit, gobbles up his supper, and then he goes out again." "Well, what about your mother?" "Oh her! she's up to her ears in work. She's got no time for me." "And your mates at work?" "We work together, and that's it! No, I've got no one to talk to." And that is what a youngster of sixteen told me!

Young people are not the only ones who experience this kind of loneliness. Many married women feel lonely even though they are living with their husbands. Very often the husband hasn't the slightest idea what is bothering his wife. And she has no inkling as to what is troubling him. And we call them a couple! In this way, we all end up living in solitude! People are all ears when our philosophers speak of the loneliness of modern man; for the simple reason that men and women everywhere are begging to be delivered from their solitude. Now this longing to escape from our isolation is very often combined with the greatest force we have within us: our sexual impulse. When this is so, we will readily ignore any restraints.

The sixteen-year-old lad will look for a girlfriend to save him from his solitude. The married man, who lives with his wife but still feels lonely, will go off for the weekend with his secretary, hoping that she will make him forget his loneliness. The student, feeling very much alone among the ten or twenty thousand young people of his university, will get involved with a female student just as lonely as himself. Thus the longing to escape from our solitude is combined with our sex drive. That is the reason why today's world is so highly conscious of sex.

In addition to this, cunning business men – film producers and novelists – make tremendous profits from the fact that man uses sex to solve his problem of loneliness. The word has gone round: no more films without at least one love scene, no more books without at least one case of adultery. And as we watch other people flirting, courting, and making love to one another, we have the impression that life is wonderful!

A young girl said to me recently, "Pastor, we have different sets of values from our grandparents. We have a new morality, a new code of ethics." When I hear this kind of thing, I am almost tempted to lift my hat (if I am wearing one) and say, "Pardon me, Miss!" But when you have been a pastor in a big city as long as I have, you no longer believe that kind of talk. And I know from experience that all this pretentious language is only put on for show. Behind it lies an overwhelming distress: of young people who have shady love affairs and who cannot cope with their problems; of married couples who try to cover up or who separate. Yes, there is overwhelming distress.

And we all know something about it. For I am not talking about other people, but about you and me!

Many years ago, I gave a talk on the same subject in a small town near Lippe. This meeting was only open to young people. When I stepped into the hall, I said to myself, "What a mess you've got yourself into! Why, it's like hell in here!" Boys and girls . . . and such heavy cigarette smoke! Some of the boys had brought along some whisky. Several girls were sitting on the boys' knees. "And I've got to speak here?" I thought. "Well, old fellow, you'll need lots of courage." Then I began speaking: "We can experience heart-breaking distress in our sex life." It was as though at that very moment someone had switched on the light. I can still see one of the boys promptly dropping the girl he had on his knee. He had been touched. There was a sudden death-like hush in the hall. I could not help thinking, "At first sight, everyone seems so happy. But it proves that I am perfectly right: we *can* experience heart-breaking distress in our sex life."

2. Where does this distress come from?

This distress arises from the fact that we no longer know the difference between right and wrong. We pretend to have new ideas about morality. But don't forget this: *sin is not a myth.* Every time I sin, and do something wrong, a weight falls upon my conscience. That is a reality! Unfortunately, we no longer know exactly what is right and what is wrong. Let me ask a few very pointed questions:

Is it right or is it wrong to indulge in sexual intercourse before marriage? If your marriage is unhappy, is adultery a need or an evil? And is homosexuality between men, or with young boys, or between boys, sinful or legitimate? Is lesbianism sin or not? Is it right or wrong to masturbate? Or to ask for a divorce?

To sum it up, what is right and what is wrong? This is the cause of our distress. Thousands of books try to make us believe that sex has nothing to do with right and wrong. So the question is simply not raised. It is evil to be a bad friend – fine. But sex is outside the consideration of good and evil, we are told. Take modern films, for instance: in a close-up, we see a kiss; then the curtain lowers and behind the curtain we can see shadowy figures in each other's arms. This kind of scene is simply part of the film. There is no question of good or evil. Is this right?

What is good? What is evil?

I remember very well how, as a young man, I suddenly saw the light. I could tell the difference between good and evil. Then this question began to bother me, "What is permissible and what is not?"

But before giving a valid answer to this question, we must first ask, "Who decides, ultimately, what is right and what is wrong?"

One day, a young couple came to see me. She was a girl of easy virtue, with make-up caked on. He, his fingers all stained with nicotine, clearly was an unstable chap. I said to them, "At least I know where I am with you. It's pretty obvious." The girl snapped back, "But there's nothing wrong with that, Pastor! There's nothing wrong with that!" I replied, "Just a moment! Who has the right to tell us whether or not there's nothing wrong with that?" Yes, who will tell us what is good and what is evil? The Church? No! I won't bow down to its dictates. When I was young, I would never have recognized the authority of the Church and its pastors over my life. And now I am one myself! Who has the right to say what is good and what is evil? Aunt Jane? My own conscience? "I follow the instructions of that small voice inside me!" some say. So, who has the right to decide what is good and what is evil?

We have now come to a very crucial point. If there *is* a living God who is the Ruler of this world, then it is for him to decide what is good and what is evil. If there is *no* God, you may do whatever seems right to you. And if that is so, I don't see why you should behave decently because of Aunt Jane either. Everyone, when confronted with this problem, must ask himself, "Is there a God or not?" I know people who live in terrible moral disorder, but who say, "I believe in God." Nonsense!

If there is a God, then he also has his say regarding sex. You have to make up your mind. You can push God out of your life. But then you will die according to your own choice. Don't try to imagine yourself saying, "I want to live without God", until the age of 45, and then suddenly deciding to become pious when old age creeps up on you. It won't work! "Seek the Lord while he may be found," says the Bible, and not "... when it is convenient for you." So I repeat: if there is *no* God, do as you please. But if he does exist, then it is he who has the right to tell you what is good and what is evil. Isn't that logical?

And I tell you that God *does* exist, that he *is* alive! If you ask me how I can say this with such certainty, my answer is, "Because he has revealed himself in Jesus Christ." I want you to understand this. Since Jesus has come into our world, all indifference and scepticism about God is only due to ignorance or to ill will.

God does exist! And because he exists, it is he who decides what is right and what is wrong. You may decide to rule him out of your life. You may say, "We have other moral principles!" But let me assure you that one day you will have to stand before God and give an account of your life.

In fact, it is a great relief to find out that God is the one who decides what is good and what is evil. And in his Word – the Bible – he states it very clearly. A man once asked me, "But does the Bible talk about those things too?" He was astonished. "Yes, it does," I replied. "God gives very precise instructions concerning what is right and what is wrong in sex."

Have you followed me? Now we must ask, "Just what does God have to say about sex?"

I shall try to summarize the teaching of the Bible on this matter.

3. What does God say?

a) God approves of sex

In one of his poems, Tucholsky writes something like this: "From my waist to my head, I am a Christian; from my waist to my feet, I am a pagan." How absurd! The Bible says: "God created man ... male and female he created them." He created us with our sexuality. I can therefore speak openly about it. It is not taboo. God created me as a man, and you too, all you male readers. So let's be men – and not mere puppets! And you ladies, he made you women. Be women, then! The desperate efforts of some women to be like men – or of certain men to be like women – are no doubt symptoms of an illness. Do you understand? You can be real men and real women! "God created man . . . male and female he created them." He didn't create a third sex! God approves of our sexuality, so we don't have to suppress it. We can trace the tension which results from my being a man or a woman back to Creation.

But we live in a fallen creation. The world is no longer as it was when it came out of the hands of God. Our sex life, so important and yet so delicate, is particularly threatened. God, therefore, took steps to protect it.

b) God protects our sex life by marriage

God approves of sex and protects it by marriage. Marriage is not merely a social contract, but an institution of God.

An American psychiatrist who wrote an important book on this topic confirms this: "Nothing has ever been written on this subject which can equal in depth what we read in the Bible, 'God created man . . . male and female he created them.'" And he continues: "I am not a Christian. But as a psychiatrist I say that marriage is exactly what we need." Provided, of course, that there is faithfulness in marriage. And not seven, eight, nine or ten marriages, as in the case of many Hollywood stars! The fact that this type of marriage is upheld as an ideal is one of the marks of the madness of our generation. It reveals our deep confusion. God instituted marriage, but the sort of marriage characterized by love and faithfulness.

So what is marriage supposed to be like? Ladies, to be a good wife, it is not enough to cook delicacies for your husband or to sew on his buttons. Men, when you have given your wife the house-keeping money, don't think you have done your duty. According to God's plan, marriage is supposed to deliver you both from solitude. Do those of you who are married have this type of married life? If not, perhaps you ought to talk the matter over together and ask each other, "What has happened to us? Our marriage was supposed to save us from loneliness!" In the beginning, God said, "It is not good for the man to be alone. I will make a helper suitable for him." Try to understand this. He wanted to take you out of your isolation.

Let me tell you a little anecdote which speaks volumes. When I was a very small boy, my sister and I were allowed one day to go to a family wedding at Stuttgart. It was the first time I had been to a wedding and everything was enormously interesting. We drove to the church in a carriage, then there was a banquet at the hotel. The last item on the menu was "bombe glacée". My sister and I were seated at the end of the table and we couldn't wait to see the "bombe glacée" arrive. But it took ever so long to come, because one uncle after another got up to make a speech. We were terribly bored. But one of the speeches has remained engraved on my memory. One of my uncles, trying to be witty, shouted, "Ladies and gentlemen! It is said that in heaven there are two chairs; they are intended for the couple who has never regretted for one second that they got married." Then he continued, "But to this day, the chairs have not been claimed." Just then he was interrupted. Over the heads of all the guests, my father shouted to my mother, who was at the other end of the table, "Mummy, those chairs are waiting for us!" I was only a youngster and I did not understand the deep meaning of those words. But my heart was filled with a great joy, for I felt the marvellous warmth of a home like ours. Is your home like this?

At my own wedding reception, one of my colleagues, an older man, made some very touching remarks about the passage in Genesis, ". . . I will make a helper suitable for him." This is what he said: "Not a despot to rule over him. Nor a slave to lie at his feet. Nor an object that he can put aside. But a helper to lavish her love on him."

On the day of their silver wedding anniversary, I was deeply impressed to see the way my father looked at my mother and to hear him say to her, "You have become more precious to me every day over these 25 years!" I could not help thinking of all those couples, who, in 25 years of marriage, have seen their love fade away little by little. It is terrifying! Many married people should be saying to each other, "Listen, let's make a fresh start." Believe me, it is possible!

There is another point I want to make. Many young people say to me, "I am not considering getting married for the moment. What do you think about it? Can we do whatever we want?" I say this:

c) God wants youth to be pure

I know that in our day and age this is considered perfectly ridiculous. But do you think God follows fashion? It is the Word of God which states this, not I. Let me put forward my arguments. In the Bible there is the story of a young man called Isaac. One day his father commissioned a servant to find a wife for him. The young man went out into the fields to pray, because he was convinced that it was God who would choose a wife for him. And although he had not made her acquaintance yet, he was already faithful to her. You young men who are not yet thinking of getting married, you may be sure that when the time comes, God will give you the young woman you need. And she deserves your faithfulness now. The same is true for girls. You young women must remain faithful to the one you know nothing about as yet. The Bible is clear on this point: God wants youth to be pure.

A psychiatrist once said to me, "I am sure that deep down in her heart, a young girl can only love once. She gives her love to only one man. If she has had a dozen lovers, she is – if you will excuse the rather strong expression – "lost" for marriage. She may marry the seventh one, but she will always think of her first love." I replied to him, "Well! what you say is extremely interesting. Using psychiatry, we come to the same conclusion as the Word of God."

I must make it as clear as possible: premarital sex, lesbianism, homosexuality, adultery, and divorce are all sins for which you will have to give account one day before God!

I could stop there. I can remember that in my younger days it helped me a lot to know what God's will was and also to realize that God is the only one who has a word to say on these matters. But it would be cruel of me to stop at this point and not to deal with another question which is of the utmost importance.

4. How can we escape this distress?

In the Bible there is a story which is wonderful and yet disturbing at the same time. One day Jesus, the Son of the living God, was surrounded by a crowd of people. Suddenly there was an uproar. The people stepped aside to make way for a troop of priests and onlookers who were approaching. They were dragging a pretty young woman with them. I have no difficulty in imagining her there before me, her clothing half torn off. They brought her before Jesus and shouted, "Lord Jesus! We caught this woman in the act of committing adultery. God's Law declares that this sin is punishable by death. You are always very merciful, Lord Jesus, but surely you will not go against the will of God! We would like to hear you say that this woman should be stoned at this very instant." Jesus looked at the young woman and then replied, "Yes, God does take this matter very, very seriously. According to God's Law, she ought to be sentenced to death." Many faces lit up. Some people picked up stones, for adulterers were stoned to death. But Jesus continued,

"Just a moment! Let the one among you who is not guilty of any sin at all – whether in thought, in word or in deed – let him throw the first stone!" Then he stooped down and started writing on the sand. I would love to know what he wrote, but the Bible does not say. After a long time, Jesus straightened up. Everyone was gone! Only the woman remained. It says in the Bible: "And the people who heard it, convicted by their own conscience, went out one by one."

May I ask you a question? "Would you have had the right to throw the first stone at that woman? Are you without reproach? Are you perfectly pure in thought, in word and in deed? Could you have thrown the first stone?" Does anyone reply? No one? Not even one person? In that case, we are nothing but a whole lot of sinners. Yes, that is exactly what we are!

On that occasion, the people made a serious mistake. "Convicted by their own conscience, they went out one by one." They should have done just the opposite and said to Jesus, "Look, we will take our place beside this woman. You didn't condemn her. Be merciful to us, too!" I know of no one else but Jesus who is able to deliver us from our sexual distress. The reason I can say that is because I myself have been helped by him. When I talk about Jesus, I am not putting forward nice theories. He intervened in my life and still does, even at this very moment. A pastor is a man like other men. He needs the Saviour just as much as you do. I have experienced the power of his salvation in two different ways:

a) Jesus forgives our sins

No pastor, no priest, nor even the angels can do this. Your first impure thought and all the downfalls which followed are irreparable sins. They will go with you into eternity right up to the judgement-seat of God, unless beforehand you have found Jesus, confessed all your shortcomings to him, and have been pardoned by him. Jesus is the only one who can grant forgiveness.

So draw near in thought to the cross of Jesus and say, "I come to lay down all the sins of my youth. I confess to you all my questionable love affairs. I don't want to hide anything from you." Then, lift up your eyes to the cross and say the words of this hymn:

> I do believe, I do believe
> That Jesus died for me;
> And through his blood,
> his precious blood,
> I shall from sin be free.

The Bible says: "The blood of Jesus, God's Son, purifies us from all sin." What a liberating word!

At the age of seventeen I was called up for military service. I can assure you that in the barracks my mates did all they could to pollute my mind. But then one day my eyes were opened and, thinking about all this obscenity, I cried out, "Who can free me from the mess I've made of my life?" Then I understood that Jesus was able to wipe out my past and forgive my sins. I turned to him. And now I would not be without him for anything in the world.

One day at a big meeting in Düsseldorf I said that, in forgiving our sins, Jesus wipes away our past. At the end of the meeting, as everyone was leaving, I saw a tall, very distinguished-looking man threading his way through the crowd to join me at the front of the hall. When he reached me, he asked excitedly, "Is it really true, as you said, that we can receive forgiveness of our sins?" "Yes, praise God! His forgiveness sustains me day by day!" I replied. He continued, "I am a psychiatrist. Many people consult me about their mental illnesses. They have complexes of all sorts. But they don't know what they are suffering from. Most of the time it can be traced back to old faults which they cannot – or don't want to – remember any more. Sometimes I have to spend hours with them, trying to draw out all these troubles from the depths of their subconscious. But there my power stops. I can bring to light the sin committed – the lie, the quarrel, the immorality – but I have often thought in despair, 'If only I could blot out each one!' And that's why, Pastor Busch, I am asking you if there really is someone who can rid us of our sins. Is it true, yes, or no?" Joyfully, I confirmed the fact once again. "Yes, thank God!" And I realized that we have an incredible, a remarkable message in the New Testament. Jesus forgives our sins!

b) Jesus breaks our chains

I said one day to a charming young secretary, "Miss, you are on your way to hell! This love affair with your boss is a terrible thing. Don't make this man and his family unhappy!" With a pained look on her face, she replied, "There's no way out! I love this man!" "I believe you," I answered, "but he has a wife and children! You are causing great harm." I could tell she was tortured by the thought of this liaison, but she could not bring herself to break it off. So I was happy to be able to say to her, "We can't break the bonds of sin ourselves, it's true. But the Bible says, 'If the Son sets you free, you will be free indeed.' Call to Jesus. He alone can liberate you."

These words of the hymn may help you to unburden *your* soul before him:

> Out of my bondage, sorrow, and night,
> Jesus, I come, Jesus, I come;
> Into thy freedom, gladness, and light,
> Jesus, I come to thee:
> Out of my sickness and into thy health,
> Out of my want and into thy wealth,
> Out of my sin and into thyself,
> Jesus, I come to thee.

As a pastor in a big city, I have witnessed the breaking of many chains.

In order to be freed from the bondage of sex and to escape the suffering caused by it, all of us, young and old alike, need the Saviour. *You* need a Saviour! Jesus offers a wonderful, a real liberation. Experience it for yourself! Otherwise you will lead a miserable existence for the rest of your life.

5. The world is thirsting for love

I must add something else. Many single women have said to me, "I am over 40 and no man has ever asked me to marry him. What should I do?" I am a convinced pacifist and I became one when I saw the distress of these single women. During the Second World War, five million young men in Germany alone lost their lives on the battle-field. Which means that five million young women have not seen their most cherished hope, that of making a man happy, fulfilled. Which means that five million young women in our country are condemned to remain single. Do I need a better reason to be against war? Just try to imagine the plight of these five million German women. The men they wanted to make happy are buried in our military cemeteries.

I would like to say to these women, "For the love of God, don't try to steal what you've been deprived of. Don't disturb the peace of married couples. This is a danger, a temptation, which is more and more frequent among our people." "So what should we do?" they ask. And I tell them, "If this is your situation, then accept it. Unmarried people are not necessarily unhappy."

The Bible tells of a single woman called Tabitha. She lived in Joppa, the present-day city of Jaffa. At the time of her death, the

Apostle Peter happened to be in the area, so they sent for him. He was amazed when he went into her room. He most likely had thought, "I'll probably find this good old lady lying on her bed, with nobody at all around." But the room was filled with people. One widow present said, "Tabitha made this dress for me." And a blind man told him, "I was so lonely and then Tabitha came to read to me every Sunday afternoon, from three to four. It was the happiest hour of the week." The youngsters there also had something to say, "When we came home from school, the key used to be under the door-mat. Nobody looked after us until the day when Tabitha came and took care of us." Peter had understood. "Tabitha had a much richer life than certain married women. Some, having to live with a boring husband, have ended up annoyed and bitter."

In Greek, the language of the New Testament, there are two words for "love". The word "eros" refers to the love which we spoke of at the beginning – physical love. This is where the word "eroticism" comes from. But there is another term which is translated by "love". It is the word "agape" which describes the love of God, that love which I can give to others.

To unmarried women I say, accept your situation – and fill your life with "agape".

The world is thirsting for that kind of love!

To sum up: it is God's prerogative to decide what is right and what is wrong; God demands moral purity of young people and faithfulness in marriage; and if our path should not lead to marriage, then it is a matter of accepting the situation.

6. A love to which we have no right

In closing, I would like to tell you something about Jesus just one last time. The subject I am dealing with is: "Our right to love". There is a love to which we have no right, but which is nonetheless freely offered to us. It is the love of the Lord Jesus. We are sinners. And we need a Saviour.

May I leave a personal testimony with you? It was at the time of the Third Reich. Once again I had been imprisoned because of my faith. The prison chaplain had just visited me and said, "You have very little chance of getting out of here this time." And then he was gone. I was left alone in my cell. It was very cramped. High up, a narrow slit let in a little light. It was cold, and I was freezing. The whole atmosphere was icy-cold. I was longing for my wife, my children, my ministry, and my young people – for I was a youth leader at the time. I was sitting there, without the slightest hope of ever being released. By the time night had fallen, deep despair had taken hold of me. I do not know if you have ever experienced such a thing. But at that very moment – I can testify to it – the Lord Jesus came into my cell. *He is alive!* He can pass through locked doors. And that is exactly what he did. He put before my eyes his death on the cross, the death he suffered because of my sins. And he whispered to me, "I am the Good Shepherd. The Good Shepherd lays down his life for the sheep." Such a stream of love flowed over me just then, that I could scarcely bear it. It was too much for me.

I realized I didn't merit that particular love, nor did I have any right to it. It had been given freely to me.

And you, too, can reach out for this love of Jesus. Why let this stream of love pass by, when it wants to flood your soul?

Can we talk to God?

A troupe of tight-rope walkers arrived one day in a village in Swabia and asked to perform that evening. Their equipment was already set up and a long rope was stretched out high above the ring, when a woman and her child passed by. In its typical Swabian accent the child inquired, "Can people really walk on a rope, Mummy?" "Of course they can," she replied, "but they have to know how. I couldn't do it myself, because I don't know how!"

Can we talk to God? Our little anecdote leads me to say:

1. We can if we know how!

Many people, like the child's mother, have to admit, "I don't know how!"

Can we talk to God? Of course we can! God is very near to us, so we can talk to him. You can talk to Mr. Smith, so why shouldn't you be able to talk to the living God? He is just as near...

But do you know *how* to talk to God?

When I was a little boy I learned this chorus:

> Little children, someone loves you,
> Away up there, beyond the blue...

And I used to think, "What's the use of praying? I could never shout loud enough for God to hear me away up there in heaven!"

The Russians are always sarcastic about this. "We have sent our sputniks into space," they say. "If God really existed, we would have seen him." Multitudes of men and women are puzzled. "Where is God?" they wonder. "Is he away up there beyond the blue? How far up? A hundred, a thousand kilometres away?"

I want to make this point as clear as possible: nowhere in the Bible is the term "beyond the blue" ever used. The Bible says something totally different. It declares: "God is not far from each one of us." In another passage we read: "You hem me in – behind and before." We cannot understand this unless we take into account the fact that our senses can only perceive a three-

97

dimensional world. God, however, is in another dimension – and yet, at the same time, he is very close to us.

Of course we can talk to God! As with walking the tight-rope, so with prayer: you can do it if you know how! The great majority of men and women today have to admit, "I don't know how to pray." What about you? Why not be completely hcnest with yourself for once? The truth of the matter is, you haven't the slightest idea about how to pray. For if you did, you would be praying.

This is one of the most alarming characteristics of the twentieth century. Our age has lost its ability to pray and as a result has lost its ability to believe. The well-known German author, Franz Werfel, wrote a novel called *Heaven Profaned*. One sentence in his book will remain engraved on my memory as long as I live: "The particular sign of modern times is man's 'metaphysical' dullness." By the word "metaphysical", he means the eternal realities which belong to another dimension. Man has become so stupefied by the radio, TV, small talk, propaganda, ideologies of all kinds, politics, neighbours, and tensions at work, that he is no longer aware of the nearness of God or the possibility of communicating with him.

Is it possible to talk to God? It would indeed be possible if people's minds over the past century had not been drugged by so much rationalism.

A sixteen-year-old boy told me about one of the most terrible incidents he witnessed as a soldier during the war. After an air-raid, he was the first one to come out of the shelter. And so it was he who found one of his mates lying on the ground, his abdomen wide open. The lad wanted to help him, but the wounded man said, "It's no use trying to help me. I'm going to die. What I need is someone to pray with me. Could you pray with me?" The boy answered, "In the Hitler Youth I was taught to curse, not to pray!" He ran to get the captain, shouting, "Captain, come quickly!" The officer knelt down beside the man, whose intestines were sticking out of the open wound, and asked, "What can I do for you, my friend?" "I'm going to die, Captain. Please pray with me!" "Good grief," exclaimed the captain, "if there's one thing I don't know how to do, it's praying!" The captain ran to get the lieutenant.

Finally all the soldiers were lined up, rank by rank, around the dying man. There they were, these tough soldiers, so sure of themselves, experts at telling dirty jokes and at swearing. Yet not one of them knew how to pray. Not one of them could even recite the Lord's Prayer.

The young lad added, "As I stood there, I vowed that the first thing I would do if I got out of this rotten war alive would be to go somewhere where I could learn to pray. I didn't want to die miserably like that poor fellow!"

This is the point we have reached today.

Social status makes no difference – the manager thinks he is too intelligent to pray, and the worker is dominated by free-thinking. We are no longer able to pray. What Franz Werfel calls "man's metaphysical dullness" is a great disaster. It's no wonder we are down and out when the slightest blow hits us.

On several occasions, when Essen was being bombed, I happened to be in the same air-raid shelter as certain loud-mouthed people who raved wildly about "the final victory", "our wonderful Führer", and "the greatness of the Third Reich". But when the bombs began to fall, these same people screamed in terror. We Christians would pray with them and sing hymns to help them stand the strain, because they themselves couldn't pray. They didn't know how! It's a terrible thing not to know how to pray.

The other day I was sitting with an intelligent, cultivated man who declared with a smile, "Pastor Busch, praying doesn't really help!" "Stop talking such nonsense!" I told him sharply. Stunned, he replied, "What's got into you?" I answered, "You remind me of someone who has had his leg amputated and who says, 'There's no point in skiing!' Like him, you don't know what you're talking about!"

I am willing to discuss the advantages of skiing with anybody, but not with an amputee. And yet, that is exactly what we do when it comes to prayer. We don't know a thing about it, but that doesn't stop us from saying, "There's no use in praying." The more miserable we are, the smarter we try to appear!

When I see the state of lethargy into which our poor nation has fallen, I am not only filled with anger but with deep sorrow. It troubles me, too, that the Church seems to assume that everyone still knows how to pray. It's probably the same in your church: at Christmas you see people there who normally never darken a church door. Our churches are crowded at Christmas! And when the pastor says, "Let us pray", – this is what disturbs me – then everyone bows his head and joins his hands together. I feel like shouting, "Stop pretending! Less than one person out of ten here really knows how to pray. You're all just putting on an act!" Am I right or wrong?

It's the same thing at marriages and funerals. The pastor says, "Let us pray", and the men stand there, top-hat in hand, thinking that looking at their hat is the same as praying. But as soon as the service is over, off they go to the local pub for a drink!

When I was serving in the armed forces in 1914, we were ordered to go to church. But before we went, the adjutant gave us the following instructions: "You will walk to your pews without making any noise. When you get there, remain standing with your hat in your hands, and slowly count to twelve. Then you may sit down." The people watching us must have thought how fervently we were praying! Actually we were just slowly counting to twelve before sitting down! I get the impression at marriages and funerals that people don't even count to twelve when the pastor says, "Let us pray"! It makes my heart ache to remember that people used to really pray, and not pretend, when they heard the words: "Let us pray!"

The world-famous explorer of Central Africa, David Livingstone – one of the greatest men in history, renowned for his courage, intelligence and learning – died like this: Accompanied by only his native porters, Livingstone had penetrated deep into the heart of Africa. One morning the boys had finished packing the material and had taken down the tents. Only Livingstone's tent remained standing. His faithful friends knew that every morning Livingstone prayed, that he talked to his heavenly "Tuan" – his God. That morning, however, his prayer-time lasted longer than usual. Eventually the chief porter ventured to take a peep through a slit in the tent. And what did he see? His master – still on his knees. They waited till noon before daring to enter into the tent. Livingstone was still on his knees. But his heart had stopped beating.

This great, intelligent man died on his knees, praying. But the small-time bourgeois, instead of humbly admitting that he no longer knows how to pray, dares to assert that it's pointless to pray. Livingstone knew how to pray. And he died praying. But we die in hospital, helped along by hypodermic injections. We could not face death if our doctors did not administer drugs to us. Livingstone didn't need them. He was used to speaking with God. And it was while he was speaking to God that he entered into eternity.

And what about family prayer? In our home – we were eight children – this is how we did things: In the morning the entire family would gather together before breakfast. After singing a hymn, we would read a passage of the Scriptures, then my father would close in prayer. Even when I had lost all interest in God, the thought that back home the family was praying for me never left me. And when as a young officer I tossed everything overboard and started out on the downward path, the prayers of my parents held me up.

Do you have family worship in your home? Fathers, one day God will take you into account and will hold you responsible for the loss of your wife and children if you have not properly managed your household. How do you begin the day in your home? By a hymn, Bible-reading and prayer?

An eminent man from Essen asked me one day to visit him at his home. There, sitting beside his wife, he said, "An amazing thing happened the other day. Our sixteen-year-old son came home one evening from your young people's meeting and asked us, 'Why don't we ever pray in our house?' 'All that,' I explained, 'is mere formality. There's nothing behind it.' He went on questioning me: 'What do you think of the Holy Spirit, Dad?' 'Why, nothing at all!' 'That,' said our son emphatically, 'is the trouble in our family. We need a father who knows how to ask for the Holy Spirit.'"

This was the story the man told me. Then I asked, "Do you want me to give your son a good talking-to for being rude to you?" "No," he replied. "If my son is right, then I'm in very bad posture." I could only reply, "Yes, you are in a serious situation. Your son is right." "That is what I was afraid of," he admitted. "What should I do?"

This man had suddenly come to realize that he had failed to fulfil a father's most basic duty. It is not enough just to clothe and feed your children. Fathers, your responsibility goes beyond that! Do you know how to pray?

There is a legend which is well known to sailors. The story goes that a phantom ship haunts the seven seas. Though it has neither crew nor captain, no storm has yet been able to sink it. Suppose another ship sees it suddenly appear in the horizon. What would the captain do? Try to contact it by radio, of course. But he would never receive a reply.

We are like that phantom ship. God tries to get in touch with us. He uses all kinds of events and experiences to reach us – especially his Word, the Bible. But we don't know how to make contact with him. Phantom ships! That's what we are!

One day when I was speaking on this theme, a child asked its mother, "Mummy, why is the man telling us off like that?" I hope you understand that my intention is not to scold anyone. It is just that my heart burns with compassion for our poor nation when I see what has become of it – the intellectuals and the workers, men and women, the young and the old. We are people who no longer know how to call upon God. Yet God is so very near – but a breath away!

Many men and women call themselves Christians and claim connection with the Church, but they know nothing about praying. I have often met people in my pastoral calls who have said, "We are good Christians, Pastor Busch. My mother knew Pastor Smith very well. Did you know him? No? My mother knew him very well."

My reply would be: "If you don't know Jesus personally, you'll go straight to hell along with your Pastor Smith. The important question is whether or not you know how to call upon the name of the Lord, whether or not you know how to pray."

I entreat you to ask yourself this question: "Do I know how to pray? Do I pray?"

Maybe you are on the point of saying, "That's enough, Pastor Busch. Tell us how we can learn to pray." I am coming to it now.

2. How can we learn to pray?

a) The cry of the new-born child

How do we learn to talk? Do you remember your first childish stammerings? No? I don't either! But if you want to learn to pray, you must first utter the cry of the new-born child. Let me explain.

On one occasion the Lord Jesus told the following story: Two men went to church at the same time. One of them was a distinguished, influential man. He went right up to the front of the church and started to pray like this: "Lord, I thank you that I am a good man..." God heard no more! Though the man went on talking to his heart's content, his speech fell on deaf ears. *God was not listening.*

The other man was not a very commendable person. More or less a crook – a black-marketeer, a smuggler, or something along those lines – he was on the fringe of society. (The Bible calls him a "publican"; in other words, a tax collector.) Struck by the solemnity of the place as he came in, the poor fellow was overcome by fear. Keeping close to the entrance, he thought, "This is no place for me. The lively atmosphere in the pub around the corner suits me a lot better. I feel at home in the pub, but I don't here!" He was just about to take to his heels when he suddenly remembered why he had come to the place. He had a deep longing for God. (Aren't we all in the same state? Longing to go back home, longing to go back to our Father?) No, he could not turn away! Nor could he go forward. As memories of the type of life he had led flooded him, he could only wring his hands and murmur this short prayer: "God, have mercy on me, a sinner." The Bible says that at that very moment the hosts of heaven began to sing for joy. A man had found life!

"I have sinned." That is the cry of the new-born child.

I was present at the birth of my eldest son. It was a very difficult delivery and I couldn't help thinking of the words of Jesus: "A woman giving birth to a child has pain because her time has come." At times it seemed that the woman I loved and whose head I was supporting was totally exhausted. Then, suddenly, I heard a faint cry. The child was there! A new life! Its wail was no harmonious melody. But when I heard it, I broke down and wept. You understand me, don't you? I was overwhelmed by that cry – the first cry of a new life.

The first cry of a person who is born again – in other words, of the man or woman who at long last has come to the light of the truth – is this: "I have sinned. Oh God! have mercy on me, a sinner." All your litanies will be useless if you do not start with the cry of the new-born child. I have never yet seen a child who started off with a long talk. To begin with there is always the cry of the new-born child. It is exactly the same for the person entering into the Kingdom of God.

Have you uttered the cry of the new-born child? No? Then go to some quiet spot and think seriously about these things. I am not out to advertise for the Church. I am out to stop some of you who are on your way to hell. You will not be checked unless you utter the cry of the new-born child: "I have sinned. Oh God! have mercy on me, a sinner."

When the prodigal son in the Bible came back home, the first thing he said upon seeing his father was, "Father, I have sinned against heaven and against you." No sooner you too will have pronounced those words than Jesus, the Son of God, will come up to you and say, "My friend, I died for your sins. I paid your debt."

b) Only a child of God can pray

The other day I met a friend who has three lovely children, a boy and two little girls. As they were walking towards me, I watched how the children bombarded their father with questions and remarks, to the point where the poor man had some difficulty answering. When I came up to them, I said, "Hello, Mr. So-and-So! Hello, little ones!" As soon as they heard my voice, as if by magic the children stopped chattering. I was a stranger, and that had been enough to silence them. A child usually feels free to talk only in the presence of his father and mother. He is embarrassed as soon as a stranger appears.

It is the same with us. We can truly pray only if we are children of God. Consequently, if we do not know how to pray, we can assume that we are not children of God.

Oh, I know, we are devout Christians! We have been confirmed, we go to church on Christmas Day, we greet the minister or priest politely. An evangelist once described certain people like this: "They are baptized hares!" When someone asked what he meant, he replied, "If you catch a hare and baptize it, it will run back into the fields as soon as you let it go. Some people do exactly the same thing. They have scarcely been baptized than they run back into the world."

When things are like this, people cannot pray. Only a child of God really knows how to pray. Only a child of God therefore can be truly happy.

This is why you must become a child of God. You were not born a child of God. You may have a Christian veneer, but you are not a child of God. We become a child only by birth. And we become a child of God only by a new birth. You must become a child of God — then you will learn how to pray. A child of God cannot live without prayer. Prayer for him is like breathing. My young people sometimes jokingly say to each other, "Now don't forget to breathe!" But *you* neglect to let your soul breathe; you forget to pray. It is essential for you to become a child of God.

How do we become children of God? In a word — only through Jesus Christ. It was he who said: "I am the gate; whoever enters through me will be saved." Out of the heavy fog of this world, Jesus comes to you — Jesus, the man bearing the nail prints on his body. He hasn't particularly interested you up to now. What you have heard about him seems so unreasonable, so senseless. Yet he comes to meet *you*. Perhaps it will strike you suddenly just who Jesus is. Then you will be able to say to him, "You are a man come from another dimension; you are the Son of the living God; you are none other than my Saviour."

The *first step* I must take to become a child of God is to recognize Jesus as my Saviour. The *second step* is to adopt an attitude of confidence towards Jesus: confidence that he can put my life back in order, deliver me from anguish, from my sense of guilt, from the sins of my youth.

An Old Testament saint exclaimed, "You take care of my soul." All of a sudden we have such confidence in Jesus that we can even break with our past and entrust our entire life to his care. That is what we call "conversion". This is what I experienced when at the age of eighteen I abandoned my life of sin and put myself into the hands of Jesus. No one could take that step for me. And I can't take it for you either. It is a personal matter between you and God. Why not make a firm decision to follow him as of now?

The very moment you take this step, you become a child of God. Though some believe we can be saved by other means, I repeat that there is only one door by which you can enter into the Kingdom of God. It is Jesus Christ who died and who rose again for you. Take a step in his direction and he will receive you with open arms. Don't hesitate any longer!

As soon as you become a child of God, you will know how to pray. Your misery will end, because you will be able to pour out your heart before God. You will be able to speak to him as a child to his father.

I have been a pastor for many long years and have had to deal with many people. I am now convinced that every individual hides deep down in his heart some secret which he drags with him everywhere. But when I become a child of God, I can open my heart to Jesus and share my secret with him: that sin I can't give up, my illicit love affair, the memory of a mistake that haunts me. I can share with Jesus things that I would never dare share with any other person.

At the close of a youth camp, several young people told us about the experiences they had had. One of them, a boy of eighteen, said this: "Though I considered myself a Christian, I was on the verge of dropping everything. One evening before going to Bible study, I prayed: 'Lord Jesus, if you don't speak to me personally tonight, I'm going to let everything drop. I can't get to grips with my problems, particularly with those I encounter in this big city, if you don't enlighten me.'" He continued his story: "When I reached home that night everything was clear to me. The Lord had answered my prayer and had spoken to me personally." This young man's story deeply touched me. In his doubt and despair, he had called upon Jesus – and had been answered!

How much more likely we are to be heard when we pray as children of God.

My mother lived in Hulben, near Urach in the Swabian Jura area. She wrote me one day during the war: "I woke up at three in the morning and suddenly began to think about my sons on the front, about my grand-children, about you in the bombing zone, and about Elizabeth in Canada, whom I haven't heard from. My heart was filled with fear. I felt as if someone was strangling me with iron gloves. Unable to bear it any longer, I began to pray: 'Lord Jesus, say something to me. I can't stand the weight of my fears.' Then I switched on the light, reached for my Bible, (happy is the person who always has his Bible on his bedside table), and opened it. My eyes fell on this passage: 'Cast all your anxiety on him because he cares for you.'" My mother's letter ended with these words: "Then I put everything into the Saviour's hands, switched off the light and fell asleep."

Isn't that wonderful? When you are a child of God you can have this kind of experience.

I remember my mother saying to me one day, "Last night I was so worn-out that I couldn't even pray. I just said, 'Good night, dear Saviour!'" As I listened to her, I thought, "That's the way for God's children to talk to their Saviour – just naturally." God really watches over his children. Night and day my Saviour is at my side because I am his child. I can count on him whatever the circumstances may be.

Is all this clear to you?

It's a tragedy not to know how to pray. So I hope you will utter the cry of the new-born child: "Lord, I have sinned; have mercy on me, a sinner." And I hope you will have no peace of mind until you become a child of God, until you belong to Jesus Christ.

Then, and only then, will I cease to be concerned about you.

I just can't believe!

1. No one can make it without faith

Now right at the outset I have this to say to you: no one can get along in life without faith in God. And I don't know what to advise; simply because nothing can be done to help the person who doesn't believe in God.

Let me explain why . . .

To some people God seems to be just a theological or philosophical concept, or some force of nature. In reality God is personal. He is very much alive and fills the whole universe with his presence. And if I have not made peace with God, if I have not put my life right with him, if I am not his child, then I am passing by the main purpose of life. This is very serious indeed.

The crunch point came in my own life when I was a young officer in the First World War. Suddenly it hit me: God is here! I felt like someone who had driven his car straight into a brick wall. Up to then I had pretended like so many other people that I believed in God. But I had not grasped the fact that God was real. Then, in the space of a second, I found myself face to face with the reality of God.

One of the psalms in the Bible describes the reality of God in very striking terms. Whatever we may do, we cannot escape God. "If I go up to the heavens, you are there." The American astronaut John Glenn declared that what had impressed him most in his space capsule was the thought: God is here too! "If I go up to the heavens," – or if I speed along in outer space – "you are there!" Or if I hide a mile below ground in the lowest gallery of a mine – I would find God there too. The psalmist even goes so far as to say: "If I go down to the place of the dead, you are there."

Recently I flew to California. My wife had slipped a little note into my suitcase on which she had written a verse of this psalm. I read it when I unpacked my suitcase in San Francisco: "If I rise on the wings of the dawn, if I settle on the far side of the sea, even there your hand will guide me."

Yes, God is a great reality.

And because God is a great reality, I cannot ignore him and get away with it. If I go on living as if God didn't exist, if I go on living in contempt of his laws – not considering the Lord's Day holy, committing adultery, lying, having no respect for my parents, and none for God's name – then I am passing by the purpose of life. Under these circumstances, it is impossible for me to cope with life.

Look around you! People simply can't find a way out of their difficulties, not even those who earn a great deal of money. Everyone is worried. Nothing is going right in their private lives and everything is going wrong in their family lives.

How can we go on living when we have no faith in God? We cannot cope with life and we are helpless in the face of death.

Not a single one of us will be living in a hundred years' time. We all shall have crossed over to the other side. There is no doubt about that! "But once in the grave, everything is all over," you may be thinking. "We shall be dead and that's that." If this is what you believe, then stop a minute and think. What should you rely on for your facts about death: your own ideas or the Word of God? How can you cope with death if this thought suddenly takes hold of you: "I can't take anything I've stored up with me"? Perhaps you have built a little house; or, like me, you have a great collection of books. But you can take nothing that you cherish with you. And you can take none of your loved ones with you, either. There is only one thing we take with us into eternity: it is our guilt before God.

Try to imagine yourself lying on your death-bed, with this thought continuously running through your mind: "I'm going to have to leave everything behind. Everything! . . . except the transgressions and sins I've committed since my youth. My wrong-doings will follow me right into the very presence of the holy and just God!" How can you be acquitted at the tribunal of God if you do not believe in the one who can justify the sinner? Never forget this: one day you will have to appear before God!

The Lord Jesus, merciful as he was, nevertheless said on one occasion: "Do not be afraid of those who kill the body." (Yet I am afraid of such people.) "They are just the small fry," Jesus implied. "Do not be afraid of them. Rather, be afraid of the one who can destroy both body and soul in hell." And, as if he had shivers down his spine at the thought, Jesus repeated, "Yes, I tell you, rather be afraid of *him*."

A well-known scholar by the name of Ole Hallesby lived in Norway a few years ago. It was my privilege to know him. He was an extraordinary person. For a whole week on one occasion, he gave a talk each evening on national radio. I find it easy to picture him sitting in front of the microphone saying, "You may drop off to sleep peacefully in your bed tonight but wake up in hell tomorrow morning. It's my duty to warn you." These words set off a storm of protests. A journalist on Oslo's largest daily newspaper wrote an editorial along these lines: "We are no longer in the Middle Ages! It is totally inadmissible that a modern invention such as the radio should be used to spread nonsense of this sort." When an important newspaper publishes an article like this, all the smaller papers follow suit. Soon the whole press was repeating: "We are no longer in the Middle Ages. How can a scholar in our day possibly talk of hell!" The controversy was hot.

Finally, Radio Oslo had to ask Professor Hallesby to clarify his position. He came back to the microphone again, and this is what he said: "I have to clarify my statements. Well, all right! Here you have it: You may drop off to sleep peacefully in your bed tonight but wake up in hell tomorrow morning. It's my duty to warn you."

That was the last straw!

Then all the bishops of Norway were questioned. "Does hell exist or not?" Even the German news magazine *Der Spiegel* took up the debate and published a lengthy article entitled: "The quarrel over hell in Norway".

Less than a year after this storm, I was in Oslo for a series of student conferences and for several public meetings in the evening as well. As soon as I arrived, I had to hold a press conference. The different newspaper reporters had gathered at my hotel. Curiously, on my right was the journalist who had been at the origin of this controversy, and on my left was Professor Hallesby representing the Protestant press. They began questioning me. The journalist on my right was the first to attack: "Pastor Busch," he said, "I am totally in disagreement with Professor Hallesby. You are a modern man. In your opinion, does hell exist? Yes or no?" "Why, of course hell exists! It stands to reason." "Come, come!" he replied. "How can you be so positive about it?" I resumed, "I shall very gladly explain. I believe that hell exists because Jesus said so. And I fully believe what Jesus said. He knew a lot more about this subject than all our so-called intelligentsia."

God's Word declares: "God wants all men to be saved and to come to the knowledge of the truth." God has showed us in his Word how we can live and die in peace. And that is why we insist upon the necessity of believing. How can I go on living and cope with my problems if I can't believe?

There is absolutely no way out!

Let me explain this another way. Let's pretend that you have a little goldfish. One day you have a bright idea: "Poor little creature," you say to it. "How terrible it must be to have to stay all the time in that cold water. Wait a minute; I'm going to see what I can do for you." So you take the goldfish out of the water, dry it with a towel and place it in a beautiful gilded cage. You give it the best of goldfish food and say, "Little goldfish, you've got a beautiful gilded cage, appetizing food and wonderful fresh air. Life is great for you now!" What do you think the goldfish is going to do? Wriggle its fins and say, "Thank you. Oh, thank you"? No! Not on your life! It is going to struggle desperately to catch its breath. And if it could speak, it would say, "I don't want your gilded cage or fancy food. I want to go back to my natural element – water."

Well, you see, our particular element is the living God who created the heavens and the earth, and who created us too. "All life comes from God", begins one Swiss patriotic song. God is our element. But as long as I have not made peace with God, the best I can do is to provide a gilded cage for my soul. You understand what I mean: man today offers his soul everything that appeals to him – pleasures of all sorts, trips abroad, good food and wine. But our soul struggles within us and sighs, "I really don't want all these things. I want to be in my element. I want to be at peace with God!" Don't be so cruel with yourself. Your heart will always be troubled until it finds rest in the living God. As a fish wants to be in its element, our soul wants to be found in God. Only then will it be in its element.

How can we get through life if we don't believe in God? I can only answer that there is no way out: neither in this life, nor in death, nor in eternity! You may object that most people seem to make it fairly well. That, in my opinion, remains to be seen! Take, for instance, a man like the German poet Goethe. He was handsome, rich, intelligent. He had everything one could wish for. But towards the end of his life, he confessed to a friend that if he were to add up the hours of real happiness he had had during his lifetime, there would not even be three days. Goethe had no peace.

How true it is that without faith we can't get through life.

2. It is vital to have true faith

What really counts is that you have true faith: faith that saves.

It is a matter of simple fact that every human being believes in something. I was at home one day during my student days when a lady came to visit my mother. As my mother had gone out, I said to the lady, "My mother hasn't come home yet, Madam, so I'm afraid you will have to put up with me." "How kind of you!" she replied politely. When I had invited her to sit down in the living room, she asked me, "And what do you do in life?" I told her I studied theology. "What!" she exclaimed. "Theology? Who believes in anything nowadays? It's impossible. We have the faith of Goethe." (This happened in Frankfurt, the city where Goethe had lived.) "Christianity is out-dated, finished!" the old lady proudly declared. We were getting into deep waters, and as I didn't want to have an argument, I changed the subject. "May I ask how your health is, Madam?" She answered quickly, patting the table gently at the same time, "Quite good . . . touch wood! But look here, young man, you shouldn't ask such questions!" "Pardon me," I replied, "but why did you say, 'Touch wood'?" "To prevent bad luck." "Really!" I exclaimed. "You have rejected faith in the living God, but you have faith in the act of touching wood. That's strange. I hope you have benefited by the exchange!"

That day I understood that everyone has some kind of faith. But it remains to be seen whether it is true faith, a faith that saves. People in our day are saying that the main thing is to believe. Some say, "I believe in the good Lord!" Others, "I believe in nature!" And still others, "I believe in fate!" or "I believe in providence!"

No, my friends, that's not it! The main thing is to have true faith, the kind of faith which brings peace: peace with God, peace of heart. I need a faith which will save me from hell, a faith whose impact I can feel right now because it has given me new life. If I have any other kind of faith, I should consider it worthless.

There was a time when many of us Germans believed in Germany, in the Führer, in the final victory. And what became of it all? Can't you see that faith can be false?

But true faith – the one that saves – is, in a word, faith in Jesus, who is none other than the Son of the living God. Faith in Jesus Christ. Not faith in the founder of a religion – there's any number of them – but faith in Jesus Christ, the Son of the living God.

A beautiful story is told in the Bible which illustrates perfectly what this saving faith in Jesus really is. In your imagination follow me back two thousand years to Jerusalem – out through the gates of the city and up to a hill called Calvary (which means "The Place of the Skull"). Pay no attention to the hysterical, screaming crowd, or to the Roman soldiers on guard who are gambling for the prisoners' clothing. But lift up your eyes. On the middle cross the Son of God is nailed, his face all blood-stained from the crown of thorns digging into his head. It is God who is hanging there! On the cross at his right they have crucified a murderer. Another murderer is on the cross at his left. Night is falling rapidly. Death is drawing near. Suddenly, one of the two murderers cries out, "Hey, you in the middle, listen! You said you are the Son of God. If this is true, and if you're not a liar, then come down from your cross and get me off mine too!"

That's easy enough to understand. When people are at death's door, they say things they would never normally say.

Then the other murderer speaks out. Turning to his companion, he says, "Don't you fear God yet?"

And that is where faith must *begin*: we must recognize that God is holy and that his wrath is terrible.

When the bombs were falling on our cities during the last war, people were shocked and bewildered. The churches were probably to be blamed for this, because they failed to warn the people that God's wrath can be terrible and that he lets individuals and nations do their own thing without his intervening.

Don't you fear God yet? This question should be shouted from the rooftops of all our cities. Don't you fear God yet? It should be shouted far and wide. Don't you fear God yet? What are you thinking about? Are you blind?

That's where you must begin: recognize that God is holy and that his wrath is terrible.

But the second criminal, the assassin, continues speaking, "We are rightly punished; we are getting what our deeds deserve."

This is the *second step* leading to faith and salvation: he admits his guilt.

I have met many people who have said to me, "I just can't believe!" I have asked them, "Have you realized that you are guilty before God?" And they have answered, "I've got nothing to feel guilty about!" I have had to tell them, "You'll never see the light if you keep on fooling yourself."

I met someone recently who excused himself in the same way. "I've got nothing to feel guilty about!" he said. "Congratulations," I replied. "I can't say as much. There's always something wrong in *my* life!" The other person said, "Oh, naturally, if you go into details." "But God does look at the details," was my answer. "Stop fooling yourself."

You will never come to have true faith – this faith which saves – unless you call sin by its name: your irregular sexual habits – *fornication*; your marital infidelities – *adultery*; your deceitfulness – not astuteness, but *lies*; your egoism – not a legitimate love of self, but a form of *idolatry*, because you have made yourself your own god.

Let me repeat again that the second step towards faith and salvation is to call sin by its real name and to admit before God that you deserve his condemnation.

It is alarming to see how so many people of our day try to convince themselves there is nothing wrong. One day God will have to remove the scales from their eyes.

Finally, the robber turns to Jesus and says, "But you, you have done no wrong. Why are you being crucified?" In a flash he understands. "It's for me he is hanging there. To take away my sin." And he shouts, "Jesus, remember me when you come into your kingdom."

He has taken the *third step*: he has believed that Jesus can save him for all eternity. He has believed that Jesus is bearing the punishment for his sins. And Jesus' answer is immediate: "I tell you the truth, today you will be with me in paradise."

This is saving faith: I become aware of the holiness of God. I realize I am lost. But I believe that Jesus, who died on the cross for me, is my only hope of salvation. Without this faith there is no way out. But with this faith you can be sure of getting out of the mess you are in. That's all I can tell you.

I have often been accused of over-simplifying matters. I can only answer that I'm sorry, but the simple fact is there just isn't any other way for us to pull through life, confront death and stand before the judgement-seat of God.

I have no choice, as a sinner, but to come to Jesus, to repent and confess my sins, then to repeat in faith:

> I do believe, I do believe
> That Jesus died for me.
> And by his blood, his precious blood,
> I am forever set free.

Never forget the words: *Jesus Christ died for me.* When you wake up tomorrow morning, they should be ringing in your heart: Jesus Christ died for me! When you are going through the daily grind at work, you should give them some thought too: Jesus Christ died for me!

The day will come, if God has mercy upon you, when you will be able to praise him and say, *"For me... Yes, I do believe!"* The instant you have grasped this truth, you will become a child of God; because Jesus said, "I am the gate; whoever enters through me will be saved."

But I must go on to my third point.

3. People who can't believe in God

Many people say to me, "Pastor Busch, what you have to say is all well and good, but as far as I am concerned, I simply cannot believe in God."

Let's examine this type of reaction more closely.

There are generally four categories of people who say this sort of thing.

First, there are the people who say *they aren't religious*. Their argument is, "I can't believe simply because I'm not religious. You are, Pastor Busch, but not me." To this objection I can only answer, "It may surprise you, but I'm not religious either!" To be truthful, I attach very little importance to church bells, incense and other such things. In these past years at Essen, it has been my joy to preach in a chapel where there is only a good brass band. No organ, no church bells – and I haven't missed them in the least. I am not against such things, but I don't need them. I'm afraid I am not very religious!

When Jesus, the Son of God, was here on earth, there were some very religious people around. There were the scribes, the priests and the Pharisees – all of them were very religious people. The Sadducees, though more liberal in outlook, could also be numbered among them. And these were the people – these religious people – who crucified the Son of God. Jesus wasn't the man for them!

Then, there were other people around who weren't religious at all: prostitutes, swindlers – the Bible calls them publicans – and the workers who struggled so hard to earn their daily bread. They were all people without faith or law! And yet it was they who turned to Jesus! Why? Because deep down in their hearts they admitted, "We are guilty before God. So many things are not right in our lives. But here is a man who will save us and make us children of God." And they believed in Jesus.

No, the Lord Jesus did not come to make religious people even more religious. But he did come to save sinners from death and hell and to make them children of God.

To those who say, "I can't believe in God because I'm not religious," I answer without hesitation, "You are the ones who are most likely to become children of God." Sinners we all are – and we all know it too!

Let me repeat this: Jesus did not come to make religious people even more religious, but to make poor lost sinners children of the living God.

The second category of people also says, "I *can't* believe in God." But if they were honest with themselves, they would be saying. "I *don't want* to believe." If these people were to believe in God, their whole lives would have to change. And that is one thing they do not want. They know only too well that many things are not right in their lives. To become children of God, they must come to the light. And that is another thing they do not want. Why, their friends would probably make fun of them! And what would all their relatives say if they were suddenly to become Christians? No, better not!

So if you meet people who tell you that they can't believe in God, look at them more carefully. Perhaps they really should be saying, "I don't want to believe."

There is a touching story in the Bible. Jesus, the Son of God, was sitting somewhere on the Mount of Olives. The city of Jerusalem was spread out below him. Facing him just a short distance away was the magnificent temple. Even the pagans said that the temple of Jerusalem should have been counted as one of the marvels of the world. This was the view before Jesus. Suddenly the disciples noticed with surprise that tears were flowing down Jesus' cheeks. Dismayed, they looked questioningly at him and then heard him sob, "O Jerusalem, Jerusalem, you who kill the prophets and stone those sent to you, how often I have longed to gather your children together, as a hen gathers her chicks under her wings, *but you were not willing*." This is one of the most moving passages of the Bible.

"But you were not willing."

The inhabitants of Jerusalem had also said, "We cannot believe." In reality they did not want to believe.

The person who does not want to believe in God is under no obligation to do so.

Let me say this in passing. In our churches there are still all kinds of restraints. But in the Kingdom of God everything is done by free will. The person who wants to live without God has a perfect right to do so. God offers himself to us, but we can reject him if we want to.

Do you want to live without God? You have the right. Do you want to live without making peace with God? You have the right. Do you want to live without ever praying to God? You have the right. Do you want to live without the Bible? You have the right. Do you want to break God's commandments? You have the right. Do you want to profane the Lord's Day, do you want to commit adultery, cheat and steal? You have the right.

The man or woman who does not want the Saviour sent by God

to save sinners is free to reject him. The man or woman who wants to jump into hell has the right to do so. God forces no one.

Only never forget that you must take the consequences of your choice. God offers pardon and peace to you through Jesus. You have the right to answer that you neither need them nor want them. And you can keep on living with this attitude. But don't suppose that in the last five minutes of your life, just before you die, you can take hold of the salvation that God has been offering to you during your whole lifetime. It is your privilege to refuse the offer of peace which God makes to you through Jesus. If this is what you choose, you will never be at peace with God throughout all eternity!

Hell is the place where we get rid of God for good. Once there, there is nothing that will ever draw you to him. You may desire to pray, but you won't be able to any longer. You may long to call upon the name of Jesus, but you won't even remember what it is.

You are under no obligation, for sure, to accept the message I bring to you. You can choose not to follow Jesus Christ. But never forget that it is hell your are choosing instead. You are absolutely free to make this choice.

"*But you were not willing*," said Jesus to the inhabitants of Jerusalem. He did not force them, but the choice that they made was horrible.

The third category of people who say, "I can't believe in God," puts up a rather curious explanation. They are never women, always men. This is what they say: "Pastor Busch, *I've seen so many things in my lifetime* that I just can't believe any longer." I usually inquire, "Now, tell me, just what has happened during your liefetime? My life hasn't been boring either!" "People have done me a lot of harm. And I simply can't believe any more." This kind of thinking haunts the world of men.

I have the rather naughty habit of teasing people who tell me this. "Do you believe what you read on the railway time-table? Do you believe what the policemen tell you when you ask for information?" I usually ask them. "Well, of course!" And so I go on: "Stop saying, then, that you don't believe in anything any longer. You should be saying, 'I don't believe in anything any longer – except what's written on the railway time-table, except what the police say...'" And we could go on and on! But I am sure you have understood the point.

Usually, with this kind of person, I end up by saying, "You see, I myself was leading a dismal life of sin, impurity, darkness and error. Then Jesus intervened. I recognized that he is the Son of God, God's Messenger, and gave my life to him. He had done so much for me. You may have the impression that you really can't believe in anybody or anything any longer. But perhaps you could at least believe the word of the one who gave his life for you? Surely you can believe what *he* says! You believe so many things. And yet you say 'No' to the only person who is worthy of your complete confidence. You say 'No' to the only person who has never disappointed anyone! And you dare to say that you've seen so many things during your lifetime. In my opinion, you haven't seen enough!"

The fourth category of people who pretend not to be able to believe in God are *those who have been shocked by the Church* or who are disheartened by its teachings.

A young student sat down before me one day and said, "I study natural science." "That's fine," I replied, "but what is your trouble, young lady?" "Pastor Busch," she answered, "I attended one of your meetings. I feel that you have something I'd like to have myself. But I can't believe. I can't accept the doctrines and traditions of the Church just like that! It would feel like swallowing a bundle of hay!" I couldn't help but laugh, but hastened to reply. "There is no need for you to swallow a bundle of hay! Have you ever heard of Jesus?" "Yes," was the answer. "What would you say," I then asked, "if I were to suggest that Jesus is a liar?" "I'd say that I don't believe it." "So, you do believe that Jesus told the truth?" "Yes," she said, "I believe that!" I continued, "Is there one single person in this world to whom you would dare say, 'I'm sure you've never told a lie'"? "Oh no," she said, "I could never say that to anyone." I continued, "From all that you have just said, it's clear that you already believe. You have confidence. That's great. You've got the right end of the stick, young lady, you believe that Jesus told the truth. The Bible says: 'This is eternal life: that they may know you, the only true God, and Jesus Christ, whom you have sent.'"

In conclusion I said, "You don't have to struggle with the doctrines and traditions of the Church. Out of the fog of this world someone has come to meet you. And as he draws closer, you will be able to distinguish clearly the nail prints on his hands and the marks of the crown of thorns on his brow. They are the proof that he took your sins upon himself and that he loved you when no one else loved you. May you see Jesus more and more clearly and may you be able to say to him, 'My Lord, my Saviour and my God!' Believing does not mean swallowing doctrine like hay, just because the pastor has said so.

"No, believing is *knowing* Jesus Christ."

Someone else may say, "As far as I'm concerned, I can't believe because I've seen a pastor who did this, that and the other thing..." And away they go! What haven't I heard about pastors! One had shady affairs with women. Another ran away with the church funds. There has been trouble with pastors everywhere. "So, how do you expect me still to be able to believe?" And I can't help blushing, for I know myself only too well. Naturally I have never run away with the church funds. But if people knew all that goes on within me, they would realize that I am not perfect either.

What can I say? Simply that nowhere in the Bible is it written: "Believe in your pastor, and you will be saved." The Bible, however, does say: "Believe in the Lord Jesus Christ, and you will be saved." A pastor is – oh, I know it's not always the case, but if he is doing his job correctly – a pastor is a signpost pointing to Christ. A signpost may be a little crooked, twisted, or washed out by the rain. It doesn't really matter too much as long as people can see what it is pointing to. As for myself, I wouldn't listen to a pastor who is not directing people to Jesus, the crucified and risen Son of God. But I'm certainly not going to get angry with a signpost, deformed though it may be, which is pointing to the right road. No, I'll just get on with going down that road.

Do you really think that you will dare to say to the living God when you come into his presence at the Last Judgement, "Lord, I didn't want your salvation, I didn't accept the forgiveness of my sins, and it was all because of that good-for-nothing pastor"? Is this the way you see yourself standing before God one day?

My friends, it is wrong to say, "I can't believe." Jesus said something which in my opinion is of the utmost importance: "If any one chooses to do God's will, he will find out whether my teaching comes from God or whether I speak on my own." The issue at stake is whether or not I am willing to obey and to put into practice, right down to the smallest detail, what I have recognized as the truth. Then, and only then, will I be able to go forward in life.

4. What should you do?

Here in a few words is what you should do if you can't believe in God.

First, *Ask God to enlighten you*. He is beside you. Say to him, "Lord, help me to believe. Help me to see the light." God answers this kind of prayer.

Second, *Count on God's presence.* Turn your thoughts to him and say, "Lord Jesus, I want to give you my life." This is what I did when, as a young man in a state of unbelief, the fear of God had become very real to me. When I heard about Jesus, I gave my life to him.

Third, *Read the Bible.* This is how you can get to know Jesus better. Every day, spend fifteen minutes or so quietly with him. Read a passage of the Bible and listen to what God is saying to you through it. Read, keeping your ears wide open to the voice of God. Then, in whatever way comes naturally, bring your concerns to God. Tell him about your unbelief. "Lord Jesus, I have so many things to tell you. I just can't find my way out. Please, help me!"

Finally, *Get in contact with other Christians.* Look for other people who are in earnest about God too. Don't remain alone. There are no solitary travellers on the road to heaven. So look for fellowship with other Christians who are walking along the same road.

How can we enjoy life if our faults and failures weigh us down?

As they say, "It's no joke any more!" That's how I want to introduce our subject, because now we are going to tackle some very serious problems.

How can we enjoy life if our faults and failures weigh us down? I ought to point out straight away that the question isn't put very well: ...*if* our faults and failures weigh us down? The truth is, every one of us *is* burdened by them. Our faults and failings follow us everywhere we go. That is why I am so glad I can tell you about something absolutely wonderful – a gift – which can enrich your life and fill it with happiness. It is something which cannot be bought in any country of the world. Even if you were a millionaire and were willing to spend your entire fortune, you would not be able to buy it! Nor can you get it through influential friends – even though a lot of people nowadays manage to get things money can't buy by pulling strings. There is absolutely no way of your getting it on your own either.

If you want it, you must accept it as a gift. This wonderful, important, incomparable thing I am talking about, which can neither be bought with money nor obtained through our connections, is nothing less than the forgiveness of sins.

Perhaps you are disappointed. Maybe you pulled a long face when you read the words "forgiveness of sins", and wondered:

1. Do I really need it?

I am convinced that most men and women reason as follows: "Forgiveness of sins? I don't need that." Recently a young man explained things to me like this: "We live in an age where our needs are created by advertising. Our great-grandparents knew nothing about chewing-gum or cigarettes. But by incessant commercials on radio, television, and posters, we have been gradually conditioned; so that now we are convinced, for instance, that we couldn't live without cigarettes. The need is created first, then they start the hard sell." The young man went on: "The Church works in exactly the same way. It tells people: 'You need forgiveness.' Then it goes on to sell forgiveness. In reality we don't need it, but you church people have created the need in order to sell your goods."

Is this really true? Let's suppose that you stop someone strolling down the street and say, "Hello! What's your name?" "Brown," he replies. "Good! Tell me, Mr. Brown, do you need to have your sins forgiven?" Mr. Brown would most likely answer, "Bah! What rubbish! What I need is a good, round sum of money, not forgiveness of my sins."

Is the young man right? Have we created a need that was previously non-existent and are we using the Bible to try and meet that need?

No, no, a thousand times no! It is the greatest of mistakes to think this. Our deepest need is to have our sins forgiven. The man or woman who thinks he or she can do without it does not know the holy and awesome God. So much emphasis has been put on the love of God in our day that we have forgotten that the God of the Bible is also a God to be feared. What shook me out of my sinful life was this thought which suddenly struck me: there is good reason to be afraid of God. The person who says, "I don't need to be forgiven", does not know the living God, who can destroy both body and soul in hell. Oh yes, there is a hell; there is eternal damnation. Jesus said so and he should know! And though the whole world may cry, "We don't believe it", the whole world will perish nevertheless. Jesus knows what is awaiting us beyond the grave. And he warns us about eternal condemnation.

Some years ago, I held a meeting in the beautiful city of Zurich, in the Congress Hall, before a huge audience. A lot of people had to stand and lean against the wall. Among those standing there, I noticed two men who were chatting away merrily. It was clear from their behaviour that they had only come out of curiosity. One of them had a nice little goatee-beard. (It had caught my attention and I had said to myself, "What a shame you can't grow one like that!") From the beginning of my sermon, I had determined to capture the two men's attention. Actually, they were very attentive until I pronounced the word "forgiveness". Immediately a mocking smile appeared on the lips of the man with the goatee. I saw him whisper something in his friend's ear. The hall was vast, and as the two men were standing at the back, I did not hear what he said, of course. But I could guess from the look on his face that it was probably something like this: "Forgiveness of sin – typical minister's blah-blah!" And perhaps he also thought: "After all, I'm no criminal. I don't need forgiveness. Come now!" (Isn't that exactly what you're thinking too?) At any rate, when I saw that man's reaction, I could feel myself getting angry. I know God doesn't like to see us get angry, but I just couldn't help it. So I said, "Now listen, everyone. We are going to have thirty seconds of silence. And I want each one of you, during those few moments, to answer 'yes' or 'no' to this question: 'Are you willing to reject the possibility of having your sins forgiven for all eternity just because you think you don't need it?'"

For half a minute a deep silence fell on this great crowd. Suddenly I saw the bearded man, leaning heavily against the wall, turn pale with fear. He must have thought, "Right now I claim that I'm not a bad chap; but when the time comes to die and things become really serious, I'd be jolly happy if my sins were forgiven. No, I'd rather not do without forgiveness for all eternity."

Would you?

If our conscience has not been totally smothered, we know very well that our greatest need is to have our sins forgiven.

A few years ago, Bill Haley gave a concert in Essen. He is among the modern musicians I call "hip rollers". Thousands of teenagers had gathered together in the "Grugahalle" to listen to him and his group. Right from the very first song, the audience went wild. They literally tore the hall to pieces. Damages were estimated at 60 000 marks. A young policeman later confided to me, "I was sitting right at the front and I had to cling to my chair so as not to join in!"

As I was walking through the centre of town the day after the show, I spied three teenagers who looked as though they had taken part in the events of the previous night. So I went up to them and said, "Hi! I bet you boys were at Bill Haley's show last night." "That's right, Pastor." "Good," I replied, "then we're on familiar ground. Tell me, what made you all tear the hall to pieces?" "We did it out of despair, Pastor Busch," replied one of them. "Out of despair? Despair of what?" "We don't know!"

The great Danish theologian and philosopher, Sören Kierkegaard, tells how as a child he often went walking with his father. Sometimes his father would stop and, looking thoughtfully at his son, would say, "My boy, you carry hidden despair within you." When I read this, I couldn't help thinking that as a city minister for forty years I have discovered that this is true of every human being.

What about you? Are you too tormented by some hidden despair? Let me tell you where it comes from. Let's take a look into the depths of your soul by means of a little illustration.

Since my parish is in the Ruhr Valley, I have often gone down the mines. It is a tremendous experience. First they give you a miner's outfit and helmet to put on; then you go down the shaft with lightning speed in a lift, to about the eighth level. Can they go even further down? Probably, but no one does because below that, it's just a pit full of mud. That is where all the water gathers which has seeped through the rest of the mine. Only once, since I have been in Essen, has the hoisting cable broken. That day the lift dropped right down to the mud-pit. It was awful.

The pit and its miry waters remind me of man. Everybody knows that there are several "levels" in our lives. Outwardly we can look very cheerful, while inwardly things are just the opposite. We can have a nice big smile on our face and yet be sick at heart. It sometimes looks as if we regard life as a big joke, but in reality dark despair is hiding deep down in the innermost recesses of our heart.

Doctors, philosophers and psychiatrists all recognize this fact. It is the subject of many books and novels. It is disturbing to see the way our despair or anxiety comes out in the open some times. A psychiatrist told me one day, "You can't imagine the number of young people who come to me for treatment." Most people, however, don't even try to find out the cause of their despair or anxiety. They simply try to get rid of it by getting drunk or by taking drugs. Isn't it more reasonable to face the facts?

Most people think that the deep-rooted despair of the human heart was only discovered this century. But, amazingly, the writers of the Bible knew about it more than two thousand years ago. The Bible speaks of a "discouraged soul". It also shows us the deep-seated cause of our despair: since the Fall, we are alienated from God, out of our element, and we dread the day when we will have to appear before him. To put it even more strongly, our greatest problem in life is our guilt before God. When we are faced with a problem of this size, we realize our inability to find a way out by ourselves. Hence the dark despair in our innermost being.

Do we need to have our sins forgiven? We most certainly do! We need forgiveness more than anything else.

Sin – what is it? Sin is anything which separates us from God. We are born sinners. A child born in England during the war, for instance, had nothing against us Germans. But he was in the enemy camp nevertheless. In the same way, having been born into the world, the camp hostile to God, we are by our very nature separated from God. As life goes on, the wall of our guilt grows higher and higher, and we get further and further from God. Each transgression of one of his commandments is like a brick we add to this wall. Sin is a terrible reality.

I'd like to tell you how I first became aware of the terrible reality of sin and of its irreversibility. I had a remarkable father. We had a wonderful relationship. One day I was nicely settled in one of the attic rooms of our house studying for an exam, when I heard a voice calling from below: "Wilhelm!" I leaned out of the window and saw that it was my father who was calling me. "What's wrong?" I asked. "Is the house on fire, or something?" "I'm going into town," he replied. "Do you want to come with me? It's much more fun to go with someone else." "But Dad," I answered, "I'm just going over a very important point for my exam. It couldn't be a worse time!" "Never mind! I'll go alone."

Two weeks later he was dead.

It is the tradition in our country that the sons of the deceased take turns at keeping vigil over the body. The night was still. Everyone was asleep. I was sitting alone by the open casket. Suddenly I remembered my father's invitation two weeks earlier to go into town with him, and how I had refused. I looked at him and cried out, "Oh, Dad! Ask me again. I'll go a hundred kilometres with you if you like."

There was no answer. His mouth stayed shut. I realized then that my lack of kindness was a terrible reality that could never be changed, even if I had all of eternity before me.

Have you ever thought about the number of times you've failed? How can we live with a burden like that? We can't cope with life if our sins have not been forgiven.

And how can we face death? Do you want to carry your faults and failings with you into eternity?

I often try to imagine my last moments. It's quite normal at my age. I can see myself holding the hand of a loved one. Then the moment comes for me to let it go; and my boat glides away into the great silence until it comes into the presence of God.

Yes, without the shadow of a doubt, you will appear before God one day. With all your mistakes, with all your failures, you will face the living and holy God. And your blood will run cold at the sight of the huge pile of faults and failings that have followed you.

Do we need to have our sins forgiven? We need forgiveness more than anything else, even more than our daily bread.

2. Where can I find it?

I just told you what happened between my father and me. There will never be a chance for me to go back on my mistake. It is impossible for us to undo the mischief we have done, and its effects abide in the sight of God. The bill is sent for payment.

A man named Judas betrayed his master for thirty pieces of silver. But almost immediately after, he was smitten with remorse. So he went back to the group of men to whom he had sold his master and said, "I've made a big mistake! Here, take your money back. I want to put things right." With a shrug of the shoulders, they replied, "What do we care? That's your business." You can talk to whoever you like; they will invariably answer, "That's your business."

Is it possible, in spite of this, to have our faults and failures washed away, to put things straight with God? Where can we receive forgiveness of sins? How can we go about getting it?

To these questions the writers of the Bible give a unanimous, warm, joyful answer. From the book of Genesis to the book of Revelation, in the Old Testament as in the New, the same theme keeps coming up again and again: our sins can be forgiven!

But where? Follow me through the gates of Jerusalem and up to the hill called Calvary. Pay no attention to the crowd which has gathered there or to the two criminals hanging on the crosses on the right and the left. Let us give our whole attention to the man nailed on the cross in the middle. Who is he? Clearly he is not like us. One day he stood before a crowd and challenged them to convict him of sin. Not a single person took up the challenge. They could find nothing wrong in him. Later he was put on trial and questioned by the Roman authorities and by the Jewish religious leaders. They could find no reason to condemn him. No, he wasn't like us. He does not need forgiveness because he has never sinned. Yet it is he who is hanging up there on that cross!

Why?

God is just. He cannot leave sin unpunished. So he placed our sin on Jesus, his Son, and his Son was punished in our stead. "But he was pierced for our transgressions, he was crushed for our iniquities: the punishment that brought us peace was upon him; and by his wounds we are healed." This is the heart of the Bible's message. God's judgement was inflicted upon Jesus so that we might find peace. This is where we can receive forgiveness of sins.

Where can I get rid of the burden of my faults and failures? Where can I make peace with God? At the foot of the cross of Jesus. "The blood of Jesus his Son purifies us from all sin." May we all take advantage of it!

An American by the name of William L. Hull published a very interesting book. He was appointed chaplain to Adolph Eichmann, the man who was responsible for the massacre of millions of Jews. Hull visited Eichmann thirteen times during his imprisonment, had long conversations with him, heard his last words, accompanied him up to the gallows and was present when his ashes were scattered over the Mediterranean.

Rev. Hull published the substance of his conversations with Eichmann in a work entitled, *The Battle for a Soul*. He wrote at the beginning of his book: "My goal was to save this loathsome sinner from going to hell." And we learn with consternation that this man who assassinated millions of people from his desk and who plunged the world into untold suffering dared to say right up to his last breath, "I don't need someone to die for me. I don't need forgiveness of sins, and I don't want it."

Do you want to follow Adolph Eichmann's example and die as he did? No? Well, if you don't, you had better turn to Jesus with all your heart. Jesus, the Son of God, is the only person in the world who can forgive sins because he died to atone for them.

During his conversations with Eichmann, Rev. Hull was almost afraid to offer forgiveness of sins through the blood of Jesus to a man like him. Could such a great criminal possibly be forgiven? Yes! By all means! "The blood of Jesus, his Son, purifies us from *all* sin." But to get forgiveness I have to confess my sins and say to God, my eyes fixed on the cross:

> I do believe, I do believe!
> That Jesus died for me;
> And through his blood,
> his precious blood,
> I shall from sin be free.

The Bible uses different illustrations to help us understand the relationship between the death and resurrection of Jesus Christ and the forgiveness of our sins; (for, as you probably know, Jesus did not stay in the grave but arose the third day and is living today).

One example the Bible uses is that of *a guarantor*. A guarantor is a person who makes himself responsible for the debts of another person. He promises to pay that person's debt for him if he can't do so himself. Somebody has to pay. It's always like that in life. Now every time I sin, I get into debt with God. The Bible says: "The wages of sin is death." This means that God demands our death in payment for our sin. But this is where Jesus intervened and died for our sins to save us from eternal death. Jesus stands surety for us before God. It is now up to you to choose: either you pay your own debt and go to hell, or you turn to Jesus and say, "Lord Jesus, I want to believe that you paid my debt. Thank you."

This leads us to the second illustration used in the Bible: *a ransom*. Supposing a man falls into the hands of a slave trader. He cannot redeem himself. Then a man full of compassion comes along and goes up to his master saying, "How much do you want for this slave? I'll buy his freedom." When does the slave get his freedom back? The very moment the last penny is paid! On Calvary, the Lord Jesus paid the price of our redemption right to the last penny. Believe it, and claim as your own the freedom he has purchased for you. Jesus redeems, Jesus liberates slaves from sin!

That's not all.

Another image which appears frequently in the Bible is that of *reconciliation*. Even the least enlightened pagan knows he needs reconciliation. That is why in almost every religion there are priests who seek to appease the gods by propitiatory sacrifices. But God Almighty accepts one sacrifice only: the sacrifice of "the Lamb of God who takes away the sin of the world". Hosts of priests have offered countless sacrifices. But Jesus is the great high priest who reconciles us to God. He is, moreover, the atoning sacrifice for our sins. He alone, therefore, can restore peace between God and us.

Another biblical picture used is that of *purification*. A Christian wrote to his brethren: "God has loved us and washed us from our sins by his blood." You probably know the story of the prodigal son who finally landed up among the pigs. Many are those – alas! – who have followed in his footsteps. But the day came when the prodigal son pulled himself together. He turned his steps homeward, then threw himself into his father's arms, just as he was. He didn't start by taking a good bath or buying a new suit of clothing and a new pair of shoes. No, he went home just as he was. And it was his father who took care of cleaning him up and getting him properly dressed.

A lot of people think they have to improve first before becoming Christians. This is a terrible mistake. We can come to Jesus exactly as we are, filthy and repulsive. He is willing to accept us with everything that has soiled our life. He himself will wash us and make us clean. He makes all things new. "The blood of Jesus, his Son, purifies us from all sin." This was the Apostle John's testimony and it can be yours too.

I cannot refer to all the many images which come up in the Bible. However, I hope you will get down to reading the Bible for yourself. And as you do, you will discover its wonderful message of forgiveness more fully.

How can we enjoy life if our faults and failures weigh us down? We can't! But everything changes when we find Jesus, when through him we come to experience the joy of having our sins forgiven. Gone our fears, our deep despair!

Surrendering our lives to Jesus is not a sad and solemn affair. Quite the contrary. It is passing out of the darkness of anguish into the light of the sun of grace.

3. How can I claim forgiveness?

You may be thinking at this stage: "It must be wonderful to know that one's sins are forgiven. But how can I get hold of this forgiveness? No newspaper has ever written a line about it. Modern novels don't deal with the subject and I don't know of a single film that can tell me anything."

How can I get forgiveness? That is the burning question!

It seems to me that the best thing for you to do is to find some quiet spot and to call upon the Lord for help – right now. He is risen, he is living. People who "believe" are described in the Bible as "those who call upon the Lord". Why not call upon him yourself?

There is a direct line connecting you to Jesus. Perhaps you have never used it before. What a shame! Why not give him a call now? You don't even have to dial! Just say: "Lord Jesus", and you'll have him right on the line! The contact with him will be immediate. That's what praying is all about.

But what are you going to tell him? Everything that is bothering you. You can say, for example: "Lord Jesus, I'm having a love affair and I just can't break it up. But I know it's wrong. Lord, help me." Or: "Lord Jesus, things are not above board in my business. For years I've been fiddling my tax returns. If I try to straighten things out, I might go bankrupt. Lord, help me." Or perhaps this: "Lord Jesus, I'm unfaithful to my wife. I can't get out of the mess I'm in. Lord, help me." You know, on this private line you can share with the Lord Jesus things that you would never dare tell anyone else. He hears you. Pour out your heart to him. Confess all your mistakes. It will liberate you.

Then say to him: "Lord Jesus, Pastor Busch claims that on account of your blood everything will turn out all right. Is that true?" Ask him. You can talk to him for hours if you want. He'll listen to you.

"Okay," you may say, "but when I have told him everything, he probably won't even answer me." Yes, he will! Listen carefully. I am going to tell you on what line you can hear him speak. Get hold of a

New Testament. Leave the Old Testament aside for the time being, because it is too difficult to start with. Open your New Testament at the Gospel of John and start reading. After, try the Gospel of Luke. Read them as you would read a newspaper article. And it won't take you long to notice that Jesus speaks throughout the entire text. This is what makes the Bible different from all other books. It is the line the Lord uses to speak to us.

Someone once said to me, "When I want to hear God speaking, I take a stroll in the forest." "That's ridiculous," I answered. "When I'm in the forest, I hear the leaves rustling, the birds singing, and the waters murmuring. And it's simply delightful. But the forest can never tell me whether or not my sins have been forgiven. Nor can it show me how my heart can be made new or how I can find God's grace. God has revealed all that to us only in the Bible."

Try putting fifteen minutes aside each day to meditate and pray. Call upon Jesus and tell him absolutely everything: "Lord, you see how much I've got to do today and that I'll never get through it all by myself." You can share everything with Jesus. Then, take your New Testament and read half a chapter, praying all along: "Lord Jesus, speak to me now." And suddenly you will come upon a word from God that is just for you. You will say to yourself, "He is saying that to me!" Underline the passage, and if you like, write the date in the margin.

When I was a young man, I was visiting a family one day. There was a Bible lying on the piano. Leafing through it, I noticed that many passages had been underlined either in green or in red. Dates had been noted in the margins. As it was a large family, I asked whose Bible it was. "It's our Emmi's Bible," was the reply. I looked at Emmi a little more closely – and I married her! She was just the kind of girl I wanted: a girl who understood that it's on this line, and on no other, that Jesus speaks to us.

I served as a telegraphist for a while during the First World War. At the time radio communications were unknown. Our instruments were small and we had to attach the wires to them. One day I had to go to an observation post situated on a hill. No shelter had been built there. So I had to lie down on the grass. As I was trying to contact our troops, I suddenly saw a slightly wounded soldier appear on the hill-top. I yelled to him. "Hey, you over there! Get down! We've been spotted. It won't be long before they shell us." He threw himself on the ground, crawled up to me and said, "I'll be given a leave with this bullet I've got. I'll be able to go back home. Say, your equipment is pretty old." "Yes," I said in a low voice, "it's an old model." "The clamps are loose." "Yes, the clamps are loose." "And look here, there's a piece missing." I flew into a temper and said, "Will you just shut up! I don't have time to listen to your comments. I've got to concentrate on getting in touch with headquarters."

It's the same thing with the Bible. I myself want to listen to the voice of Jesus. But when people come along and say to me, "The Bible is just a book written by men", and other such foolish remarks, I can only answer, "Do shut up! I hear the voice of Jesus in the Bible."

Do you see what I'm getting at? Don't let yourself be led astray. Jesus speaks to us on one line only – the Bible.

You should also get in touch with other people who study the Bible. When I mention things like this to people, they always answer, "All that is so old-fashioned. Only old people go to church these days." I have been a youth worker for over thirty years, and have met countless numbers of young people who can testify that forgiveness of sins is a reality, that we can talk to Jesus and that he answers us.

Seek the friendship of men and women who have experienced these things. Yes, it *is* possible to find people who want to travel on the road that leads to heaven.

Jesus is standing before you today and he says: "Come to me, all you who are weary and burdened, weighed down by your faults and failures, and I will give you rest for your souls. Yes, I can forgive your sins."

"You get on my nerves!"

We all find that other people get on our nerves, don't we? It's part and parcel of everyday life. Scarcely a day goes by without someone annoying or irritating us. But it's the same for others – we get on their nerves too! Everyone annoys everyone else. Well, almost everyone! My wife, for instance, never irritates me. But there are some people who really exasperate me. Don't you find the same thing? Of course you do!

This way of looking at others is the root cause of the constant frictions in our families, our neighbourhoods, our businesses and industries – and even in our churches. The whole world is suffering from the "you-get-on-my nerves" syndrome.

Many people think, "I would enjoy life if So-and-So were not around!" So-and-So is a thorn in the flesh for them. He is their pet aversion.

So it seems it is high time we dealt with the question: How can we stop people getting on our nerves?

This is actually part of a much bigger problem. It's a bit like when someone coughs. He could be suffering from a serious lung infection. If so, cough sweets will do no good. What the sufferer needs is a thorough check-up and the proper treatment. Do you see what I am getting at? The fact that we get on each other's nerves is only a symptom of a more serious disease the world is suffering from. The reasons go deeper than, let's say, our neighbour's unpleasant character!

The real cause is a sickness which affects the whole world.

1. The world we live in

I owe my view of the world to the Bible. To my mind, the Bible's approach is the only valid one. Most philosophies usually go out of date within twenty years.

The Bible states that in the beginning, when God created the world, it was perfect. Adam didn't get on Eve's nerves and Eve didn't get on Adam's. There was perfect harmony between them – perfect harmony, too, between mankind and God. They were all one: God and mankind; man and woman. There was not the slightest flaw in their relationships.

But, according to the biblical account, a disaster happened right at the beginning of mankind's history: the Fall. Man was put to the test. He was not supposed to eat the fruit of a certain tree. God had forbidden him to do so. But it was too tempting! So, of his own free will, he chose to disobey. Adam ate the forbidden fruit; and as a result of his fall, a great rift was opened up.

On the one hand, his relationship with God was broken. God chased man from the Garden of Eden and placed two angels to guard the entrance. Our separation from God dates from that moment. Since then we irritate God and he irritates us. To demonstrate this, you only have to talk to people about God. They immediately get all worked up and start yelling, "Oh, stop it! We don't even know whether God exists!" Between God and us there is a great gulf.

On the other hand, human relationships were also broken. You only have to look at Adam and Eve's children to see that even then men had already started to get on each other's nerves. There were two brothers. Relations between brothers, as we all know, are often strained. These two brothers, Cain and Abel, were very different from one another. One day, Cain, who was a farmer, was working in the fields with his hoe. He saw his brother, Abel, walking by. I have no trouble in picturing his reaction: "I hope he won't come hanging around here. I can't stand the sight of him!" But Abel came up to him and said a few words. Suddenly Cain grasped his hoe and began to hack at the face he hated, hitting it again and again until at last Abel was lying at his feet, dead.

We are civilized people; we do not kill each other with hoes! But if you read the papers, you know that things like this still happen now and then. When I think back to the trials of Nazi war criminals, I can't help saying to myself, "They had exactly the same mentality as Cain; they were full of hatred for their fellow-men." It was in the name of this hatred that they massacred hundreds of thousands of men, women and children.

We human beings seem to think that if no one saw it, nothing happened! How many of us are haunted by memories of sinister deeds which no one saw!

Cain fled. He was worried. Suddenly he heard a voice calling: "Cain!" Who could it be? "Cain!" the voice repeated. A chill of fear went through him. It came to him in a flash that it was God who had called his name. God had been there all the time! God had witnessed the whole thing and hadn't said a word! "Cain!" came the voice again. "Where is your brother Abel?" On the defensive, Cain answered, "I'm not my brother's nursemaid! No one ever asked me to keep an eye on him." But Got replied, "Cain, your brother Abel's blood cries out to me from the ground."

This story is a perfect example of the rift that opened up at the Fall. Human relations have not been the same since: something was broken. We annoy one another. But the rift also affected man's relationship to God. God annoyed Cain – and he annoys some of you too. The trouble is, we cannot get rid of our fellow-men. Nor can we get rid of God!

This is the world we live in.

2. Words can't help

It's no use talking about the "good Lord". Between God and us there is a wall, a gulf. During the war, when my house and half the city of Essen were on fire, a woman came rushing up to me, screaming, "How can your God allow all this!" "Maybe it's because he is your enemy," I replied.

Since the Fall, the relationship between God and man has been broken. Having wandered far from God, our relations with other people are no longer the same either. This is the deep reason why other people get on our nerves. In the final analysis, if your neighbour bothers you, it is because of the Fall, because we are fallen men separated from God. And the best advice in the world will not change a thing.

The other day I happened to be at the Swiss border. Hanging on the wall inside the customs-hall was an attractive poster with these words: "Togetherness is better". I thought to myself, "No doubt it is; but that's no help when someone gets on my nerves." I read on another poster: "Be nice to others". The Americans have put stickers on every street corner of our towns with the slogan, "Keep smiling". But nothing changes, in spite of it all.

I remember a family I used to visit frequently when I was a student at the Faculty of Theology. There was no unity in this family. They all lived in the same village, but there had been a lot of quarrelling and hard feelings between them. In my optimism as a student minister, I had gathered the whole family together one evening with the praiseworthy intention of reconciling them to each other. I talked my head off . . . By eleven o'clock I had put everything straight, and they all shook hands. Overjoyed, I gave myself a pat on the back: "You're going to be a good minister. You're getting off to a great start!" So I went home happy and slept soundly. The next morning I happened to meet one of the young women of the family. I said to her, "It was wonderful to see the way things got sorted out last night, wasn't it?" "Wonderful?" she questioned. "Don't you know what happened afterwards?" "No . . . What?" I asked, turning pale.

On the way back home, apparently, the quarrel had been taken up again. And things were worse than ever! You think that's funny? Well, I didn't find it funny. That day I became keenly aware of the brutal reality of the Fall; our relationship with God and with our fellow-beings is broken.

People write to me quite often, saying: "Dear Rev. Busch: At such-and-such a place, I have relatives who are not getting on with each other. Could you go and visit them?" I always refuse, because I know how useless it is to advise others. Just think for a moment of all the people who irritate you. I could tell you what you should do, but it would be absolutely pointless. It's tragic.

Let me illustrate this.

Suppose I am calling on a family. And then in comes their seventeen-year-old son. He is totally relaxed, is wearing worn-out jeans and has the latest hair style. The father – a conscientious, well-mannered civil servant – suddenly gets furious and explodes, "Look at him, just look at him!" The sight of his good-for-nothing son makes the father's blood boil.

Or take the case of a nice Christian mother with a tendency to be legalistic. Her daughter dares to put on some lipstick, and the mother exclaims, "Oh, how that girl gets on my nerves!" Meanwhile, her daughter is thinking, "Does Mother ever get on my nerves!"

Isn't it like this everywhere?

One day a man in the process of getting divorced, to whom I was explaining that divorce is a sin, snapped at me, "Pastor Busch, stop it! The way my wife eats her soup is enough to make me lose my temper."

Do you find that funny? I don't. It horrifies me. Do you think these are small, insignificant things? Well, they aren't. They are symptoms of the sick, fallen, rebellious world in which we live as men and women without God.

Exasperation can take on some very serious forms at times. I know a young girl in Essen who is totally paralysed with multiple sclerosis. She lives in a small house. Next door lives a selfish, cruel young man. He watches TV every evening and turns the sound up very high. Each evening till late at night the sick girl can hear everything through the thin wall dividing the two houses. One day she begged him to turn his television set down a bit. But he did just the opposite: he turned it up full blast. And so, year after year, night after night, hour after hour, the poor girl has to put up with this situation.

That is how cruel we humans can be.

When I was a young pastor, I had to prepare 150 youngsters for their confirmation. I decided to visit each one of them in their homes. They lived in tenement-houses. In the first home I called at, I found them quarrelling. In the second, they were quarrelling. In the third, it was no different. Some time later I asked the children at catechism if those who had no fighting at home would stand up. Only three or four stood up. "Does that mean that in all the other families there is quarrelling?" I inquired. "Yes." Turning to the children who had stood up, I asked them, "How come there are no squabbles in your house?" "It's because we live alone," was their reply.

That is the situation.

And we are expected to be courageous, cheerful and hard-working when all the time we live in a perpetual state of nervous tension. When something falls on our foot, it hurts. But when other people continually get on our nerves, it is unbearable.

3. God intervenes!

If that were all I had to say, then it would have been better to say nothing. But I have incredible, amazing news for you: in the midst of all this nervous tension, this mutual irritation, God in his great mercy intervenes. The sad state of the world does not leave God indifferent. No! He gets involved.

And he does so in a marvellous way. This is the message of the Bible – a breath-taking message. God broke down the wall which separated us from himself, and he came to us in the person of his Son, Jesus. Men and women today reject the Bible's message because they feel it is irrelevant. This attitude only shows the blindness of our generation. In rejecting Jesus, they turn down their last hope.

What great fortune for people like us, on bad terms with both God and man, that God destroyed the wall which separated us from him. What great fortune for us that Jesus came to bring about a radical change in our situation!

But how can he do it?

a) Peace with God

All perfections are combined in the person of Jesus. There has never been any rift between God and him. He is the Son of God.

The other day someone said to me, "Jesus was just a man like us; he was the founder of a religion, nothing more." I answered, "We are probably not talking about the same person. I am talking about the one who said, 'You are from below; I am from above.'" The person I am thinking of is the Son of the living God, the Unique One, the extraordinary being who came into our poor, lost and cursed world.

There has never been any rift between God and Jesus. And no one ever got on his nerves; not even Judas. And yet Judas betrayed him. Jesus, for his part, loved Judas right to the end. I want you to see Jesus from this angle: as the only man whose nerves were never set on edge by other people.

Take, for instance, the account of the last supper, on the eve of Jesus' crucifixion. In the East, as you know, in Bible times, people didn't sit on chairs; they lay on big cushions all around the table. How on earth they managed to eat in that position is beyond me! One thing I'm sure of is that it is impossible to use a knife and fork lying down. But that was the way they ate.

It was also the custom before settling down for everyone to take off his sandals and wash his feet. Now on that particular day, the disciples had walked a long way with Jesus. Completely worn out, they took off their sandals and threw themselves on the cushions. And I can just picture Peter looking at John meaningfully as if to say: "Well, one of us will have to go and get some water and a sponge to wash our feet. For once, you can do it. After all, you're the youngest. You're always trying to get off lightly, John, and it's starting to get on my nerves!" But John only shrugs his shoulders and thinks to himself, "That Peter really annoys me. He's always picking on me just because I'm the youngest. Why can't James go and get the water?" Meanwhile James, in his corner, is thinking, "Why me? I'm one of the Master's favourite disciples. Let Matthew look after it for once!" And so, because everyone was trying to get out of the job, they were getting on each other's nerves.

Just then Jesus got up. The disciples turned pale. "He isn't going to do it, is he?" Yes, he is going to do it! Jesus came back with a servant's apron tied around his waist, carrying a basin full of water and a sponge, and began washing the disciples' feet. The feet of Judas, of Peter, of John, of James, of Matthew... (I almost added... and mine!)

How true it is that all perfections are combined in the person of Jesus, the Son of God. God was in him. And he loved other people.

But now I want to show you Jesus in the place where I most love to look at him: on the cross. Let me lead you out of the gates of Jerusalem and up a hill. On that hill a crowd is clamouring; Roman soldiers, armed with their spears, are on guard; and three crosses have been raised. The man I have been talking about is nailed to the cross in the middle, a crown of thorns on his brow. Don't take your eyes off him, because it is for you he is suffering. He is dying so that you may be delivered from your misery and be reconciled to God.

Would you like the obstacle that has come between God and you to be taken away? Then come to the cross of Jesus. This Jesus, who died and rose again for you, was sent by God as his envoy of peace. Do not allow your doubts, however numerous they may be, to stop you. Place your confidence in Jesus. Lay down the burden of your sins before him. And tell him: "From now on, I want to belong to you."

If you take this step, I can assure you that God will grant you the gift of his peace.

In his letter to the Romans, the Apostle Paul declares: "Therefore, since we have been justified through faith, we have peace with God through our Lord Jesus Christ." Yes indeed, Jesus is God's envoy of peace. Accept him. How terrible to think of all the men and women who have heard about Jesus but have refused his offer of peace. Do not follow their example. I plead with you: for love of your own soul, say "yes" to the peace offering God has made you through Jesus.

I was talking to some journalists today. They had reached the point where they were wondering whether there was still anything in our day and age worth believing in. "Frankly," I told them straight out, "having gone through two world wars and lived under the Nazi regime, I have to admit I really don't know what I can rely on any more. Our thinkers and politicians don't take their own flowery speeches seriously – so why should I? No, I don't know what to believe in on this earth... excepting the offer of peace God extends to me through Jesus Christ."

We can take God's offer seriously. It is the only thing that is still sure. It is worth giving the matter some thought.

If you are one of those disillusioned people who say, "You can't trust anyone any more", then the Gospel is just what you need. For God, in Jesus Christ, took you very seriously. And now it's up to you to consider his offer of peace seriously.

Jesus restores the contact between God and you. Perhaps you may object, "But I go to church regularly. I put money in the collection plate every Sunday!" What good is that to you, I ask, if you do not have peace with God? Let me repeat this: Jesus died for you. He took all your wrongdoings upon himself so that you might be able to throw yourself at his feet, saying, "Lord, I come to you, totally aware that I'm a poor, lost sinner. But I believe in you. I accept you as my Saviour."

This is how you can lay hold on life, and find peace with God.

b) Peace with others

When Jesus breaks into a life, he brings peace with God and peace with our fellow-men. We stop getting on each other's nerves.

Some of you readers may be wonderful Christians. But as long as other people continue to get on your nerves, there is something wrong with you. Is that clear? Perhaps you will say, "But you don't know my neighbour – she's a real meanie!" And I would answer, "As long as you don't love her, there is something wrong in your life. Because when Jesus has come into our life, we should stop being so sensitive and so easily irritated by those around us."

Jesus offers us peace with God and peace with the person who gets on our nerves. So, if you can't stand certain people, you need Jesus. Apart from him, nothing else can help you. Your nerves will be shattered in the long run by all these tensions. You need Jesus to give you peace with God. Then, and only then, will things be all right with other people.

I have a very good friend who lives in a lovely flat. The landlord, however, is not easy to get along with and is a real penny-pincher. One day he wrote my friend an insolent letter: "You will do this and you will do that, and you will pay such-and-such a sum." My friend told me what happened: "When I read that letter, I flew into a rage. I sat down at my desk with the intention of answering it then and there. But just as I was about to do so, the sight of Jesus on the cross, dying for me – and for my landlord – flashed before me. I couldn't write the letter! Instead, I went to see him and said, 'Mr. So-and-So, do you think it is necessary for such offensive language to be used between us? It seems to me that both of us are men who are open to discussion. So why don't we just sit down and talk things over calmly? I like you, and I really don't think you need to speak to me like that.'" The landlord was completely disarmed – and there was no more trouble. The two of them – the hard landlord and the disciple of Jesus Christ – eventually became good friends.

Let me tell you another touching story. I know a man by the name of Erino Dapozzo who was an evangelist in France. He came home from the war, after his internment in a concentration camp, with a badly injured arm. Dapozzo told me once of an incident in his life which I have never forgotten: "The commandant of the concentration camp where I was interned called for me one day about noon. They led me into a room where the table was set for one person. I was starving. The camp commandant came strutting in. Then he sat down at the dinner table and had a royal feast served to him. I had to stand at attention all the time and watch him devour one course after another. He was licking his lips . . . and I was dying of starvation. But the worst was yet to come. When his coffee was being served, he took out a small parcel and placed it beside his cup. Then he turned to me and said, 'Do you see this parcel? It's from your wife who sent it to you from Paris. It's full of biscuits.' (I knew there was very little to eat in France, and that my wife must have deprived herself in order to bake those biscuits.) Then the man began eating them, one after another! I begged him, 'Please, give me one, just one, to keep as a souvenir from my wife. I promise you, I won't eat it!' But he only laughed, and gobbled them all up, right to the last one."

In an infuriating situation like that, our exasperation can reach a climax and turn into hatred.

Dapozzo went on with his story: "Suddenly I understood what the Bible means when it says: 'The love of God is shed abroad in our hearts.' And I felt there and then real affection for this man. I thought, 'Poor man, nobody loves you. You are surrounded by hatred. How privileged I am as a child of God.'" Dapozzo was filled with compassion for the commandant! He did not allow the man to irritate him. And the commandant must have felt it, for he got up hastily and left the room.

When the war was over, Dapozzo went to visit him. The man turned pale when he saw Dapozzo at his doorstep. "You have come for revenge?" he asked. "Yes," replied Dapozzo, "I've come for revenge. Let's have a cup of coffee together. I've got a cake in the car. It will make a nice little snack for the two of us." The ex-commandant was terribly upset. Then suddenly he understood: the man who is submitted to Jesus Christ is no longer under the domination of hatred. He has been liberated from his seething anger because God's love has been shed abroad in his heart.

As an old minister working in a big city, time and again I have heard people complain: "I feel so lonely. Nobody loves me." I can't stand listening to that sort of thing any more! I always feel like asking them, "What about yourself? How many people do *you* love?" When we ourselves are a block of ice, it's not very rational to say there is no love in the world!

When this dawned on me, I immediately said to myself, "I'd better start being kinder to other people." But very soon I realized it was impossible. Our heart is so full of "self"! I know we feel particularly drawn to certain people because they are likeable. But what about the others, those who get on our nerves?

I remember a conversation I had with a communist worker. He said, "We demonstrated in favour of the coolies of Shanghai." "That's great," I replied. "And how are things going with your next-door-neighbour?" He exploded: "When I see that fellow, I'll smash his face in!"

No, it's not very difficult to love someone at the other end of the world. But things get complicated when it comes to loving someone who lives next door.

I believe that the world will never change unless each one of us personally learns to love his neighbours – including the one who is hard to get on with, the one who is violent, and the one who wishes us no good. *It can't be done alone.* It is a gift of God. From personal experience I know it is not easy. When Jesus takes over our life, he not only gives us the gift of peace with God, but he wants to help us find peace with our fellow-men too.

But it hurts! For in the process Jesus shows us that we get on other people's nerves even more than they get on ours, that it is harder for them to put up with us than for us to put up with them. Since I have known Jesus, he has often put his finger on wrongs I have done to other people. And I appreciate more and more the fact that Jesus bore my sins on the cross and grants me forgiveness of sins.

Jesus is able to start the greatest revolution the world has ever known. If this is to come to pass, each one of us must accept him. I beg you, therefore, not to be content with just listening to my words. Put your trust in Jesus.

How I would love you to be able to say, "I have found Jesus and he has found me."

Things have got to change – but how?

When I was young, the writings of Max Eyth, an author who has long since been forgotten, were all the rage. He was an engineer by profession, and his novels usually centred upon the beginning of the industrial era. The title of one of them was *Professional Tragedy*. In the story we meet with a young engineer who one day, through a series of curious coincidences, is offered a very important contract. The project consists of constructing a bridge over a river at the very point where the river develops into an arm of the sea. The difficulty of the enterprise is increased by the fact that the bridge will have to stand up to the pressure of the in-going and out-going tides. Our modern technology didn't exist at the time either!

The young engineer gets to work and builds a huge bridge. When it is completed, there is an official opening with music, flag-waving and full press coverage. The officials present at the ceremony are invited to cross the bridge on a train. The young engineer is the talk of the whole country. His name is in big letters in all the newspaper headlines. His reputation is made.

Soon afterwards, he opens a large architect's office in London and marries a rich woman. He has everything he wants in life. Yet, a strange secret, shared only with his wife, clouds his life. One day in early autumn, he suddenly disappears. That night, as the storm rages and the rain pours down, the young man can be seen wrapped in his rain-coat, standing at the foot of his bridge. He is afraid. He can literally feel the fury of the storm battering against the pillars of the bridge. Again and again he goes over his calculations to reassure himself that his pillars are solid enough and that he estimated the pressure of the wind correctly. As soon as the storm is over, he goes back to London. Once again he is the great celebrity, an important figure in the social life of the city. No one can detect the hidden fear that is gnawing at him: "Did I construct that bridge properly? Is it solid enough?" These agonizing questions torment the young man day and night and darken every minute of his life.

Max Eyth goes on to describe in very striking language how one terribly stormy night the engineer, overwhelmed with fear, once again goes to have a look at his bridge. He sees a train about to cross it. He watches the red lights on the last wagon intensely. And then, suddenly, he can see them no longer. The train, he realizes, has just disappeared into the deep waters of the raging sea. The bridge has collapsed in the middle!

When I read this novel for the first time years ago, this thought went through my mind: "Actually, this is the story of every human being." Each and every one of us is working on the construction of the bridge of our life. And from time to time, during a sleepless night or after some traumatic experience, fear takes hold of us: "Have I built the bridge of my life properly? Is it solid enough to resist the storms of life?" Instinctively we know that something is wrong: the bridge of our life is not quite perfect.

Therefore, the first point I would like to make is this:

1. Something is wrong

As a minister working in a big city, I have often asked people: "Tell me, is everything perfectly all right in your life?" Never yet have I met a single person who has not ended up admitting, "Perfectly all right? No! Things should be different in many areas of my life." Of course, I cannot tell you where the weak point is in your life's bridge. But you yourself are aware that many things should be different.

That is why we make good resolutions now and then: "I am going to change. I absolutely must improve in such-and-such an area of my life." Be honest – do you really believe a person can change? No, in reality man is incapable of changing. The Bible says this with brutal realism: "Can the Ethiopian change his skin or the leopard its spots? Neither can you do good who are accustomed to doing evil."

The world is full of lessons in morality and good resolutions, but no human being can change by himself. This is a strong word.

Some people I meet are perfectly aware of the weaknesses in their life's bridge. Occasionally I am asked, "But what can I do? It's impossible for me to change." That is true: the unchaste person cannot give himself a pure heart; the liar cannot make himself truthful; the selfish person cannot suddenly become altruistic (for even if he succeeds in putting on a show of a little love, that little bit of love will be tainted with selfishness); and the dishonest man cannot be transformed into an honest man. If only I knew you well enough to be able to show you the weak spot in the bridge of your life! But God knows, and he can show it to you.

This is a very disturbing truth that the Bible reveals to us. I am not talking about my own ideas. I am simply passing on to others what the Word of God has to say.

The Bible has a terrific message for you right now, a message which will take your breath away. Here it is: the living God sent someone into this world who can transform you and change your entire life. This person is none other than his Son, the Lord Jesus Christ.

2. Everything can change

My friends, I do not know whether it is the Church's fault that people think the Gospel is just a lot of fairy-tales. For my own part, I find its message extraordinary. God sent his Son into the world to give me a chance. And Jesus made this astounding declaration: "Behold, I make all things new." He alone can change a human being.

I have known alcoholics who have been delivered from their addiction; selfish old women (selfish to such an extent that they pestered everybody to death) who were changed from one day to the next and began to think of others; and men, obsessed by sex, who have been given the purity of a child. Jesus transforms. He appears, and suddenly all things become new.

That is why we need a Saviour, we who know that the bridge of our life is not what it should be. We need the Lord Jesus – not the externals of Christianity, but the Christ himself. It's not religion, not dogma, not membership of some denomination that we need, but the living Saviour. And he is right here. You can call upon him at this very moment and confess to him all the misery in your life. That is the extraordinary message I have to share with you.

Recently I spent a week in the city of Munich. There is a huge park right in the centre of the city called the English Garden. As my hotel was only a short distance from this park, I went there for a walk every morning. Near the entrance gate there is a wooden bridge spanning a river. To the left of the bridge, the water flows over a dam and turns into a water-fall. At the bottom of the water-fall I saw, one day, a piece of wood bobbing in the water. I wasn't in a hurry, so I stopped to watch how the log turned round and round in circles. At times it looked as though it were going to be swept along by the current and continue on its way. But the swirl of the water always snatched it back again. When I came back the next day, the piece of wood was still there. Each time, just when it looked as though it would be swept along by the current, it would be dragged back by the eddy of the water. Can you picture the scene? There was a fairly swift current – but the piece of wood kept going round and round and round!

Most of us are just like that. Our lives turn endlessly in the same vicious circles: the same sins, the same anxieties, the same ungodliness, the same despair in our hearts. Day after day, it's the same monotonous life, the same routine. We turn round and round in circles. But not far from us is the current. It flows from Jesus, the Son of God.

This Jesus died for us on the cross. Believe me, if God allowed his Son to die such a cruel death, there must have been some reason for it, even though you may not yet see the reason. In your mind's eye, look at Jesus in agony on the cross. There *must* be a meaning to his death! For that reason alone you cannot simply pass by without at least trying to understand what it's all about.

Because he died and rose again, a liberating current flows from Jesus. Alas, we are just like that piece of wood in the English Garden. We are turning around in endless circles. That time in the park, I thought, "All the piece of wood needs in order to be swept along by the current is a slight push." Try as I may, I couldn't reach it without running the risk of falling into the water.

We are not a piece of wood however! To get out of our old vicious circle and to get into the liberating current flowing from the Son of God, we have to give ourselves a push. And when we have done so, we discover that God helped us along!

But at this point I prefer to emphasize the fact that we all, each one of us, must personally take this step towards the liberating current. No one else can do it for us. Some people, though, are deeply aware right from the start that God is working in their heart, and that it is he who will enable them to take that step which will get them out of the old vicious circle and sweep them along into the liberating current flowing in Jesus.

3. It's either this or that!

Two Bible stories will illustrate what has just been said.

The Apostle Paul had been imprisoned in Caesarea, the city where the Roman Governor had taken up residence. The new procurator of Judea was a Roman by the name of Festus. One day, the Jewish King Agrippa and his sister Bernice arrived at Caesarea to pay their respects to Festus. They said to him, "Festus, a very interesting prisoner named Paul apparently is in your custody.

We'd like to hear this man for ourselves." So the next day the audience room was prepared. Festus, Agrippa and Bernice made their entrance in great pomp and ceremony, followed by high-ranking officers and the leading officials of the city. At Festus' command, the accused was brought in. But within minutes, the roles were reversed. The accused was no longer Paul, but all the aristocracy gathered around him. Paul stood there before them all and delivered a speech of great spiritual power. He strove to make his audience understand who Jesus is. Rather than concentrating on their sins, he described to them the Son of God – the one who said: "If a man is thirsty, let him come to me and drink." Paul said something like this to them: "You, with your thirst for living, your guilty conscience, your longing for God, your fear of death, listen to me! Jesus stretches out his hand to you and says, 'Come to me, all you who are weary and burdened, and I will give you rest.'" With words like these, Paul spoke in praise of Jesus whom he had met personally one day on the Damascus road.

When he had finished speaking, the Governor Festus said to him, "Paul, you are a good orator. But what you say is madness! You let yourself get carried away by your enthusiasm!" Festus hadn't understood a thing. The Bible says of certain people: "Their heart is as fat as grease." Some hearts are as if covered with grease, so that everything slides off. At any rate, Festus' heart was like that.

Agrippa, on the other hand, was quite upset. He said something which always deeply moves me: "You almost persuade me to become a Christian!" With those words, the king rose and left the room. And things remained as before! Like the piece of wood in the English Garden, Agrippa's life went on tracing the same circles, in the same swirl, in the same humdrum life, in the same kind of existence – until his death, until hell.

What about you? Are you too going to leave things as they are? If so, then Jesus died in vain for you. And his resurrection will be of no use to you. For you, there will be no forgiveness, no liberation, no peace with God. For you, as for Agrippa, only a step separates you from being a Christian: "You *almost* persuade me to become a Christian."

There are men and women today who call themselves Christians, and yet they have never become children of God. There are men and women today who call themselves Christians, and yet they are on their way to eternal damnation. There are men and women today who call themselves Christians, and yet they have no peace. It's tragic!

Now I am going to tell you the second Bible story which is just the opposite of the first one. The Apostle Paul arrived one day in the city of Philippi, a European city where everything was to be found: places of entertainment, theatres, night-clubs; in a word everything to be found in any city worthy of the name. And as in every real city there is a prison, there was also one at Philippi. The establishment was under the direction of a former Roman officer who may have been appointed to this post because of some wound received in battle. One day the jailer was put in charge of two unusual prisoners: the Apostle Paul and his companion, Silas. They had preached the Gospel with rare power in the city. Their preaching had caused a riot to break out and the local authorities had ordered them to be flogged and thrown into prison. So both Paul and Silas were placed in the care of the jailer, with the order that they were to be kept well under guard until the next day. The jailer, an old stick-in-the-mud for whom orders were orders, nodded assent: "Keep them well-guarded? Don't worry! I'll see to it!" Deep down in the heart of the prison was a cell with water trickling down the walls. It was to this dungeon that he brought his two prisoners, and locked their feet in the stocks.

If you asked me what this man's religion was, I would say: the same religion that most of you have! He believed in the "good Lord", or maybe even in several "good lords". At that period, everybody in the Roman Empire had some kind of religion, but nobody bothered much about it. Just like today. Can you identify with this man?

Suddenly something strange happened, something we will never be able to explain completely. To begin with, towards midnight, Paul started to sing a hymn of praise in honour of Jesus. Probably it had taken him all this time to accept the unjust treatment he had received: the blows, the imprisonment, the stocks. This sort of treatment is very difficult to take. But a thought flashed into his mind: "The Lord Jesus, the Son of God, has redeemed me by his blood. I am a child of God. I have peace with him. And even here in prison, he holds me in his hand." So he struck up a song of praise; and Silas joined in, singing the alto or the bass. It was beautiful! The other prisoners listened to them, full of amazement, for never before had such sounds been heard in the prison. And with good reason!

In the course of my imprisonments, I have come to know what police state prisons are like. All that can be heard is the swearing, screaming and groaning of the prisoners, and the yelling of the guards. When I started singing a hymn one day, they immediately came to stop me. In our day they have come to understand how dangerous it is to allow someone to sing God's praises. But in those days it wasn't so.

Paul and Silas went on singing. Of course, the jailer was very surprised. "By jove!" he thought to himself, "what are they singing?" He pricked up his ears. "Why, those are religious songs," he exclaimed, "and here in prison too! In that hole down there, there's good cause for one's morale to be very low. And these fellows are singing in honour of their God!" The jailer went back to bed. But he had hardly settled down when he felt the tremors of a violent earthquake. It was God who brought it about. All the prison doors burst open. The prisoners' chains broke. The jailer jumped out of bed, got dressed as fast as he could, and discovered that the doors were opened. "Good heavens! The prisoners have escaped," he cried. "I'll be disgraced. I'm in for it!" He was on the point of committing suicide when he heard Paul's voice coming up from below: "Don't harm yourself. We are all here!"

The Bible gives no details as to what went on in the depths of the man's soul. But in a flash he had understood this much: "There must be a living God who intervenes for his servants. All my life I have insulted that God by my way of living and acting. He'll turn me away, reject me, because he knows my sin. He knows all about the dirty tricks I've played. Yes, there is a living God – and as for me, I'm lost." He dashed downstairs into Paul's dungeon and cried, "Sirs, what must I do to be saved?" He had just realized his life was like that piece of wood in the English Garden. It did nothing but turn in circles. Things always remained at the same point. But now the situation was critical: "What must I do to reach the liberating current?"

If the Philippian jailer had asked us such a question, we probably would have preached a sermon to him or moralized. If we had been in Paul's situation, it is possible that we would have begun by asking him to let us out of prison. But Paul answered immediately, in a single sentence: "Believe in the Lord Jesus, and you will be saved, you and your household." The jailer's knowledge was very limited. He was vaguely aware that this Jesus saves us from the wrath of God, from judgement, from hell – and from our former way of living. But in a mere moment he got that salutary shock which tore him from his former life and swept him along into the liberating current. From then on he belonged to Jesus.

The Bible goes on to relate how this man took Paul and Silas out of their dungeon and washed their wounds, listening attentively to all that Paul was teaching him about Jesus. He was baptized that very night, testifying in this way that he belonged to Jesus. The story ends with these words: "The jailer brought them into his house and set a meal before them, and the whole family was filled with joy, because they had come to believe in God." The jailer was now being swept along by the life-giving current. He had found peace with God.

One man said that he was almost persuaded to be a Christian. The other man found himself pushed into the liberating current coming from Jesus. What will become of you?

4. Take Jesus' offer seriously

Things have got to change – but how? To begin with, you've got to get to know Jesus.

It was shortly after the war. A college principal telephoned me one day, saying, "Pastor Busch, I've got fifteen young men here. They passed their 'A' levels in the army. But they have to take one term's extra tuition for their diploma to be considered valid. They are former air force lieutenants, infantry and artillery captains, and other lower-ranking officers. Needless to say, they're furious about having to go back to school. Would you agree to give the course on religion?" I accepted, and went to my first lecture in fear and trembling.

I found them all sitting there in their worn-out uniforms, these young warriors who had become grey-haired on the battle-field. "Hello," I said as I entered. "I've come to give you some lectures on religion." My introduction was cut short, for immediately one of them stood up and opened the debate. "Why did God allow this horrible war?" Another one went on, "Where is the love of God? He stayed silent when millions of Jews were dying in the gas chambers." Similar questions were coming from all sides. In the end, I raised my hand and said, "One moment, please! You are going at it like a blind man at the helm of a ship in heavy fog! It's senseless talking about God in that way! God is totally unknown and hidden to us. He has revealed himself in only one way – in Jesus. And before going on, we must first learn who Jesus is. Gentlemen, we will take up the discussion again only after having looked first of all at the revelation of God. That will be our subject in the next few weeks. The next time, bring your Bibles with you."

They brought them, and we started reading the book of Genesis: "In the beginning God created the heavens and the earth." Then we went on to the story of the Fall, then to the account of God's judgement on a fallen humanity. They were all very impressed by this statement in the Bible: "Your wickedness will punish you; your backsliding will rebuke you. Consider then and realize how evil and bitter it is for you when you forsake the Lord your God and have no awe of me, declares the Lord, the Lord Almighty." Nations and individuals have discovered how true this can be.

After that, we read the story of Jesus together. Without interruption we listened to the account of his death and resurrection. That particular hour will forever remain engraved on my memory. While one of the young men was reading the passage out loud, a great hush suddenly fell over the class-room. We held our breath as we listened to the great things that God had done through Jesus Christ. And such a change was brought about in these young men's hearts that never again did they get involved in the kind of sterile discussion that had started in the first lecture. These lads all called themselves Christians, but they knew nothing about the living God who came to us in the person of Jesus Christ and who accomplished all that was necessary for our salvation.

Yes, you must get to know Jesus. And then? You must take his offer seriously.

Jesus told a parable one day. A king organized a wedding banquet for his son. He sent his servants to inform the guests: "Come, the banquet is ready!" But all of them, one after the other, excused themselves. The first one explained, "Sorry, but I'm just in the process of concluding a very important deal, and I have to sort it out immediately."

The second guest had another excuse: "Thank you for the invitation, but I just got married. I'm sure you understand that as I'm right in the middle of my honeymoon, I can't very well do anything else."

In the end, no one came. I have often tried to imagine how these people felt later on. They must have thought to themselves: "Really, I ought to have accepted the invitation to the banquet of the king's son; however, the circumstances weren't at all favourable."

Isn't that what you say to yourself too? "Really, I ought to become a child of God, but somehow I just can't make it! I really can't..." I implore you, accept by faith the invitation of the Son of God!

So many people say to me, "I believe too." I know that we Germans believed in a whole lot of things during the Third Reich: in the Führer, in the final victory, in the miracle weapon, and so on.

But what we are most in need of is not some ordinary kind of belief, but peace with God. This peace can be obtained through Jesus alone. By way of a few illustrations, I want to explain what it means to believe.

At the beginning of my ministry, I used to do door-to-door visitation in a very select district. At almost every house, the people would slam the door in my face, saying, "We don't want to buy anything!" I would put my foot in the door, whenever possible, and reply, "I'm not selling anything. I am a pastor." "We've no need for a preacher here!" the answer would invariably come.

One day I went into an apartment which opened right into the kitchen. A young man was pacing back and forth in the room, with a furious look on his face. "Hello," I said. "Hi!" "I am a Protestant minister," I continued. "What? A preacher?" he yelled, as he stopped dead in his tracks. "That's the last straw! Get out of here as fast as you can! I have no faith in anything any more. I've lost faith in humanity." He had probably just received a hard blow. I replied, "Young man, let's shake hands. I've lost faith in humanity too." Astonished, he asked, "What did you say? As a minister, you should be trying to keep up faith in humanity." "Do you think so?" I retorted. "I'm sorry, but I've given up on humanity. I have gone through the war. And when I think of the obscenities, of all the filth, and of the desert of selfishness which this world has become, no thanks, I just can't believe in humanity any more." "You are right," he agreed, "but, how come you are a pastor then?" To which I replied, "Oh! that's because I received a new faith, a faith nothing in the world can shake." "Ha!" he exclaimed, "I'm really curious to know what kind of faith it is."

So I announced the Gospel to him: "It is an absolute faith in Jesus Christ, who came to this world as a Saviour." He was astounded. "Jesus Christ? But that's Christianity. I thought Christianity was done with, out-dated!" he exclaimed. "Not in the least. Christianity starts where all other beliefs end."

How I wish that you would get rid of all your false beliefs so that you too could come to saving faith in Jesus Christ.

Right after the war, as I intended to travel a lot, I bought an old Opel P4. It was a real antique! When I first came along in my shaky little P4, a friend shouted, "Look at that! The pastor driving a car. We'll have to put padding around all the trees!" Somewhat hurt, I answered, "You seem to think I can't drive." "Of course you can. You've got your driver's licence." "Get in, then," I invited him, "and we'll go around the block." "No thanks!" came the hasty reply. "I haven't made my will yet!" Just then, my wife came along. "Emmi, do you want to come for a ride?" I asked. Without the slightest hesitation, she climbed into the car. And – I assure you – she is still alive! When she moved from the solid ground into my car, she placed her life into my hands. Do that very thing with regard to Jesus: place your life whole-heartedly and without fear into his care.

Not long ago, I read the moving story of an incident which took place during the Second World War in Stalingrad. At the time the city was completely surrounded by Russian troops. The last German aircraft maintaining the link with the non-operational zone had just landed. They had loaded the aircraft with the wounded. But other soldiers arrived – slightly wounded or half-dead from cold – and they wanted to get on board too. So they clung to the plane, holding on to whatever they could find: the door handles, the undercarriage. Then the plane took off. When it landed later, none of those who had clung to the aircraft were there. Having hands that were frozen, they had simply been swept away by the storm. Only those who were inside the aircraft were saved.

When I read this incident, I could not help drawing a parallel between the Gospel of Jesus, the Son of God who died and rose again for us, and this life-saving aircraft. For us, Jesus is a means of escape from eternal damnation. With him there is plenty of room. But – sad to say – so many men and women are not on the inside. They have never got on board. They are content with simply hanging on to the fuselage. They go to church once a year, at Christmas. They have been baptized – but that does not hinder them from thinking and acting like the rest of the crowd. And when they die, the minister will certify that they were good people. In reality, however, they were always on the outside. And one day they will be swept away by the storm. There isn't the shadow of a doubt about that! Only those who are on the inside will be saved.

Are you among them?

Hell will be swarming with people who had heard about Jesus, but who never got on board with him. To get "on board with him" means "to believe in Jesus". Do it!

In Lübeck Cathedral, a very beautiful and very old church, there is a fine altar-piece representing the crucifixion, painted by Hans Memling in the fifteenth century. In 1942, when the church was on fire after an air-raid, an unknown soldier, with a few friends, ran inside the sanctuary at the risk of his life to save this work of art.

Shortly after the war, I held a series of meetings in Lübeck. One day the curator of the Museum of Fine Arts came to see me and said, "I have the famous Memling altar-piece stored in the cellar. If you are interested, I would gladly show it to you." Of course it was a wonderful opportunity. So the curator took me, along with a friend, down to the cellar. It was a magnificent painting: soldiers with spears on horses, gambling mercenaries, a motley crowd, women in tears, Pharisees with their mocking look. And there, high above the crowd, three crosses.

Suddenly a very strange detail caught my eye: right in the middle of the throng, at the foot of Jesus' cross, there was a blank space. I remarked to the others, "How strange that in the middle of the throng, directly at the foot of the cross, there should be something like an empty space. I wonder what the artist could have been thinking of?" Those medieval painters always tried to convey some message through their paintings. My friend suggested an explanation. "This is what I think he wanted to say: at this spot, right at the foot of Jesus' cross, there is a free space. You may place yourself there, if you wish."

I often think of that painting when we sing this hymn:

> Upon the Cross of Jesus,
> Mine eye at times can see
> The very dying form of One
> Who suffered there for me.
> And from my smitten heart, with tears,
> Two wonders I confess –
> The wonder of His glorious love,
> And my own worthlessness.

How I rejoice that beneath the cross of Jesus there is a free spot – a place for me.

There is one for you too.

Are you going to wait much longer before deciding to stand there?

"Not for me!"

Every generation invents its own slogans and expressions. People use and repeat them on the slightest pretext as though they applied to every circumstance. One such saying is the negative expression "not for me". It means: "I don't want it at any price. It is out of the question!"

It is used as an excuse for a quarrel, for hurting others, and sometimes even for doing harm to ourselves. So this stock saying can become extremely dangerous – even to the point of putting someone's life in jeopardy. But it can also produce positive results. It all depends on the way people use it.

We are going to have a look at the issues now.

1. We don't use it when we should

There is a story in the Bible which, though centuries old, is still relevant today and illustrates clearly this aspect of the question.

You have probably heard about Abraham, the man of God of whom this is said in the first book of the Bible: "Abraham believed the Lord, and he credited it to him as righteousness." Abraham was the kind of man who was keenly aware of his shortcomings. But he lived so close to God that the instant he became conscious of a sin in his life, he immediately confessed it and seized by faith the forgiveness which God offered him.

Now one day Abraham found himself in an awkward situation with regard to his nephew, Lot. The Bible tells us that Abraham was rich in sheep and cattle. Lot, who accompanied his uncle, also had large flocks and herds. What was bound to happen did happen! "Quarrelling arose between Abraham's herdsmen and the herdsmen of Lot." An open conflict was on the verge of breaking out between the uncle and the nephew – all because there wasn't enough pasture land for everyone. The quarrels between the shepherds of Lot and the shepherds of Abraham were becoming more and more serious. After each new incident they would run to their respective masters and heatedly report the words and deeds of their opponents. Obviously the situation was degenerating.

If you had been Abraham, who was a lot older than Lot, what would you have done? If I had been Abraham, I probably would have told him, "What a way to act! Things have gone too far! You'd better pack up and leave." And Lot, more than likely, would have flashed back, "Not on your life! I maintain my rights. You are the one who should leave!"

The squabblings would never have been stopped with reactions like that.

Then things came to a head and it seemed that a rupture between Abraham and Lot was inevitable. But the pious old man lived close to God; and as he gazed at his nephew, he thought to himself, "A conflict? A split? No, not for me! It is out of the question!" Placing his hand on Lot's shoulder, he said to him, "Let's not have any quarrelling between you and me, or between your herdsmen and mine, for we are brothers." Abraham went on to suggest a settlement of the difference which might very well turn to his own disadvantage. But what did that matter? "A quarrel? No, not for me!"

You too have probably known this kind of situation when someone has strongly provoked you. Did you, like Abraham, think, "A quarrel? No, not for me"?

Is that the way you reacted? I doubt it. You probably preferred to pick up the gauntlet, with the result that even today you are still at odds with Mrs. So-and-So or with your neighbours. How many times this short saying – "not for me" – would have been the right thing to say. Didn't the Lord Jesus himself say, "Blessed are the peacemakers"? If our Christianity has such little impact, isn't it because when situations become critical we do not manage to say, "A quarrel? It's out of the question!" Isn't it because in this type of situation we fail so miserably?

Let me tell you another Bible story that I like very much. It is the story of a young man named Joseph. He had been sold by his brothers, so it was as a slave that he arrived in Egypt, a very vast and highly civilized country at the time. A rich man by the name of Potiphar, the owner of many slaves and several magnificent residences, bought him.

In his early teens, Joseph had resolved to serve the living God. He had said to God, "I want to belong to you." And then young Joseph found himself all alone in Egypt. He saw how the other slaves stole and told lies. But he refused to follow their example. Naturally, they made fun of him.

Potiphar, however, soon discovered that Joseph could be relied on, so he began to entrust important duties to him.

You see, even though people do defy Christians, they like to call upon them for certain jobs, because they know that Christians are honest and dependable.

By the time Joseph reached manhood, his master had appointed him as attendant of his household and of everything he owned. The Bible goes so far as to say, "With Joseph in charge, he did not concern himself with anything except the food he ate." Perhaps Potiphar would have liked to give that job to Joseph as well! It was the only thing he had to look after himself.

Joseph developed into a well-built, handsome young man. He dressed with taste and elegance. It is not surprising, therefore, that the master's young wife finally took notice of him. Mrs. Potiphar was a pagan. And an idle woman too, for she had a host of slaves at her beck and call, and they took care of everything. There is a proverb which says: "Idleness is the mother of all vices."

One day the young woman laid eyes on Joseph and started to flirt with him. But Joseph took no notice of her. It was on another such occasion that the terrible scene took place when, all alone in the house with Joseph and the prey to unbridled passion, she suddenly stood before him and, clutching him by his cloak, begged him to make love to her. The Bible relates in words of touching beauty how, after a moment of thought, Joseph answered her.

"It's out of the question! No way! Adultery? Not for me!" That's how we talk...

But people in the Bible had a nicer way of saying things. Joseph chose his words carefully: "No one is greater in this house than I am. My master has withheld nothing from me except you, because you are his wife. How then could I do such a wicked thing and sin against God?"

This was Joseph's way of saying, "Not for me!"

All of us, at some time or other, have found ourselves in this type of situation, when we have been tempted by one particular sin which people today no longer like to consider as a sin – the sin of adultery. Have we reacted by saying, "God sees me. Commit adultery? Nothing doing"?

How does Joseph's attitude affect you?

I am afraid that if we had been in his situation, we would never have dreamed of answering – simply out of respect for God's commandment to be pure in word and in deed – "Not for me! It's out of the question!" This saying rarely comes to mind in those moments. God does not forget this. The day will come when he will remind us of all our sins. It's unfortunate that just when we most need it, the words "not for me" don't even enter our head! Yet, this is by far the best way to react in the hour of temptation, when we are just about to trample one of God's commandments underfoot. One of the characteristics of the twentieth century is that people no longer take the laws of God into account.

At the consecration of the present bishop of Hanover, I had to address all the ministers of the city. The bishop himself had suggested the theme of my speech: "What are the pastors and parishes of our city lacking?" This is what, in substance, I told them: "I have but one thing to say. What we all lack (pastors and people alike) is the fear of going to hell, the fear of seeing God take things seriously, and the fear of his inflexibility where his commandments are concerned."

"Not for me!" is an excellent reply to use when the spirit of this age tempts us to trample God's laws underfoot.

The Bible describes a very gripping scene: Jesus, the Son of God, was on the summit of a very high mountain. The Devil – (oh, you don't believe he exists? He is none the less very real, let me say in passing) – was standing at Jesus' side, showing him all the kingdoms of the world and their glory. He said to Jesus, "All this will I give you if you bow down an instant, just an instant, and worship me." But the Son of God replied, "Not for me! The whole world may bend the knee before you, but for me it is absolutely out of the question." In reality he put his answer much better: "Away from me, Satan! For it is written: 'Worship the Lord your God, and serve him only!'"

Wouldn't it be great if the saying "not for me" *always* came to our mind at the right time? It's a pity we don't use it when we should.

2. We use it when we shouldn't

Alas, my friends, most of us use this expression at the wrong time.

For example, before me is a young man – a really nice chap, as some would say. I say to him, "You could make something great out of your life if you surrendered it to God!" And he replies, "Not for me! It's out of the question!"

We treat God as though... I'll use an illustration to explain. As my doctor prescribed a one-hour daily walk, the other day I took a path which runs along the edge of the southern railway station of Essen. And there, right in the middle of the way, I suddenly came upon an old chesterfield. Needing it no longer, the owners had simply left it in the public park under cover of night. They must have thought, "It's the city's problem to get rid of it!"

This is how I see the story of the old chesterfield. A young couple had probably inherited it from a grandmother who had passed away. But having a modern flat and new furniture, the husband had said to his wife, "What are we going to do with this old chesterfield? It doesn't match with our other furniture. And who knows, it could have fleas in it! The best thing is to get rid of it." So they took it to the public park and left it there.

That is exactly how men and women today treat the living God. He just can't fit in with our lifestyle. And he doesn't suit our modern pluralist society either! Neither does he conform to the mentality of our age. So what are we going to do with him? Let's leave the old chesterfield in the church! It's closed all week anyway!

My friends, the living God is not an old chesterfield! Is that clear? God is not some old object we can discard as we please just because we find it old-fashioned. Do you have any idea just who the living God is? Maybe the Church is partly responsible for the fact that God is a problem for many of us. In reality, the mere mention of his name should be enough to give us the shivers. But we take refuge behind a wall of indifference – not for me!

Let's try to retrace the effect to the cause. Almost everywhere we hear that the whole Western world is sick. Not physically sick only – with the increase of cancer, leukemia, heart-disease, and all kinds of other ailments – but spiritually sick as well. It has the worst of all diseases. Modern man is suffering from spiritual deficiency. This is the only explanation for the alarming increase of depression cases. As a shrewd Swiss medical doctor put it: "Our generation is suffering from a lack of God." In the Middle Ages, people still reckoned on God – the cathedrals they built make that plain. But as time went by man tried to get rid of God. Marxism is nothing else than a gigantic attempt to put God on the shelf. They have tried to replace him by technology. Scholars, in their attempt to prove that God does not exist, have resorted to the pen. And the masses have shouted, "Religion is the opium of the people." Even the most simple youngster has wondered where God could be hiding; and while still sucking his thumb, he has exclaimed, "I haven't seen him – so he can't exist!"

Yes, everything has been done to try to rid us of God!

And what is the result? All these attempts have ended in failure. We have not been able to get rid of God. I am still looking for an honest atheist courageous enough to declare with conviction that God does not exist. This type of person is nowhere to be found nowadays. And even if one were to be discovered, he would be so uninteresting that he could not be taken seriously.

Shortly before his death, one of the founders of modern nuclear physics, Professor Max Planck, published a booklet entitled, *Religion and Science*. In it he declares: "For us scientists, it stands to reason today that God is the ultimate end of all knowledge." It is obvious that man has not been able to eliminate God.

I held a series of conferences not long ago in a small town in the mountains. As I came out of the church one evening, I spied a group of young boys, all about twenty years old, who were hanging around not far from there. "Why don't you come in?" I asked them. "H'm." "That's no answer! Tell me," I said, turning to one of them, "do you believe God exists?" "I don't know," came the reply. "But that's terrible. Either he does exist – and you should commit yourself to him – or he doesn't exist – and you should leave the Church. Say, have you had your name taken off the church roll yet?" "No!"

Looking at another lad, I continued: "What about you? Do you believe that God exists?" "Yes, I do!" "Tell me, then," I asked, "do you observe his commandments?" "Oh no!"

I went from one to the other, questioning; and not a single one dared to deny the existence of God. Yet not one of them wanted seriously to surrender his life to God either. And it is the same everywhere.

Many men say to me in the course of my pastoral calls, "I believe there is a God, but I leave it to others to go to church." These men do not deny God, but they nevertheless do not want to get involved with him.

And so the problem of God remains unanswered. Problems that never find a solution can create serious complexes, and nervous or mental disturbances. They can eventually bring a person to his ruin. We do ourselves a lot of harm when we do not bother to clear up the problem of God.

In our churches, there are ten women to every man attending our services. Where are the other men? I can assure you that long before you even step into hell, you are going to decline inwardly; and this will be because you have neither the courage to put your life into God's hands, nor the means to get rid of him.

In the face of this particular situation, we Christians have a tremendous message to announce: This God we treat so terribly tore down the wall which separated us from him and came to us in the person of Jesus. A divine Saviour came to earth! Not only did he live among us, but he also died in our place on the cross. Is it possible for God to do more than that for us? Then he rose from the dead – overcoming death and opening up the way of life.

And you? All you manage to say is, "Well, all that is quite interesting. It's worth hearing, but it's not for me!"

Such inconsistency fills me with nausea. It makes me literally sick.

In the early years of my pastorate, there was a worker in my parish who, every time I tried to speak to him about Jesus, would always send me packing, mocking me as he did so. One time I asked him, "How do you expect to face death?" He answered, "Oh you pastors, you are always trying to scare us by talking about death. Count me out!"

He carried on in this way until the day he lay on his death-bed – he wasn't even forty years old. His wife phoned me in the middle of the night. I rushed to his side. "The moment has come," I said to him, "when Jesus is calling you for the last time." It was terrible. He wanted to pray, but couldn't. I repeated one Bible verse after the other – words of forgiveness – but he simply couldn't grasp them. He had said, "Count me out!" Now it was God who was no longer willing. The man died in the torments of deep despair and never found peace with God.

There is a solemn verse in the Bible which goes like this: "How shall we escape if we ignore such a great salvation?"

I beg you, take this extraordinary message seriously. "For God so loved the world that he gave his one and only Son, that whoever believes in him shall not perish but have eternal life." But Jesus does even more than that. He speaks a comforting word to us all: "Here I am! I stand at the door and knock. If anyone hears my voice and opens the door, I will come in and eat with him, and he with me."

There are all kinds of "Christians". There are those who are content to give their church offering – nice people, but terribly boring. There are those who only go to church at Christmas – I feel sorry for them, these special-day Christians. Then there are those who send their wives to church, but who never set foot in it themselves – it doesn't cost them a thing. Others say, "I've been baptized" – well, at least that is something; but if there's no more to it than that ... And finally there are those who, having heard the living Saviour's call, have answered, "Count me out!"

It's really terrible! "Lord Jesus," people say, "I'll take a little bit of Christianity. But allow you to take over my life? That's really going too far. Not for me!"

That is how we can use the saying "not for me" at the wrong time.

If you do want to know the reality of Jesus personally, then you must take heed to his call, open the door and let him into your life.

3. Someone who doesn't use it

There is someone who would have many reasons to say "not for me!" but who doesn't – God be praised! It is the Lord Jesus himself.

I have another story to tell. A Danish author by the name of Jacobson wrote a moving novel entitled, *Black Death at Bergamo*. Bergamo is a small town in Italy, not far from Ravenna, built on a mountain-side. It is accessible only by a stony path. In Jacobson's story, the pestilence broke out one day in the Middle Ages in this small town. It was horrible! Day and night the bells tolled. People cried to God, imploring his help. But nothing happened. The pestilence struck all the harder.

The townsfolk were filled with dismay and said to one another, "God is dead." Then they threw all constraint to the winds. The barrels were rolled out of the wine-cellars, and everyone started drinking freely and heavily. It was not long before drunk men and women could be seen pairing off to indulge in sex – with no concern as to who their partner might be. The drinking-bout degenerated into a real orgy – an orgy of despair. For days and days nothing else counted but to follow one's instincts. At times, right in the middle of a dance, someone would collapse, struck by the disease. But no one took any notice. The orgy went on . . . "Let's eat, drink, and be merry, for tomorrow we die!"

Then one day, all of a sudden, everyone stopped short. Far off in the distance singing could be heard. Everyone ran to the city gate. They saw, to their great surprise, a procession of penitents coming up the path leading to the town. As they made their way up the hill, they chanted a litany: "Kyrie eleison – Lord, have mercy upon us!" Leading the procession was a young monk bearing a heavy wooden cross. The cortege finally arrived at the city gates, but the inhabitants of Bergamo just stood there and laughed. "Bunch of idiots!" they shouted. "Here, God is dead. Stop your stupid chanting. God is dead! Come and join us. Let's all eat, drink and be merry, for tomorrow we die!"

The monk heading the procession paid no attention and walked on. Although no one had been inside the church for days, the doors were wide open. The procession made its way into the church. The monk leaned his cross against a pillar. Then the wild, frantic horde of desperate, death-bound townspeople overran the church with shouts and loud laughter. An apprentice-butcher wearing a blood-stained apron, completely beside himself with despair, marched up to the altar. Snatching a golden chalice, he held it up and shouted, "Let's drink and get drunk, for here God is dead!"

Meanwhile, the monk had gone into the pulpit. He was very pale, but with a wave of the hand he signalled to the crowd to be quiet. Silence was restored. Then he began to speak: "I want to tell you something. When they hung the Son of God on the cross and pierced his hands with nails, everybody there started sneering at him, defying and ridiculing him. Even the two thieves, crucified at his left and right, joined in mocking with the mob. It was then that the Son of God thought, 'Is it for those people, who aren't even touched by my approaching death, that I must die? Do I have to give my life for such repulsive and callous people?' And shouting loudly, 'Not for me! Count me out!', he tore the nails out of the wood by his divine strength, jumped down from the cross, and snatched his cloak away from the soldiers with such force that the dice went rolling all the way down the hill of Calvary! He threw his cloak over his shoulders and went back to heaven, repeating all the way, 'Not for me! Count me out!' The cross was empty. So now there is no possibility of redemption, of salvation or of eternal life. Only death and hell await us."

The monk finished with these words. A deathlike silence fell over the church.

In the meantime, the apprentice-butcher had stepped down from the altar and was standing directly underneath the pulpit. The chalice slipped out of his hands. "There is no possibility of redemption, of salvation..." Taking three steps forward, he pointed his finger at the monk and shouted in a sharp tone, "Hey, you up there! Put the Saviour back on the cross, put the Saviour back on the cross."

My friends, the monk didn't relate the facts the way they really happened.

You see, one of the most astonishing things is that the Son of God did *not* say, "Not for me!" In a certain way, Jesus continues to allow himself to be crucified by those who say, "Work, pleasure and health are of more importance to us than salvation."

Yes, the Lord would have every reason to declare, "Not for me! Do what you like!" Yet, to this very day he has not ceased to be interested in you.

If I had been Jesus, I would have let the world run on to its destruction. But the Son of God did not say, "Not for me! Count me out!" On the contrary. He continues to search us out. How much longer will he have to look for you? When will you come to understand that he wants you to be his? When will your eyes open? When will you say to him, "My Lord, my Saviour"?

Briefly, my last point...

4. We cannot cope alone

To those who reject him saying, "Not for me! It is out of the question!", Jesus answers, "Without me you can do nothing." This is absolutely true. All that you may do in life without the Saviour is of no value in the light of eternity.

I watched some youngsters fighting in the street one day. A little fellow, who happened to be passing by, also got his share of the blows, probably by accident. Just as I was wondering whether I should intervene, I witnessed a touching scene. Somehow the little fellow managed to get clear of the scuffle. His eyes were watering, his nose was runny, but he started running as fast as his little legs would carry him. When he was sure he was far enough away, he stopped and yelled at the top of his voice, "You'll see, I'm going to tell my big brother!" Immediately the fight broke up. He had a big brother! A big brother to whom he could tell everything and who was ready to help him. And I thought to myself, "My little friend, it's great that you have a big brother!"

My heart overflowed with joy that day – for I too have a big brother who stands at my side. Jesus! It is wonderful to see how this big brother powerfully intervenes on behalf of his own. And he reminds us: "Without me you can do nothing."

Why not say to the one who has done so much for you, "Lord Jesus, I don't want to do anything without you from now on"?

Is there any certainty in religious matters?

No! It is clear that in religious matters we can have no assurance. Religion is, by definition, man's search for God. Worry and continuous uncertainty are necessarily part of this pursuit.

It is not so with the Gospel, which is God's search for man. Perhaps it would be better then to put the question another way: Does the Gospel give us any certainties?

1. People are content to be uncertain about God

People are funny nowadays! As soon as a strong healthy chap has some little ache or pain, he runs to the doctor's and says, "Doctor, it's really sore here. What's wrong?" He wants to know exactly what is wrong.

Or take the case of a family which is looking for a maid. A young girl applies for the job. "Well," says the mistress of the house, "you'll have a room with hot and cold water, television and a hi-fi. You'll also have a whole day off each week." "That's fine," the girl answers, "but I'd like to know how much money I'll get at the end of the month." The lady replies, "We'll come to an agreement on that point only after I have seen how you work!" "Never!" retorts the girl. "Under those circumstances, I'd rather not take the job. I want to know in advance how much I'll be earning!" Wasn't she right? Of course she was.

When we apply for a job, obviously the most important matter is what our salary and status will be. We want to know where we stand. Where money matters are concerned, we tolerate no uncertainties. And so it is with all areas of our life – except the most important one of all: our relationship with God. There we tolerate the most unbelievable ambiguity.

Many years ago, I held a series of meetings in the city of Augsburg. A tent had been erected on Plärrer Square where the annual fair is held. The committee organizing the meetings had an excellent idea. On Saturday night the city's places of entertainment were usually packed. So they decided to hold a meeting on Saturday night – at midnight! The meeting was not publicly announced. They didn't want to see a lot of Christians swarming in out of curiosity.

On the stroke of half-past eleven, my friends jumped into their cars to pick up the people out on the town as they left the cafés and cabarets closing at midnight. Waiters and waitresses on their way home from work were also taken along. One after the other, the cars dropped off their passengers in front of the tent door. And when at midnight I got up on the platform to speak, a most unusual audience was there before me. Some people were a little tipsy. Seated in the very front row was a big fat man with a half-chewed cigar clamped in his mouth and a bowler hat on his head. "Well," I thought, "let's hope things go off all right!" Then I started to speak. The moment I mentioned the name of God for the first time, the fat fellow with the bowler hat yelled out, "Doesn't exist!" Everybody burst out laughing. But I leaned over the pulpit and asked, "Are you sure about that?" He scratched his head, and his bowler fell on his nose; then, rolling the stub of his cigar to the other corner of his mouth, he finally answered, "Well, I guess no one really knows anything certain about God." I just laughed and said, "Sorry, but I have some sure information." "What do you know about that!" he exclaimed. "And what is your source?" I answered that it is Jesus who gives us all the facts about God. A deathlike hush at that moment fell on the hall.

Do you have certainties about God? And you Christians, can you say, "I *know* I have life in him; I *know* that in his love he has saved me"? Most of you would probably answer, "I hope so!"

Isn't it surprising that where God is concerned, believers and unbelievers alike are resigned to living in doubt and uncertainty. If I walked from one end of town to the other, asking this question to everyone I met on the way, "Tell me, do you believe God exists?" they would all reply, "Yes; there must be a God!" But if I continued with this question, "Do you belong to him?", these same people would say, "I don't know."

In a realm as vital as this one, men and women are willing to accept the haziest situation!

One of our young people had an interesting experience just recently. He is a student; and in order to make a little pocket-money, he got a summer job as an unskilled worker in a construction company. One day his fellow-workers discovered that he was active in a Protestant youth group. "Good Gracious!" they exclaimed. "Are you in with Pastor Busch?" "Yes." A regular round of ribbing followed. They started to jeer at him. "You probably go to church on Sunday?" "Of course I do!" "Every Sunday?" "Yes, every Sunday." "But, you must be crazy!" they exclaimed. "Of course not! I even go to Bible study during the week." "Are you kidding?" was the reaction. "Why, it's pure insanity!" Then they spat all their poison at him: "Preachers only aim to make their congregations stupid!" "Christianity has failed miserably after two thousand years of effort." "The Bible is just a heap of rubbish."

The young man came under very heavy attack. But he had a hide like an elephant's, and simply let everything slide over him. Then he said to them, "If that is your attitude towards Christianity, I presume you have all left the Church." Silence. One of the older men took up the conversation, "What do you mean by 'left the Church'? Hell! I believe in the good Lord too. You seem to think you're the only one who is a Christian. I believe in the good Lord just as much as you do!" The others chipped in, "You have a way of making yourself look better than others. We're Christians too. We believe in God, just like you do." Suddenly the roles were reversed. They began to yell all together: "We believe in God too. We are Christians just as much as you are." When they quietened down, my young friend asked them, "Well then, why are you making fun of me?" They replied, "You get on our nerves. There's no way of discussing with you."

Those construction workers were husky chaps and after a lot of hard work they could gulp down a couple of pints of beer at once. They didn't care a hoot about Christianity; but when they were cornered, all they could find to say was, "We're Christians too!"

What should we think of it all? Isn't it disturbing?

Where God is concerned, it doesn't bother us to be in the dark. People act sometimes like pagans, sometimes like Christians. Am I wrong? I am afraid that most of you live in the same uncertainty, the same confusion.

2. The Bible gives us wonderful certainties

You may protest: "But Pastor Busch, the Christian faith has nothing to do with certainties! Doesn't the genius of Christianity lie in the fact that we know nothing but that we believe everything?"

Not long ago, a man gave me one of those stock arguments I've heard so often throughout the years: "I know that two and two make four; but as to Christianity, we can know nothing, we only have to believe." According to this viewpoint, it seems that where biblical truths are concerned we are supposed to put our logic to sleep and have a blind faith. Most people believe this.

Someone else may say, "But you Christians don't even agree among yourselves. There are the Catholics, the Protestants, and the sects. And among Protestants, there are the Anglicans, the Lutherans, the Presbyterians, and so many others. Which group is right?"

It seems to me that even Christendom is convinced that the Christian faith is, in its essence, something particularly vague, particularly uncertain. But this is a serious mistake.

In fact, it is only through the New Testament that we can learn just what the Christian faith is. Every single phrase contains certainties. That is beyond all doubt! It's not normal that Christians should live in such uncertainty. But it isn't Christianity's fault – absolutely not! The New Testament is full of wonderful certitudes, from beginning to end.

One of them is the fact of *the existence of God*. He is not presented as the Supreme Being, Providence, Destiny, or the good Lord, but as the *Father of our Lord Jesus Christ*. That God does exist! How can we know it? Because he revealed himself in the person of his Son. We can be absolutely certain about that. Open your Bible at any page. The Bible does not speak about religious problems. It testifies that God exists and that he revealed himself through Jesus Christ. It shows too that the man who lives without God is not living right.

Another certainty is the fact that this *God* (who is capable of destroying nations and of administering justice) *loves me deeply*. We are not reduced to guesses. We read in Romans 8:38: "For I am convinced that neither death nor life, neither angels nor demons, neither the present nor the future, nor anything else in all creation, will be able to separate us from the love of God that is in Christ Jesus our Lord." This is something we do not suppose; it is something we *know*.

How is God's love made known to us? It is manifested in Jesus Christ. Therefore the believer can sing:

> When peace, like a river, attendeth my way,
> When sorrows, like sea billows roll;
> Whatever my lot, Thou hast taught me to say,
> "It is well, it is well with my soul."
>
> Tho' Satan should buffet, tho' trials should come,
> Let this blest assurance control,
> That Christ hath regarded my helpless estate,
> And hath shed His own blood for my soul.

My sin – oh, the bliss of this glorious thought!
My sin – not in part, but the whole,
Is nailed to His cross; and I bear it no more:
Praise the Lord, praise the Lord, O my soul!

For me, be it Christ, be it Christ hence to live!
If Jordan above me shall roll,
No pang shall be mine, for in death as in life
Thou wilt whisper Thy peace to my soul.

But, Lord, 'tis for Thee, for Thy coming we wait;
The sky, not the grave, is our goal:
Oh, trump of the Angel! oh, voice of the Lord!
Blessèd hope! blessèd rest of my soul!

Do you know something of this? Are you sure about this?

The different believers mentioned in the Bible also had *full assurance of their salvation* and they knew they were God's children. "For he has rescued us from the dominion of darkness and brought us into the Kingdom of the Son he loves." Jesus' disciples experienced a radical change in their lives – and they knew it! Paul wrote: "We know that we have passed from death unto life." Can you say that? Elsewhere we find this: "The Spirit himself testifies with our spirit that we are God's children." Here we have a present tense: "we *are*".

The Bible is full of certainties.

Where, then, does this absurd statement come from: "I know that two and two make four. But as to Christianity, we can know nothing, we only have to believe"? I too know that two and two make four. But I am even more certain that God exists. I know that two and two make four. But I am even more certain that God loves us in Jesus Christ. All those who have surrendered their lives to the living God can go a step further: we know that two and two make four. But we are even more certain that we are children of God.

Tell me, in what churches today do they preach such absolute certainties? Where, I ask? Doesn't this demonstrate that we have deviated from the biblical position and that it is high time we came back to it? Let's get rid of our watered-down Christianity! A touch of Christian faith is of no use. What we need is a faith that is thoroughly biblical, a faith that takes God at his word. This is what we all need to be sure of: that God exists, that he loves us and that we are his children. Everything else is secondary.

There are two aspects to the certainties of the Christian faith. I know *objectively* that God exists and that his revelation in the person of Jesus Christ is authentic – even though the whole world rejects it. I know too that Jesus died to reconcile the sinner with God and that he rose from the dead to save him – even if no one were to take advantage of it. On the other hand, I know *subjectively* that God exists, that he revealed himself in Jesus Christ, that he died and rose from the dead. I know it because I have personally claimed it for myself by a deliberate act of faith.

If ten thousand scholars were to declare to a young believer that Jesus did not rise from the dead, he can say this, "Gentlemen, in spite of the respect I owe you, I *know* that my Redeemer is living." Were the whole world against him, the believer can firmly declare, "I know in whom I have believed." Were you to drown me in scientific arguments, I would answer, "I know more about it than you do!" And even if the whole universe were to doubt it, I would still say, "I am certain of it."

When our faith is founded on the Bible, it is just as solid as that!

3. Do you have this certainty?

Now I have to ask you a question. Do you personally have assurance like that? Or is it still missing in your life? I will not have spoken in vain if you come to admit, "I thought I was a Christian, but I can't be, because everything is so vague in my mind..."

I remember a young people's camp I attended in Holland. Around two o'clock in the morning I was awakened by a knock on the door. I opened it and saw there before me the whole group in their pyjamas. "What brings you here at such an hour of the night?" I asked. One of them answered, "We thought we were Christians. We've just come to realize we were wrong." They were so troubled about it that they wanted to clarify the matter then and there in the middle of the night!

We have taken a great step in our life when we admit that, though we call ourselves Christians, we are far from having the assurance the Bible gives.

Charles Haddon Spurgeon, the famous London preacher who was at the origin of a powerful revival in the last century, once said, "Faith is a sixth sense."

As you know, we have five senses which allow us to perceive the outside world: taste, smell, hearing, touch and sight. By their means we are able to find our way in this three-dimensional world.

A man who accepts only what can be perceived by the senses reasons like this: "Where can God be? I can't see him. I can't see Jesus either. So how can you expect me to believe?"

But when God enlightens us by his Spirit, he causes a sixth sense to develop within us. This means that we are not only capable of seeing, touching, hearing, smelling and tasting, but we can perceive the spiritual world as well. As the Bible puts it: "This is eternal life: that they may know you, the only true God, and Jesus Christ, whom you have sent." Only a sixth sense can grasp this truth.

Recently I went to visit an industrial magnate in Essen. His office was situated in a big commercial building overlooking half the city. After passing through several offices and waiting rooms, I found myself at last seated in front of him. I explained the reason for my visit, and in a few seconds the matter was settled. So we started to chat... He said, "How thrilling to have a pastor in my office for once!" "Oh, I'm sure it must be very exciting!" I replied teasingly. "You know," the man went on, "after the war, from time to time I attended some conferences on theology. What struck me at those meetings..." "Go on," I interrupted to encourage him, "I'm not easily shocked." "What struck me most at those meetings," he repeated, "was that Christianity seems to lack clearness. Subjects like *The Christian and the Economy, The Christian and Disarmament, The Christian and Money, The Christian and the Church*, were dealt with. But they never explained what a Christian is! Obviously those people didn't know themselves!"

Seated in that magnificent office, I hit hard, "Oh, that's not true! You must be mistaken." He then asked me, astonished, "Can *you* tell me what a Christian is?" "Of course," I answered, "I'll make it very clear to you. There can be no possible confusion on that point." "Well now," he said in a slightly mocking tone, "some people say that a Christian is someone who has never been in trouble with the police. Others think that a Christian is anyone who has been baptized and buried religiously." "Sir," I replied, "let me tell you what a Christian is. Hold on tight! A Christian is a person who can say from the depths of his being, 'I believe that Jesus Christ – true God of true God, begotten by the Father from all eternity, but also true man of true man, born of the Virgin Mary – is my Lord and that it was he who saved me, a poor, lost and condemned sinner.' Sir, you are a poor, lost and condemned sinner!" He nodded in agreement. He had understood that much – and was willing to admit it.

"Good," I replied. "... It was he who saved me, a poor, lost and condemned sinner, who bought me and liberated me from sin, from death and from the Devil's hold. Sir, bought and liberated from the power of the Devil!" He nodded assent once again. He obviously was not ignorant about these matters. I continued. "...It was he who bought me and liberated me from sin. The Bible says: 'For you know that it was not with perishable things such as silver or gold that you were redeemed from the empty way of life handed down to you from your forefathers, but with the precious blood of Christ, a lamb without defect or blemish.' Listen to me carefully," I said. "Only the man or woman who can say, 'I belong to Jesus; he has liberated me from sin, from death and from hell by his own blood. Of that I am certain' – only that person is a Christian!"

There was a moment of silence in the office. Then the man asked, "But how can it be done? How can it be done?" I replied, "Your secretary told me just before I came into your office that you are going away on holiday. I'll send you a New Testament right away this afternoon. Take it along with you and every day read a chapter of the Gospel of John. Read it in an attitude of prayer. That's how it will be done!"

To sum up, the Christian position as described in the New Testament carries a double certainty: one, *objective*, that the biblical truths are trustworthy; and the other, *subjective*, that I can claim them by faith and be saved. Do you have these certainties? For my part, I couldn't go on living if I were not certain that God had accepted me.

I asked a young man one day, "Do you love the Lord Jesus?" "Yes," he answered. "Do you know whether he has accepted you and whether you are his child?" "I'm not altogether sure," he replied. "I still have many doubts." "I for one," I retorted, "couldn't bear to live in such uncertainty. I need assurance that I am God's child."

The person who calls himself a Christian yet who doesn't even know if God exists – although he knows right to the last penny what his financial situation is – that person is not a Christian at all. According to the New Testament only the man or woman who can declare, "I know that Jesus has become the Master of my life", is a true Christian.

Let me illustrate this by means of an anecdote that you have perhaps already heard. General von Viehban tells that one day during manoeuvres, as he was riding through the forest on horseback, his uniform got caught on a branch and was torn. It is against the regulations for a general to walk around with a tear in his uniform. When he arrived at the army quarters that night, he spied a few soldiers sitting on a stone wall. He drew his horse to a stop and called them, "Is there a tailor among you?" One of the soldiers rushed up to the general, saluted, and said, "Here, Sir!" General von Viehban barked out this order: "You will come immediately to my room at the Golden Lamb Hotel and repair my uniform." "But I don't know how to sew, Sir," came the reply. "What! You don't know how to sew? But aren't you a tailor?" "Forgive me, Sir," answered the soldier. "My name is Taylor, but I am not a tailor!"

So it is with the majority of men and women. They call themselves Christians, but in reality they are not Christians at all. What a dreadful and extremely serious situation, because it means that these people are not saved.

I must, therefore, go a step further and ask this question:

4. How can we get assurance?

If you want to be sure about these things, I advise you first of all to ask God for assurance; then start reading the Bible for a few minutes every day.

I draw your attention to an important point: we do not come to assurance of salvation by means of our logic, but by means of our conscience.

Every time I start a discussion on the Christian faith these days, somebody always comes up with this: "You know, I just can't believe! There are too many contradictions in the Bible." "Contradictions?" "Yes, contradictions!" they declare. "For instance, the Bible says that Adam and Eve had two sons: Cain and Abel. But Cain killed Abel. And so Cain was the only son left. The Bible goes on to say that Cain went into a far country and found a wife there! Now, if they were the only people on earth, how could Cain have found a wife elsewhere? It just doesn't make sense!"

Have you ever come up against this objection? It seems to me that this is a key argument used by men here in Germany to escape from God. Usually I answer them like this: "What you say is very interesting. Here's a Bible. Show me where it is written that Cain went into a far country and took a wife." They usually start to blush. I continue: "If you have rejected the Bible, the means by which multitudes of reasonable men and women have come to the faith, if you consider yourself more intelligent than they are, you have probably studied the Bible thoroughly! Please, show me the passage where this is found!"

It always turns out that they don't know a thing about it. So I show them the passage in the Book of Genesis myself. It says: "Cain went out from the Lord's presence and lived in the land of Nod, east of Eden. Cain lay with his wife and she became pregnant and gave birth to Enoch." Cain had simply brought his wife with him! Who was she? In the context it is said that Adam "had other sons and daughters". Cain, then, had married one of his sisters. It is clearly stated in the Bible, on the other hand, that God wanted all humans to be descended from the same blood. Consequently, it was necessary in the beginning for brothers and sisters to marry among themselves. God later prohibited blood-relations to marry. Is this clear?

Then I draw my conclusion. "Your objections," I remark, "fall down like a stack of cards!"

Do you think this man is going to open up to the Gospel now? No way! He already has another objection on the tip of his tongue: "Yes, Pastor Busch, but tell me something . . . " And away he goes again! Even if I were to answer ten thousand similar questions, he obviously wouldn't budge an inch.

No, faith does not spring from our logic but from a troubled conscience.

One of my predecessors in Essen, Reverend Julius Dammann, was at the origin of a great spiritual awakening in our city. A young man came to see him one day to ask him questions like the one about Cain's wife. With a wave of the hand, Julius Dammann evaded the question by saying, "Young man, Jesus Christ didn't come to quibble over trivialities, but to save sinners. When you are convinced that you yourself are a sinner, you may come back."

It is people with guilty consciences, people who are willing to admit deep down that their lives are one big mess and that they'll never get out of it by themselves, who come to believe in the Saviour. Logic follows.

One day I walked into a hospital room where six men were in bed. I received a warm welcome. "It's really nice of you to come and see us, Pastor Busch," they said. "We'd like to ask you a question." "Okay. I'm listening." From the very first glance, I knew they were going to ask me a trick question. One of them, under the watchful look of his room-mates, asked, "You believe that God is all-powerful, don't you?" "Yes, I do." "Well," he continued, "here is my question: Could your God create a rock that would be so heavy he couldn't even lift it himself?"

Have you seen the trap? Whether I answered "yes" or "no", the conclusion would be the same – God is not all-powerful.

I thought the matter over for a moment, and wondered if I should explain this to him, but it all seemed so stupid to me that in turn I asked him a question: "Young man, before answering, I'd like to know whether you have sleepless nights over this question." "Sleepless nights?" he asked, a look of blank astonishment on his face. "Oh no!" "Well, it's like this," I continued, "my time is limited, so I can answer only those questions which are depriving people of their sleep. Tell me, young man, what is hindering you from sleeping?" The answer was immediate: "I've got a problem with my girlfriend. She's pregnant, and we can't get married yet." "Well," I said, "if that's what is causing your sleepless nights, let's talk about it." "All right, if you want," he agreed, rather surprised. "But what does all that have to do with religion?" he asked. I answered, "Your question about the rock has nothing whatsoever to do with Christianity. But it's not so for the affair with your girlfriend. In that instance, you were at fault. You broke one of God's commandments in having sexual relations with her. So now you are racking your brain trying to find a way out – an even greater sin. You see, you are stuck in the mud. Your only chance of getting out is to turn to God, and to repent, by confessing to him, 'Lord, I have sinned.' Then, and only then, will the Lord be able to do something for you." The young man listened attentively. And suddenly he saw the light: "Jesus is interested in the burden which is weighing on my conscience. He can help me and repair my wasted life."

The young man tried first of all to resort to reason. But he just talked nonsense. Only when he became aware of his guilt did he see things clearly.

Have you understood now that to gain assurance of salvation there is no sense wasting time on thorny questions like the ones we referred to? No. The only way to get assurance is to listen to your conscience and to cry out, "I have sinned." At that moment, the crucified Saviour will make himself known, and you will *know* that your sins have been forgiven. The way of salvation passes through our conscience and not through our logic.

If you want to get this certainty, then you must be willing to run a risk. Let me explain. Most churches have multi-coloured stained-glass windows. When you look at them from the outside, even in full daylight, they seem dark, and you can scarcely distinguish the colours. But as soon as you go inside the church, the colours take on life. It is exactly the same for the Christian faith. Seen from the outside, it appears obscure, dull. But you have to get inside – that is, you have to risk taking the step towards Jesus. You have to surrender your life to the Saviour and trust him. *Then* everything becomes clear and bright. It is a step from death to life. And in a second all the beauty of the Christian faith is unfolded before your eyes.

One day Jesus was preaching. Thousands of people were listening to him. As he spoke, Jesus clearly said that unless there was a radical change in their life – brought about by God himself – they could not enter into the Kingdom of God. Thereupon several men stood up, saying, "Come on, let's go. He exaggerates. We can't accept what he says." And so they left. Some women, who saw them get up and leave, decided to do the same. Then a gang of young people followed on their heels. Finally the whole crowd began to break up. It must have been terrible.

Imagine that I am preaching a sermon and that suddenly the people start leaving the hall one after the other. Well, that's just what happened to Jesus! All of a sudden he was alone. Thousands of men and women left while he was speaking. They didn't want to listen to him any longer.

Only the twelve disciples remained.

If I had been in Jesus' place, I probably would have pleaded with the Twelve: "You at least, please stay with me. You my faithful friends, don't leave me!" But Jesus' reaction was quite different. Do you know what he said to them? "You may go too, if you want." In the Kingdom of God there are no restraints. It is the only kingdom where there is no police force. True liberty of choice is part of it. "You may go too, if you want." That is what Jesus said to his disciples. They must have been torn. When six thousand people get up and leave, it is tempting to do the same. Probably they felt like following the crowd – especially when Jesus offered them the possibility: "You may leave too . . . " The way was wide open. "If you want, you may be lost. You may choose to live without God. You may run straight into hell." But Peter started to think: "Where could I go? But where? Should I throw myself into a job and work like a slave? Or live in the filth of sin? And find myself in the end facing death and hell? That would be stupid!" Then he glanced at Jesus. And he became absolutely certain of one thing: only a life lived with Jesus was a life worth living. He said, then, to Jesus, "Lord, to whom shall we go? You have the words of eternal life. We believe and know (which is the equivalent of: we have the certainty) that you are the Christ, the Son of the living God. We will stay."

My friends, that is how we get absolute certainty. After looking carefully at the different paths open to us, we come to the conclusion that Jesus is the one and only way out. I hope you, too, will come to share this wonderful assurance of the disciples: "We have believed and know that you are the Christ, the Son of the living God."

Before closing, I would like to say a special word to those among you who have already taken the first step of faith – by surrendering your life to Jesus Christ – but who think deep down: "I'm not sure of my salvation. How can I get assurance? There's still so much sin in my life!" I'd like to say this to you, "Do you really think it is necessary to wait until we no longer sin before we can be sure of our salvation? In that case, we'll have to wait till we are in heaven!" We will need the blood of Jesus for the forgiveness of our sins up to our very last day, up to our very last breath!

You no doubt recall the story of the prodigal son who fell into his father's arms uttering these words: "I have sinned." His father received him with open arms and had a great celebration in his honour. Now, try to imagine the following scene: the next morning the boy accidentally lets his cup of coffee fall to the floor. In the far country, among the pigs, he had lost the habit of being at table. So when he hears the cup breaking into a thousand pieces, he begins to swear: "Damn it! It slipped out of my hands." Is his father going to throw him out the door because of that, and say, "Go away! Go back to your pigs!"? Never. He'll say just the opposite: "Never mind; it's all right." Turning to his son, he may even add, "Son, try not to let that happen again. We'll do our best to help you learn again how to put your coffee cup on the table properly, to stop swearing, and little by little to get used to the ways of home." But the father will never send him back to the pigs.

When a man surrenders his life to Jesus, it is not long before he makes the sad discovery that his old nature has not disappeared and that he still falls into sin from time to time. When you have suffered defeat after your conversion, don't despair. Get down on your knees and say three things to God: *first of all*, "Thank you, Lord, because I am yours forever"; *secondly*, "Forgive me by virtue of your blood"; and *thirdly*, "Liberate me from the hold of my old nature."

But above all, let him know how grateful you are for the fact that you are still his child.

To sum things up, being certain of my salvation allows me to say, "I have come back home; I have come back to my father. I'll strive for holiness like a son who has come back home for good, and not like a son who is put out the door each time he blunders and who is forever coming back."

Those who preach that we have to claim salvation afresh every day proclaim a terrible message. My children don't have to stand every morning before my desk and ask me, "Daddy, can we be your children again today?" They *are* my children. And the man or woman, boy or girl, who is a child of God, is God's child for ever. He (or she) will battle against sin while being and remaining a child of God.

May each one of you come to the full assurance that you are a child of God!

Is religion a private affair?

Most people think so. Are they right? Does Christianity in particular have something private about it? Or, to put the question more clearly, does the Christian's faith concern himself only?

Before answering, I am going to ask you a very simple question: What do you see engraved on coins? An image or an inscription? Both, of course. Every coin has two sides. So does the Christian faith. If the Christian faith is authentic and alive, it has two sides to it. There is the strictly personal, private side; and there is the public, open side. If one of these aspects is missing, there is something dubious about it.

Let us now consider these two aspects of genuine faith.

1. The personal aspect

To illustrate this, I am going to tell a story. Someone once told me that I was just a story-teller. I replied, "There is nothing wrong with that. I'm always afraid of seeing people drop off to sleep in church. So if I tell a little story from time to time, it keeps them awake!" Anyway, our whole life is made up of experiences – not of theories!

A preacher by the name of Johann Heinrich Volkening lived in the region of Ravensburg in the nineteenth century. This man of God was behind a powerful revival movement. The whole area around the city of Bielefeld was completely transformed as a result of his preaching. One evening Volkening was called to the bedside of a wealthy farmer who owned a very large farm and was known as an honest and hard-working man. But he had a very strong dislike of evangelistic meetings. The fact was, the man was unwilling to admit he was a sinner, and couldn't understand why he needed a Saviour. His motto in life was: "Do what is right and shame the Devil." As I said, one evening Volkening was called to his bedside. The old farmer was dying and he wanted to take communion one last time. So Volkening went to the farm. He was a tall man and his sparkling blue eyes attracted people's attention. Coming up to the dying man's bed, he looked at him for a long time without saying a word. Finally he spoke, "Heinrich, I am worried, very worried about you. The road you've been travelling on so far doesn't lead to heaven; it leads straight to hell." Then Volkening turned around and walked out! The farmer, hot with anger, yelled after him, "And you're supposed to be a preacher! And you dare to preach about the love of God!"

Night fell. But the poor farmer, who was seriously ill, couldn't get a wink of sleep. His conscience was tormenting him: "You are not on the way to heaven, but to hell ... What if, after all, it were true?" The numerous sins he had committed flooded his memory. He had not honoured God as he ought to have done. At times he had managed to deceive others in very sly ways.

As one night after another slipped by, a deadly fear took hold of his whole being. He could find no rest. He came to realize that he had committed a multitude of sins throughout his life and that he had absolutely no grounds for assuming he was a child of God. He got to the point where he longed to make an about-turn in his life. So three days later he called his wife and said, "Go and get Volkening." It was late at night, but Volkening came immediately. The old farmer said to him in an anxious tone, "Pastor, I think it's high time for me to change my life." "Yes," replied Volkening, "as we get older, we get wiser. But a hasty repentance isn't necessarily a true one! You need something deeper than that." Once again the preacher turned on his heels and stamped out of the house. Once again the farmer flew into a rage. Wouldn't you have been angry too? Wouldn't it have been better for Volkening to be kinder to the farmer? After all, the man was at death's door! But Volkening lived very close to God, so he knew what he was doing.

Three days later, the old farmer was in agony and deep despair. He knew his days were numbered. He asked himself, "What place has there been in my life for love, joy, peace, patience, kindness, goodness, faithfulness, meekness, and self-discipline?" His whole life through he had despised the Saviour who had died for him. Every time God in his love had spoken to him, he had turned him down. And now here he was on the brink of hell – desperate. He implored his wife, "Go and get the minister!" "No," she replied. "I won't go any more. It won't be any use anyway." "Please," he implored, "please, go and get him. I'm on my way to hell." So off she went.

When Volkening arrived, he found a man who had grasped the meaning of this passage in the Bible: "Do not be deceived: God cannot be mocked. A man reaps what he sows." He brought his chair up to the bed and said, "You are going straight to hell, aren't you?" "Yes," was the reply, "I'm going to hell." Volkening's tone became imploring. "Heinrich," he said, "let's go together to Calvary. That's where Jesus died for you." Then he went on to explain with compassion how Jesus goes about saving a sinner. First of all, we ourselves must become aware of our sinful condition; then we have to stop repeating our favourite motto in life; and we have to stick to the bare facts. Then, and only then, can Jesus grant us his salvation.

At last the farmer understood: "Jesus died for *me* on the cross. He atoned for *my* sins. He can fully justify me by offering me the only justice which is acceptable in God's sight." For the first time in his life he really prayed: "O God, be merciful unto me, a sinner. Lord Jesus, save me from hell."

Volkening left the room quietly. He could go back home with his mind set at rest, because the dying man had called upon the name of the Lord. Three times in the Bible we find this verse: "Everyone who calls on the name of the Lord will be saved." The next day when Volkening came back to see him, he found a man at peace with God. "How are you, Heinrich?" he inquired. "Jesus has accepted me – by grace," was the answer.

A miracle had happened.

Now I am going to tell you another story.

A learned Jew found Jesus one night and said to him, "Master, I'd like to have a little talk with you about religious questions." But Jesus replied, "There's nothing do discuss. Unless a man is born again, he cannot see the Kingdom of God." "What's that you say?" exclaimed the visitor. "I can't go back into my mother's womb and be born a second time!" But Jesus held his ground and declared, "Unless a man is born of water and the Spirit, he cannot enter the Kingdom of God."

Here we have the strictly personal aspect of the Christian faith: the man or woman who wants to lay hold of eternal life must go through the narrow gate, by being "born again" through the miraculous action of the Holy Spirit.

We're not talking theological subtleties here. No. Your eternal lot is at stake. You may not have the chance of having a Volkening at your bedside when you are at death's door. So you would be wise to listen to what I have to say.

To be "born again" implies that I have at last come to recognize that God is right; that I admit I am lost and that my heart is evil. To be "born again" requires that I acknowledge my need of Jesus, the world's only Saviour. To be "born again" entails my making a forthright, honest confession of my sins: "Lord, I have sinned against heaven and against you." To be "born again" also involves my making an act of faith: "The blood of Jesus purifies me from all sin. He paid my debt and offers me the only justice acceptable in God's sight." To be "born again" calls for a total surrender of my life into the hands of Jesus. Finally, to be "born again" means that the Holy Spirit makes it clear to me that I am a child of God: or, to use biblical terms, that God has put his seal upon me. Without the experience of this "new birth", you will not enter into the Kingdom of God. The man or woman who has become a child of God can be absolutely certain of it. If I am drowning and someone pulls me out of the water, I know for certain that I have been saved when I feel the ground under my feet and when my breathing comes back to normal.

Let me repeat: this is the strictly personal aspect of the Christian faith. The "new birth" is an experience each one of us must go through personally if we want eternal life. Looking back at the way I became a child of God, I am forced to admit it was a real miracle. I was living far from God, committing all kinds of sins. But then Jesus came into my life, and now I belong to him. I wish I could have ten lives to live in order to snatch men and women from everlasting damnation by bringing them to Jesus Christ. Have no rest until you are "born again" and can say:

> His for ever, only His;
> Who the Lord and me shall part?
> Ah, with what a rest of bliss
> Christ can fill the loving heart!
> Heaven and earth may fade and flee,
> First-born light in gloom decline;
> But, while God and I shall be,
> I am His, and He is mine.

The new birth is not the end of the Christian's experience. It is only the beginning. Throughout the Christian's entire life, his faith will have a personal character to it.

Right from the beginning of my Christian life, I knew it was indispensable to listen every day to my new friend's voice. So I started to *read the Bible*. Many people today seem to think that only pastors read the Bible. Not far from my house in Essen there is a public park. That is where I like to go to read my Bible in the morning, walking to and fro as I do so. People in the neighbourhood sometimes watch me. One person said to me the other day, "I see you reading your prayer-book in the mornings." It's Roman Catholic priests, you know, who read their prayer-book. The man could not imagine my reading a book that any ordinary person might also read. Contrary to general opinion, the Bible is a book for everybody.

In the camps I organize for my group of young people in Essen, we gather together in the morning before breakfast for a fifteen-minute time of meditation. We begin by singing a hymn, then we look at the day's reading in *Daily Light*. Afterwards, I suggest a passage of the Scriptures and everybody goes off to read it for himself in his own little corner. Those who have taken the first step of faith towards Jesus continue this practice at home, because they cannot do without hearing the Good Shepherd's voice and talking to him. If you have decided to follow Jesus, be sure to cultivate the personal aspect of your faith by beginning to read the New Testament. Have your fifteen-minute quiet time every day, morning or evening.

And when you have finished reading your New Testament, close your eyes and pray: "Lord Jesus, now I have to talk to you. I've got so many things to do. Help me to get through them. Deliver me from my favourite sins. Give me love for others. Fill me with your Spirit." Talk to Jesus. He is very near and can hear you. *Prayer* is also one of the private elements of the Christian faith.

A while ago, I said to a man who had just been converted, "You need to spend a quarter of an hour every day in the presence of Jesus." To this he replied, "Pastor Busch, I'm not a pastor like you. You've got time for that. I haven't. I've got a very tight daily schedule." "Listen to me carefully," I said. "You never manage to get through all your work, do you?" "No," he admitted, "never." "You see," I explained, "that's because you don't put aside a time for meditation and prayer. If you took the habit of talking every day to Jesus – reading a few verses of the Bible methodically, followed by a moment of prayer – you would soon see that you can get through your work as if it were child's play. The more work you have, the more you will need that fifteen-minute quiet time. You may even need to stretch a quarter of an hour into half an hour in order to have enough time to bring all your preoccupations before the Lord. And you'll see that things will get better. If I tell you this, it's because I've experienced the truth of it myself. Sometimes I've scarcely got a leg out of bed when the telephone rings. Then I go and get the paper at the front door. Then the phone rings again. Soon after that, someone comes for a visit. All day long my nerves are on edge. Nothing goes right. Then suddenly I remember: 'Why, you haven't taken a minute off to talk to Jesus today; and he hasn't had a chance to talk to you. No wonder things are going wrong!'"

This time spent in the presence of Jesus is also one of the private aspects of the Christian life.

Another one is what the Bible calls *"crucifying the flesh"*. In the course of my life, I have talked to numerous men and women. Almost all of them have told me about their woes and grievances. Wives have complained about their husbands; and husbands have complained about their wives. Parents have criticized their children; and children have criticized their parents. But it never occurred to them that when they pointed a finger at someone else saying, "It's his (or her) fault that I'm not happy", they were actually pointing three fingers at themselves!

If you make a habit of meditating and praying, it will not be long before Jesus shows you that you yourself are responsible for your woes. Your marital and family problems are due to the fact that you are not living in the presence of God. Things are not going right because you are not walking with God. The Christian must learn, day after day, to crucify his old nature.

I would like to share with you a personal experience I had recently. Along with about fifty other people working among the young people in Essen, I was able to attend a retreat of several days. It was wonderful, so wonderful that it was beyond description. We were all so happy to be together; and God richly blessed us. In spite of this, there were some tensions. But the last day, before celebrating the Lord's Supper together, one person after another could be seen getting up and going over to someone else and saying, "Please forgive me for this or for that." As for me, I had to go to three co-workers and say, "Will you forgive me for speaking so harshly to you the other day?" "But you were right," replied one of them. "Forgive me all the same," I implored. It is not easy for a man of my age to humble himself before a twenty-year-old, but I would have had no peace if I had not done so.

If you form the habit of coming regularly into Jesus' presence, you will learn to crucify your old nature each day. And you will see that things will improve. This is one of the elements of the strictly personal side of the Christian's faith. If you know nothing about this aspect of the Christian life, then – I beg you – stop calling yourself a Christian!

Often, when I am walking along the street, I reason like this to myself: "The people rushing past me in this street probably all consider themselves Christians. If I stopped someone at random and asked, 'Excuse me, are you a Christian?', he would more than likely say, 'Of course I am. You don't take me for a Muslim, do you?' And if I continued to question him, 'Tell me, have there ever been times that you haven't been able to sleep because of your joy of being a Christian?', he would probably remark, 'Are you crazy, or what?'"

Am I not right? Present-day Christianity gets no joy at the thought of the faith it professes. We complain about the Church – that's all! Not the slightest sign of joy! But from the moment we experience the miracle of the new birth, we understand the significance of this word from the Apostle Paul: "Rejoice in the Lord always. I will say it again: Rejoice!"

Lately I read a magnificent passage of the Bible to my young people: "For you who revere my name, the sun of righteousness (a prophetic allusion to Jesus) will rise with healing in its wings." Isn't it beautiful? The text continues: "And you will go out and leap like calves released from the stall." This passage puts it so beautifully yet I rarely meet Christians who, in their joy at belonging to the Lord, "jump like calves released from the stall". Why is it we don't feel this joy?

The answer is simple: we are not real Christians.

I can't help thinking of my mother. Her deep joy in the Lord was visible to everyone. I have known many other Christians who, like her, were shining with joy. I hope that as the years go by I too will come to feel the joy of the Lord more and more. This means taking the Gospel seriously and not being satisfied with a thin veneer of Christianity.

So much for the first side of the Christian faith – its strictly personal aspect.

But there is another side – seen by all.

2. The public aspect

First and foremost, *a Christian has fellowship with other believers.* This is a very important point. The true Christian joins up with other Christians who, like him, are yearning for the full accomplishment of their salvation.

There is the Sunday morning worship service, for example. Why don't you go? "But I listen to the Sunday morning broadcast service!" you may exclaim. Now, I am not talking about the sick. For them it is an excellent thing to be able to tune in to a service of worship. But if you don't feel like taking part in person in a real worship service, in a real gathering of believers, then your Christianity does not go very far. The Sunday worship service is an integral part of a genuine Christian life.

Around the year 300 A.D. – a very long time ago – an extraordinary man by the name of Diocletian ruled over the Roman Empire. Formerly a slave, Diocletian had progressively climbed up the social scale until at last he sat on the throne of the great Roman Empire. By that time, Christianity had permeated throughout the whole empire. The Emperor Diocletian knew, of course, that his predecessors had persecuted Christians. But he thought to himself, "I won't be so stupid. I'm not going to persecute the best people in the empire. They can believe whatever they want. Under my rule, everyone can freely choose his own religion." It was quite unusual for an emperor to have such a tolerant attitude. The world's rulers, in general, want to have control over our consciences.

Now, Diocletian had taken as a close associate a certain Galerius, a former shepherd. He later succeeded Diocletian on the throne. One day Galerius said something like this to him: "Diocletian, you'll see that when these Christians are in the majority, there will be a lot of public unrest. They keep on talking about Jesus – their king. We have to do something to stop them!" "Come on," replied Diocletian, "you are talking nonsense. For 250 years, my predecessors continually persecuted the Christians and never succeeded in stamping them out. As for me, I'd rather leave them alone." Diocletian had a lot of common sense. But Galerius went on nagging him: "Those Christians are a strange lot, you know. They claim that they are filled with the Holy Spirit, and that others are not; and they claim to be the only ones for whom salvation is available. They're a proud people and you'd be wise to get rid of them."

Diocletian continued to refuse. Galerius, on the other hand, was not easily defeated; so he came back again and again until at last Diocletian gave in: "Okay, but all we'll do is to prohibit the Christians from meeting together."

An edict was proclaimed to the effect that henceforth all Christians were forbidden to worship together under penalty of death. They had the right to follow their own beliefs on a strictly personal basis, but not as a gathered group of believers. Their elders met together to consider the situation: "What should we do? Wouldn't it be wiser simply to obey? After all, we can do what we want behind the walls of our homes. Nobody will lay a finger on us at home." Their conclusion is highly instructive: "Meeting together for prayer, singing, preaching, instruction and the giving of our tithes is an integral part of our Christian faith. We shall continue as before!" And they continued to meet in their churches.

Galerius exulted. "You see, Diocletian," he said, "those Christians are enemies of the state. They will not submit." And he launched one of the most cruel persecutions that the Christians had known up to that time. Many Christians submitted, thinking: "We can stay at home and still be Christians! We won't go to the meetings any more." But this was not the opinion of the Christian Church in general. "Those people are apostates," it declared. "The man or woman who ceases to attend Christian assemblies is considered as an apostate."

We should be saying the same thing to the Christians of our generation. There are indeed a great number of apostates in present-day Christianity. The Christians of that period were totally right in opposing the imperial edict, for the Bible clearly says: "Let us not give up meeting together, as some are in the habit of doing." Nowadays, we might say, ". . . as *almost everybody* is in the habit of doing." That is why I insist that those who earnestly want to be Christians ought to join an assembly of believers.

There are different ways for believers to meet together: there are the regular church meetings, Bible studies in private homes, prayer cells, youth groups. I beg you, get in contact with other Christians. A Frenchman said to me one day, "Some people like to eat herrings; others like to go to church!" Sorry, but that's simply not true! It's far more serious than that! Some people are on their way to hell; others look for the fellowship of other believers. That is a matter of fact.

If you are really serious about living as a disciple of Jesus Christ, then you must make some effort to find a group to join where you can learn more about Jesus. This is very important. You must go only where they talk about Jesus. No one can say, "In my area, there's nothing." People who love the Lord Jesus can be found everywhere. They may not be numerous. They may even be a little strange. But that doesn't matter! Your Christian faith is a dead faith if you do not have fellowship with other believers.

A Christian service of praise consists of at least four things: singing, teaching, prayer, and offering. They should be a part of every meeting. This was the practice of the early Christians; and that's how every Christian's God-given new life should be expressed.

There is only one type of Christian faith. It's the kind that finds its expression in the fellowship of other believers. The Bible goes so far as to say: "We know that we have passed from death to life, because we love our brothers." This verse implies that the person who is not attracted to other Christians is still spiritually dead.

I shall never forget the extraordinary beginnings of my ministry at Bielefeld where I was assistant-minister in one of the districts of the city. There were only a handful of us at the Sunday morning services which were held at the local parish hall. One Saturday night God allowed me to have a long discussion at the House of the People – a communist-owned hall – with some militants and free-thinkers. It lasted until one o'clock in the morning, when the bar-tender finally put us all out of the door.

It was raining outside. I had managed, for the first time, to gather around me an audience of about a hundred men – all factory-workers in my area. We formed a circle under a street light. The men asked me questions, and I answered them. We spoke about Jesus and about his coming into this world. After a while, they came to the point where they were honest enough to admit they were unhappy, that they were only fooling themselves in claiming not to have sinned, that deep down they really believed in eternity and in the coming judgement of God. Around two o'clock in the morning, I finally said to them, "Now, my friends, it's time for me to go home. In the morning I am holding a church service at 9:30. I'm certain you'd all like to come ... if you weren't so scared of each other!"

Just in front of me was a worker whom I will call B. At the time he must have been around thirty-five; and he was a real Westphalian. "Who, me?" he asked. "Scared? Not on your life!" "Okay, okay," I replied, "don't get excited! But if you do go to church on Sunday, you'll get a lot of remarks at work Monday morning, won't you? And that's what you're all afraid of!" A second time he said, "No, I'm not scared!" And a second time I said, "Come on, now! You'd like to come, but ... " "All right. I'll be there tomorrow morning, with a hymn-book under my arm!"

And that Sunday morning – only a few hours later – who should come strolling down the street, a hymn-book tucked under his arm, and walk right into our hall, but this good old Westphalian! He was well-known in the district. Monday evening, he came to see me and said, "You were right. My pals at the factory were really mad at me for going to church. But I've seen through the bluff of our pro-paganda. We cry 'Long live liberty', but actually we are slaves of other men. I've thrown everything overboard, including their old book on free-thought. Now, tell me about Jesus ... I want to know more about *him*."

He was my first convert. And it all started because one Sunday morning he attended the worship service of our humble little body of believers. He persevered, and others followed his example. A breach had been made. As time went by, God continued to work among us. But the thing that struck me most at the time was the fact that the turning point for these workers arrived when they started attending our meetings – and came under the influence of Christian fellowship and teaching.

I beg you, for the sake of your soul and your eternal salvation: get in touch with other believers. I'm not campaigning for any specific church or any particular preacher. My first and foremost concern is the salvation of your soul.

Then too, every Christian is called upon *publicly to confess* what he has found in Jesus. This is the second aspect of the open, visible side of the Christian faith.

Have you ever witnessed to Jesus Christ, if only by remarks like this: "It's true, Jesus is alive"? Or: "You are insulting the name I love above all by your blasphemies." Or: "With your obscene stories, you are dragging one of the greatest marvels of God's creation in the mud." Have you ever testified to him simply by saying: "I belong to Jesus"? People just wouldn't believe their ears if we all started witnessing!

As long as we don't have the courage to talk to others about our Saviour, we are not true Christians. Jesus said: "Whoever acknowledges me before men, I will also acknowledge him before my Father in heaven. But whoever disowns me before men, I will disown him before my Father in heaven." It will be tragic on the Judgement Day to see so-called Christians stand up and say, "Lord Jesus, we believed in you", and to see Jesus turn to his Father and exclaim, "I never knew them"! "But Lord, I was really . . . " "I do not know you," will be the reply. "Your neighbour never knew he was going straight to hell. You never warned him, even though you yourself knew the way leading to eternal life. Every time you ought to have opened your mouth and taken a stand for me, you remained silent." "I know, but my faith was so weak." "You ought to have confessed even that weak faith. A weak faith still has a powerful Saviour. Anyway, I never asked you to proclaim your faith, but to proclaim *me*. I do not know you."

"Whoever acknowledges me before men, I will also acknowledge him before my Father in heaven. But whoever disowns me before men, I will disown him before my Father in heaven." That is what Jesus says. And Jesus never lies. When will we get the courage to open our mouths and acknowledge him?

I must tell you another story. I was speaking a few weeks ago in one of the cities of the Ruhr Valley. The meetings had been organized by a young friend of mine, Gustave. Gustave is head of the repair shop of one of the city's large garages. He has become a joyful and effective witness of Jesus Christ because he learned to take a stand for his Saviour at the right time. One Monday morning in the shop, each worker, one after the other, began bragging about his "Sunday exploits". One of them said, "We were so drunk that the beer came running out of our eyes!" Another fellow described in detail an adventure with the opposite sex. "And you, Gustave," they asked, "where were you?" At the time he was still an apprentice mechanic. "In the morning," he replied, "I went to church. In the afternoon I went to Pastor Busch's young people's meeting at the Weigle House." Then followed a regular round of teasing and mocking. And the young apprentice stood there, crestfallen. But suddenly, while everyone – apprentices, mechanics, and even the foreman – was attacking him, a hot anger surged up within him. "Why is it," he thought, "that among people who call themselves Christians it is possible to boast about the most shameful things, but it is not possible to take a stand for the Saviour?"

He determined then and there to endeavour to win the whole shop to Jesus Christ. Beginning with his fellow apprentices, he took each one aside in private and said, "Listen, if you go on like that, you will end up in hell one day. Why not come with me next Sunday to the young people's meeting at Weigle House? You'll hear all about the Lord Jesus there!"

By the time Gustave left the shop after having successfully passed his mastership exams, things had totally changed. I witnessed this for myself. All the apprentices belonged to my group of young people. Three of the mechanics went to the meetings at the YMCA. In the shop, nobody dared to make any obscene remarks any longer. When a newcomer would start to talk smut, the others would signal for him to be quiet, or else someone would whisper in his ear, "Shut up! Gustave might hear you."

And so Gustave gained everyone's respect. Today he has a very responsible position as head mechanic in an important garage. God has clearly blessed him in every way.

Once again I repeat my question: Where are the Christians today with the courage to speak out and publicly declare themselves for their Saviour? Yet, it is only as we confess Christ that we grow spiritually.

Is the Christian faith a strictly private affair? No, it is not! We have an obligation towards the world to testify to our faith in Jesus Christ. So, put an end to your contemptible silence. Otherwise Jesus will disown you on the Judgement Day.

During the Third Reich, a good number of my young people, all teenagers, were enrolled by force in Hitler's "Arbeitsdienst", or "Labour Force". Shortly before their departure, I gave each one a small Bible with this recommendation: "When you have joined your unit, on the very first evening lay your Bible on the table, open it and read it in the sight of everybody. This will be like a bombshell. But the next day, it will be over. If you don't take your stand right at the start, you'll never do it."

They did what I suggested. They put their Bibles on the table the very first day. "What are you reading there?" "The Bible." If a hand-grenade had exploded in the room, the reaction would not have been worse!

Sad to say, in our German society you may read any kind of dirty book, but not the Bible!

One of my young friends, Paul, (he did not come back from the war) discovered the next morning on opening his locker that his Bible had disappeared. He looked around the room. One of the boys burst out laughing; the others soon joined in. "Did you pinch my Bible?" he asked. "H'm...," was the reaction. "Where did you put my Bible?" he insisted. "The sergeant-major's got it!" Paul knew then that things were going to be tough.

When he had finished his chores that night, he looked for a spot where he could be alone, and prayed: "Lord Jesus! I am alone. I'm only seventeen years old. Please, don't let me down. Help me to take a stand for you." When he had finished praying, he went to the sergeant-major's office and knocked on the door. "Come in!" The sergeant-major was sitting at his desk. And there on his desk was Paul's Bible! "What do you want?" "Please, Sir," Paul implored, "give me my Bible back. It's mine." "H'm...," was the only reply. He picked up the Bible and started leafing through it. "So, it's to you this Bible belongs?" he remarked. "Don't you know the Bible is a dangerous book?" "Yes, Sir, I know it is. It's a dangerous book even locked up in my locker. It stirs up trouble even there!" The officer straightened himself up in his chair and said, "Sit down a minute." Then he blurted out, "At one time, when I was younger, I planned to study theology." Paul asked, "Sir, have you denied your faith?" A deep conversation then followed during which the sergeant-major, a man of about forty, admitted to the seventeen-year-old, "Actually, I'm a very unhappy man. But I can't go back – the price is far too high." "Poor man," Paul said, "but Jesus is well worth all the sacrifices!" The officer dismissed the youngster with these words: "You are a fortunate lad, my boy." "You are right, Sir," agreed Paul as he walked out of the office with his Bible tucked under his arm. From then on, no one ever made the slightest remark about his Bible.

Where are the Christians today who have the courage to stand up for their convictions?

Is the Christian faith a strictly personal matter? Yes, it is. The new birth and the Christian life take place in the depths of the believer's heart.

Is the Christian faith a strictly personal matter? No, it is not. Christians unite in church to worship God together. Together, they participate in home Bible studies, young people's meetings, and fellowship groups. They open their mouths and publicly declare that they follow the Lord.

The world must see that God has lit a fire on earth in the person of Jesus Christ!

When will the end come?

Some time ago, I talked with a businessman. He slapped me on the back and said, "Pastor, what you are doing to encourage young people to live decent lives is good." "To be very frank," I answered, "I don't expect much to come of it. The Bible says that man's heart is evil from his youth. So I don't think that moralizing is much use. I would like something different." "Oh . . . ! Exactly what would you like?" "I'd like to see these young people turning to the Lord Jesus and becoming children of God for now and for eternity." "Pastor," he said, "what you say there is fine, but you've got to come down to earth."

Now isn't that a word of wisdom? "You've got to come down to earth!" I burst out laughing. "My dear friend," I asked jokingly, "I've got to come down to *what* earth? Haven't you noticed that the earth has been wobbling under our feet for a good long time?"

You don't have to be a big boss in industry to realize that the world is no longer a safe place. And this is what frightens people today. Everyone is looking for security, but everyone knows it's nowhere to be found. Some people open a bank account in Switzerland; others have a nuclear shelter built in Bolivia. After all, security must be somewhere! But deep down we all know one thing: there is no security. Little wonder people today are anxiously asking, "What is our world coming to?" Undeniably, one of the characteristics of our times is the fact that many people are wondering when the end of the world will come.

A few years back, a play by the Swiss author Dürrenmatt, *The Physicists*, appeared on the stage. The play ended with a scene in which one of the physicists made a very gloomy prognosis: no one can prevent humanity from using the atomic bomb and exterminating itself. The author concluded: "And there somewhere in space, the radio-active earth will continue to turn indefinitely and uselessly."

The vision of a deserted world turning endlessly in space, without life or purpose, seemed very real. When a modern writer speaks in such startling terms about the end of the world, it demands our attention. Personally, I do not believe that Dürrenmatt was right. I do not believe that some day there will be no more than a radio-active earth turning round and round in space. If I tried to explain this to the author, he would probably ask me, "Why don't you accept my theory? It stands to reason that's what will happen." But I would reply, "This is not the Christian viewpoint. The Lord Jesus implied that the human race would not disappear before the end of the world. In spite of the probabilities, things will not come to pass as you imagine."

The question is, who can you believe and whose prognosis can you trust?

There are two wrong ways of considering the future.

There is the way Joseph Goebbels had, which simply consists in fantasizing about what the future might be like. Even now I can hear him ranting, "Five years from now, German cities will be standing more beautiful than they have ever been!" This way of thinking really amounts to projecting one's own fantasies onto the veil which hides the future.

Jehovah's Witnesses use this method with skill. Some older people may remember the posters that were stuck at every street corner in 1925: "Millions of people now living will never see death!!" This slogan originated with the International Bible Students. Ironically, more people died a few years later than ever before in the history of the world. The International Bible Students had simply dreamed up a rosy picture of the future. Later they changed their name and became known as Jehovah's Witnesses. And they are still probably inventing new mental images today.

Second, there is the way of the fortune-tellers. I have to admit that I don't understand a thing about it. And I don't want to learn a thing about divination, spiritism, radiesthesia, cartomancy, horoscopes, and the like. Let me tell you why. God has said quite plainly in his Word, the Bible: "Do not practice divination or sorcery." He has also said this: "Do not turn to mediums or seek out spiritists, for you will be defiled by them." Another passage reads: "Let no one be found among you who sacrifices his son or daughter in the fire, who practices divination, or sorcery, interprets omens, engages in witchcraft, or casts spells, or who is a medium or spiritist or who consults the dead. Anyone who does these things is detestable to the Lord."

As my greatest desire in life is to be a Christian and to be part of God's people, I shall take care not to get mixed up with those things. If by any chance you have fallen into this trap, then I beg you for your soul's sake and for your salvation: take time to search your heart; then cry to Jesus, confess this sin to him and ask his forgiveness.

For my part, I am determined to put my trust in the Bible, in the Word of God. I cannot do otherwise, because the Bible bears the stamp of authenticity. It is not mere speculation. Time and again its writers claim: "Thus speaks the Lord!"

The surest way of finding out about the future is to refer to the Bible.

At the height of the war, the Gestapo ordered me to stop my itinerant ministry. I was authorized to hold meetings only in the city of Essen. The city was devastated by bombs. Nevertheless, every evening I held a Bible study in a cellar. Having lots of spare time during the day, I took this opportunity to study the last book of the Bible, the Revelation of John, thoroughly. What struck me most in my study was its relevance. And I decided then to share with others the lessons I drew from it.

1. Jesus is coming back

The Bible states this clearly. The return of Jesus Christ in glory is the crowning event towards which the expectations of all Christians converge. When Jesus ascended into heaven forty days after his resurrection, the disciples kept their eyes fixed on him. And they saw him disappear into another dimension. "A cloud hid him from their sight." Then all of a sudden two messengers sent by God appeared to the disciples and said, "This same Jesus, who has been taken from you into heaven, will come back in the same way you have seen him go into heaven."

Yes, Jesus is coming back again! Some day, coming from another dimension, God's dimension, the Lord Jesus, in a cloud of glory, will burst into our three-dimensional world. *This is the Christian hope.*

I must tell you how this extraordinary truth impressed itself upon me more than twenty-five years ago. I was a young pastor at the time and had just moved into a mining district of the city of Essen. I was only twenty-seven years old and I found myself alone among 12,000 miners, none of whom were the least interested in my message. In the heart of the district, surrounded by miners' apartment blocks and shaft towers, was a large desolate square. On one of the corners of the square a small house was still standing. I was able to fix up a modest meeting-place in it and then I began holding regular Bible studies. It was wonderful to see the people come one after the other for the first time: a few miners (communists and free-thinkers) who were curious to hear what this young preacher had to say, some dear old grandmothers, a handful of children and two or three young people. Strange as it may seem, this modest embryo of a church exasperated all the population of the area. We were disturbed at every meeting. One day they broke the windows. So we had shutters put on. But then they began throwing stones at the shutters. The noise was deafening. After that, they began playing football with tin cans right in front of the door so that no one could hear a word that was being said. On another occasion, they paraded with pipes in front of our little hall and began singing lustily. Inside, our little group began singing a hymn.

Those were heroic times!

Then one day the situation became alarming. It seemed as if all hell had been let loose. Something strange happend. A heavy object was hurled against the door, and fell to the ground with a great crash. "They've thrown a bomb!" I thought. I could hear the sound of people running away. Our hearts stopped beating. Then it was silent again outside. I slowly opened the door and saw, there on the ground, in the middle of a puddle of water, a huge metal crucifix. It had been torn off a neighbouring Catholic clubhouse and thrown against our door. It was as if our enemies wanted to say to us, "Here's your Christ! Let him lie in the mud!"

It was a dreary November evening. It was raining. And there at our feet was the cross in a puddle. I was standing at the edge of that desolate square. Behind me our small group was huddled together, trembling and quivering with fear; and before us all, in the puddle, was the image of the crucified Saviour. I could not help but think, "God could have left the world to its awful fate for a thousand reasons. Yet he didn't. He even sent his Son, who did an extraordinary thing: he took our sins upon himself and allowed himself to be nailed to a cross. And what has man done? Instead of falling down and worshipping the Saviour, he has taken his image and thrown it into the mud. It's as though he has spat at the hand God has stretched out to him."

Mind you, at least those people in Essen had some hatred for Jesus. People nowadays don't even bother to hate him! They just throw the crucifix in a puddle out of pure indifference.

A smouldering anger overwhelmed me that day. "What will God do now?" I thought. "Surely fire will fall from heaven!" But no fire fell. It continued raining. And the image of the Saviour on the cross stayed lying in the puddle.

I could hear mocking laughter from afar. They were making fun of me! "Things will not always be like this," I suddenly thought.

"The Son of God, who died for this world, will not always be an object of contempt. No, it will not always be like this. For the moment his power and majesty are still hidden. But the day will come – and this is absolutely certain – when the world that despised him will have to recognize him as the only way of salvation and as the Lord of the universe. He will come again in his glory."

That evening in the rain, on the deserted square with the crucifix in the mud, my small group of believers close by, I was able for the first time, as I walked back to our modest meeting-place, to rejoice at the thought of Jesus' return. When I was in the pulpit again, I opened the Gospel of Matthew, chapter 24, and read: "They will see the Son of Man coming on the clouds of the sky, with power and with great glory." I have not stopped rejoicing about his return ever since.

When I see to what extent my Saviour is despised – this Saviour who delivers from death, forgives sins, brings happiness and who saves – I am glad to know that the day is coming when the cloak of contempt will fall from his shoulders and he will appear in all his glory.

The first time I went into the main hall of the Weigle House, a Christian youth centre in Essen, my attention was caught by a painting on the wall. In this hall, where hundreds of young people gathered together, was a unique painting. It represented the return of Jesus Christ: at the bottom of the painting, a city; above it, clouds; on these clouds, a white horse on which the King was mounted. His hand was lifted up and on that hand the nail prints could still be seen.

I said to Pastor Weigle, my predecessor, "Is this the only picture you have on the walls? It doesn't seem very appropriate here in a youth centre." "My dear friend," he answered, "these young people spend all week at school, at work, in the factory, or down the mine. When they testify to their faith in the Lord Jesus, they encounter nothing but sarcasm and mockery. And if they speak out against evil, they get mocked and criticized. It's not surprising that they are often discouraged. This painting is intended to remind them, when they gather here, that Christ is victor and that by eternal decree the world *will* be his."

I have personally experienced the power of this marvellous hope. Under Hitler's rule, I was arrested after holding a big meeting in the city of Darmstadt. They pushed me into a police car beside an official of the Gestapo. Hundreds of people crowded around us. The SS soldier at the wheel was ordered to start driving. But the motor would not start. The car was probably in good condition, but it just wouldn't work. "Get going!" yelled the SS officer. But the engine still stalled. Just then, from the midst of the crowd, a young man standing on the church steps began singing with a loud voice:

> Rejoice! the Saviour reigns –
> The God of truth and love;
> When he had purged our stains,
> He took His seat above:
> Lift up your heart, lift up your voice:
> Rejoice again, I say, rejoice.
>
> Rejoice in glorious hope:
> Jesus, the Judge, shall come,
> And take His servants up
> To their eternal home:
> We soon shall hear th'archangel's voice:
> The trump of God shall sound: Rejoice!

The young man immediately disappeared into the crowd. And then the car started! Turning to the Gestapo official, I said, "My poor friend! I am on the victor's side." He started at my words then whispered to me, "A long time ago I used to be a member of the YMCA." "Well!" I said, "and now you are arresting Christians! Poor man, I wouldn't want to be in your shoes." We continued talking until we reached the prison, but in that short time the hope of Christ's return had opened up before me.

And as the days darken, the expectation of Christ's coming takes on greater importance.

Jesus Christ's return in glory will be, in fact, his third coming to earth. He came the first time at his incarnation. Born of Mary, he lay in the manger of Bethlehem. It is this event we celebrate at Christmas; that is, if we still know what it's all about. It was then that the Son of God became a man, so that we might become children of God and that he might become our brother.

Jesus comes for the second time right now, this very day – in the person of his Spirit. He says, "Here I am! I stand at the door and knock. If anyone hears my voice and opens the door, I will come in and eat with him, and he with me."

Why do we evangelize? To prepare the way for the Lord Jesus to come to people today. The Bible says: "To all who received him, to those who believed in his name, he gave the right to become children of God."

When Jesus comes for the third time, it will be in all his glory. The Bible has disclosed something of the circumstances which will lead up to this momentous event. At the time of his return, we will have exhausted all the various systems of government: constitutional monarchy and absolute monarchy; presidential democracy and popular democracy; dictatorship and who knows what. And we will have recognized that none of these systems is worth much.

This will be the opportune time for Jesus to come back.

2. Events preceding Christ's return

The Bible states that the course of the world's history will run for a good long time throughout the ages. Then, in an almost imperceptible way, will come a period of time when its course will, as it were, draw to a close. To designate this period, I shall use an expression which is not found in the Bible. I will refer to it as "the period of the end". The Bible tells of a time of wide-spread chaos when men will be unable to resolve their problems. Panic-stricken, they will look for help but will find none. The Lord Jesus emphasized that four factors would characterize this "period of the end".

He alluded to the *political confusion* of this period when he said, "Nation will rise against nation, and kingdom against kingdom." No era such as ours, when diplomats have held so many costly conferences, has ever been known. No era such as ours, when rearmament is being carried out to the detriment of the peoples in such a senseless way, has ever been known. The money put out for atomic weapons could be used to build several big cities and thus bring an end to the housing shortage. But instead of that, politicians the world over are saying, "We must rearm!" Even the smallest state must have its atomic bomb. Yet, never before has there been such longing for peace! Every country wants peace. No one wants war. But each country enters like a madman into the arms race. Could this not be the political chaos of "the end"?

Secondly, Jesus mentions the *economic confusion* of this period: "There will be famines and earthquakes in various places." The earth produces enough food for all men to eat their fill. And there have never been so many qualified economists as in our days. Never has world economy been so sophisticated. Yet in spite of this, according to United Nations reports, more than one-half of humanity never eats its fill. In a society as highly civilized as ours, shouldn't we be able to satisfy the hunger of all men? But somehow we can't manage it. And the economic disorder grows.

The third distinctive sign of "the period of the end" to which Jesus alluded is *religious confusion*. Jesus described it in these terms: "At that time if anyone says to you, 'Look, here is the Christ!' or, 'Look, there he is!' do not believe it. For false Christs and false prophets will appear and perform signs and miracles to deceive the elect."

I was recently confronted with a young man who said to me, "I don't know who to believe. There are the Roman Catholics, the Orthodox, the Protestants, the Jehovah's Witnesses, the Mormons, the Moonies, the Buddhists, the Muslims, and all the others. Who am I to believe?" I laughed and answered, "Young man, muster your courage for things are going to get worse and worse. The Bible says so!"

This is indeed one of the signs of "the period of the end". Because people refuse to be guided by the Word of God, they are being misguided by the Devil. And God allows it. "Look, here is the Christ...! Look, there he is!"

There is terrible confusion in religious matters. I am alarmed when I observe the way people run from one religious spectacle to another. But let me tell you right now that no great preacher can ever save you. If you do not meet the Saviour personally you are eternally lost.

There is one last sign of "the period of the end": *the return of the Jews to Palestine*. The existence of the State of Israel seems to me to be one of the most amazing signs of the times. Some people see no sign at all in it.

But recently when I was queueing at the Swiss border and saw a car with a "State of Israel" licence-plate in front of me, I could not help but think, "Biblical prophecies are being fulfilled and even licence-plates are proclaiming it!"

My father told me that in 1899 the Jews were offered Madagascar as a land of refuge, but they refused. "Nothing doing!" they said. "We have received a promise: the promise of returning one day to the land of our ancestors." World opinion at the time was that it was impossible for such a thing ever to come to pass. And yet, the State of Israel does indeed exist today.

What characterizes "the period of the end" is the fact that in spite of all its progress mankind is more and more bewildered. Man's helplessness is obvious. How long "the period of the end" will last I cannot say. The Bible does not mention the number of years. But it does warn us to "watch". The Apostle Paul gave this advice to Christians: "So then, let us not be like others, who are asleep, but let us be alert and self-controlled."

When this period of confusion before Christ's return is at its peak, *the time of the Antichrist will begin.* I shall call it "the last days". It is true that we are now experiencing the confusion of "the period of the end". And this confusion even now clamours for the appearance of "the strong man". Yes, our present-day world is demanding this strong man. And when distress is at a climax, this powerful man will appear and proclaim himself as the liberator of the world. He will not be the Christ, but the Antichrist.

The Bible tells us that out of the ocean of the nations a dictator will emerge who will dominate the whole world: he is the one we call the Antichrist. Under his rule, the world will be united for one last time. This era of history will be marked by man's obstinacy. It will be man's last attempt to rescue the world by a political and economic programme set up by himself. It is fascinating to read the description the Bible gives of this last dictator. It describes him in metaphorical language. To understand it, the Holy Spirit must enlighten us. The Apostle John saw the vision and wrote: "I saw a beast coming out of the sea. He had ten horns and seven heads, with ten crowns on his horns, and on each head a blasphemous name."

How can we explain this impressive description?

The sea is the symbol of the nations of the earth. Those who have ever been at the sea know how rough it can get. It is never perfectly calm. The nations of the world are never altogether at peace either. There is always a hot spot somewhere.

The last "liberator" of the world will emerge from the sea of the nations. All the great political leaders of the last two centuries stood as liberators. And they all had their origins in the people: Napoleon, the little Corsican; Adolf Hitler, the little corporal of the First World War; Stalin, the shoemaker. All of them were precursors of the Antichrist. Each one of them came from among the people, and the people, delighted, acclaimed them saying, "They are one of us!"

Jesus Christ, my liberator, does not come from the sea of the nations, but from the world of God. For he is the Son of the living God.

The Antichrist is called a *beast*. What does this mean? The Bible states that man was made in the image of God. The closer I am to God, the more human I become. The farther I turn away from God, the more bestial I become. Nietzsche, the great enemy of Christianity, declared on one occasion: "The most noble man is the fair-haired beast." He had understood perfectly. The Antichrist shall be a man completely estranged from God. He will have turned his back upon God. This is what will make a beast of him.

He will be a beast *with seven heads*. What does this mean? It means that he will be no fool. People will certainly be able to say of him, "He has got a good head on his shoulders!"

The Antichrist will have *a mouth like a lion's*. This signifies that he will drown the world with his propaganda. Our generation has already had a foretaste of the lion's growl blaring through all our public address systems. It is not difficult to imagine that once the Antichrist is here his absurd propaganda will have a levelling effect on all aspects of our lives.

This ultimate attempt by man to save the world without seeking the help of its Saviour, the Lord Jesus, will nevertheless meet with success. Salvation will be offered to man without his having to repent and change his ways. And all his problems will be resolved for him: in the political field by the creation of a world empire; in the economical field by the distribution of food rationing cards; and in the religious field by the worship of the Antichrist himself.

It is alarming to observe how rapidly our world is heading towards "the last days".

And when that time is here, the whole world will submit to the Antichrist. Christians will be the only ones to say, "We refuse to adore you!" Everyone, whatever his social status may be, will have to bear a mark on his or her forehead. But Christians will say, "No! We have a Saviour. He is Jesus!" Because of this, they will be persecuted. The Bible states: "No one could buy or sell unless he had the mark." Concerning this verse, a Swabian Bible commentator named Auberlen wrote the following remark one hundred and fifty years ago: "We do not understand very well what this means, but the unfolding of the events themselves will help us to see clearly." We who have lived under totalitarian regimes can understand these things to some extent. We know what it means: Mr. X receives no certificate of registration, no food ration card, no work permit; he can believe what he wants, but he no longer has any country or any rights. This is happening right now in our days.

I was upset when I first read this verse. "So many people believe the Bible is out-of-date," I could not help but think. "It isn't the Bible which is out-of-date, but our ideologies. The Bible guides us towards the future."

The Antichrist will tolerate anything, except a testimony borne to the real Saviour, the Lord Jesus Christ. That is why Christians will be persecuted.

One day, when I was talking to my children about these things, my little girl started to cry. "Honey," I said, "why are you crying?" Sobbing, she replied, "But it might happen any day!" "Yes," I said, "it's possible." "And what will happen if I can't stay true to Jesus?" "This would be terrible," I explained, "but what matters is that you follow him day by day right now."

The period of "the last days" could take us by surprise at any time. When it does, we will no longer have any chance of finding Jesus. For there will be no more church services. Church bells will be melted down to make statues to the glory of the Antichrist. Churches will be turned into museums and used to exhibit pictures of the Antichrist's earlier years.

At this stage, people will be crying out for comfort. But having rejected Jesus, the only Comforter, they will find no other comfort. In their distress men and women will be at the mercy of their fellow-beings. Christians, however, will consider themselves fortunate – even if they do have to face death – for in these difficult days *they* will have a Comforter.

I have also been troubled by this statement Jesus made: "Men will faint from terror, fearful of what is coming on the world." The book of Revelation seems to suggest that the Antichrist will fill the world with fanfares and flags. I used to wonder how these two statements could be reconciled. On one hand we read of terror and expectation; and on the other hand of great success. But having lived through the year 1933, I have learned that the world can be filled with cheers, fanfares and flags, and yet be gripped with terror and fear of the future.

When the Antichrist is at the pinnacle of his power, when he is certain that Jesus has been eliminated for good – God will intervene! Jesus will come back in all his glory. Little is said of the Antichrist, except that Jesus will destroy him with the breath of his mouth.

As the times become darker and darker, the frightening signs of humanity's distress and of the Antichrist's future reign become more visible. But people who read the Bible take courage, because they are expecting the return of Jesus Christ.

3. Events that will follow Christ's return

Here again the Bible traces only the outline.

First of all, we are told that Jesus will reign for a thousand years on the earth. Once again the Bible uses figurative speech which probably indicates simply that Jesus will rule for a long period of time. All this seems perfectly coherent to me: first of all, man's hopeless state will become evident; then, obstinate man will make his last attempt to save the world; but after that, Jesus must rule. And he knows how to govern!

If you want proof of this, visit a home where Jesus is King – for they do exist even today – and you will be conscious of a different atmosphere as soon as you have crossed the doorstep. I think of a young couple I know. The husband came to see me one day and said, "I'm ready to surrender to God. I've denied his existence up to now. I've even spoken publicly against him. I can't bear it any longer!" He went on to unburden himself about all the things which were weighing him down. He admitted his marriage had gone sour. He said, "I wanted to show everyone that you can be happily married even without God." And then everything went wrong. Their first child died and standing beside his dead body he and his wife had a bitter quarrel. In the end he had to admit, "God is against us. I surrender." The funeral service, which I took, was distressing. In the middle of the room was the coffin of the child. On one side, the young man and his family. On the other, a pretty young woman, biting her lips, surrounded by her family. Two worlds, two sides. And separating them, the dead child!

It took more than a year for the woman to come to believe in the Lord Jesus. I shall never forget the short note she sent to me on Easter morning: "He is risen in my heart too!"

After that they got married – they had been living together – and started afresh. Though both of them were very independent by nature and proud of their intelligence, they nevertheless came to experience real harmony as a couple. The husband explained to me one day how this had come about. "Before," he said, "everything used to go wrong in our home . . ." "And how come everything is fine now?" I interrupted. He replied, his face aglow, "Because now Jesus is the head of our home. My wife and I don't fight to prove who's boss any more. But together we ask, 'What does Jesus expect of us?' And it works!"

As he talked, an idea suddenly struck me: If it is so beautiful, so wonderful, when Jesus rules over a home, what will it be like when he is King of the world?

The world will go through a second period of testing after the reign of Jesus. Hearts will be tried, to prove whether or not they have been really changed. Satan will be literally unchained, and it will be seen that the heart of man has not changed a bit and that mankind is still what it has always been.

The Bible gives us to understand that there will be a last revolt against God, and that after this the end of the world will come. All the solar systems will disintegrate. The heavens and the earth will pass away. Then, as John the Apostle wrote, recording his vision of "the last things": "I saw a great white throne and him who was seated on it. And I saw the dead, great and small, standing before the throne, and the books were opened. Another book was opened, which is the Book of Life. The dead were judged according to what they had done as recorded in the books. And if anyone's name was not found written in the Book of Life, he was thrown into the lake of fire."

Someone once asked me, "Where will the throne be if everything has disappeared?" I answered, "Don't worry about that. You should rather be concerned about the way in which you will appear before that great white throne!" We can be damned! I would prefer that this terrible truth were not found in the Bible. But the Word of God does confront us with this terrifying eventuality: of being eternally damned.

I am going to tell you a short story. A dinner party was once being given in a castle in Scotland, and the conversation turned to the subject of Christianity. The guests were all sitting round the fireplace in which a big fire was burning. An elegant elderly gentleman turned to the hostess and said, "From your remarks, Madam, I gather that you are a Christian. Do you seriously believe everything that is written in the Bible?" "Yes." "And that each one of us will be judged?" "Yes." "And that the person whose name is not found written in the Book of Life will go to hell?" "Yes, I believe this." The man arose, crossed the room and took a budgie out of a cage hanging in a corner. Then he came up to the fireplace and pretended to throw the bird into the fire. Shocked, the lady leapt up to stop him. "What are you doing?" she shrieked. "The poor little bird!" The man began to laugh. "You see, Madam, you feel sorry for this poor bird, and yet the one you call a God of love would cast millions of human beings into hell. What a strange God of love!"

There was a moment of silence, then the lady resumed, "I'm afraid you're wrong. God throws no one into hell. We jump into it ourselves. God wants all men to be saved."

The Bible paints a fearful picture of the Last Judgement. We are given a description of the tribunal of God. "And I saw the dead, great and small, standing before the throne, and the books were opened. Another book was opened, which was the Book of Life. The dead were judged according to what they had done as recorded in the books." People are strongly opposed to the message of a judgement. "It isn't true!" they say.

One of my young friends was asked at work, "Do you really believe in the Last Judgement?" "Yes, I do." "Come off it," his work-mates said. "How many people are living now? And how many have already died? Well, just try to imagine everyone being individually judged. Can you count the time that would take?" The young man answered back, "When that moment shall come, we'll have plenty of time. We won't have anything else to do!"

Yes, God will have lots of time for us. By judging us individually, he shows us for the very last time how seriously he takes each one of us. God already made this clear to us when his Son died in our place. You may not take your own life seriously, you may choose to waste it in sin and thoughtlessness – but God will take you seriously on the Day of Judgement nevertheless.

The Bible concludes its outlook on the future with this statement: "We are looking forward to a new heaven and a new earth, the home of righteousness." And it describes this new world in words which transcend our understanding. The description emphasizes one grand and unique reality: God has attained his goal. Those whose names are written in the Book of Life will inhabit this new world. They will be in his likeness, in the likeness of the Son of God. In this world there will be no police, no prisons, no courts, no evil spirits, no wars, no pain, no sin, no death.

Read for yourselves the marvellous chapters 21 and 22 of Revelation.

These tremendous images are far beyond our understanding, living as we do in a world of sin, death and suffering. As for me, when I think of what God has in store, I long to be in that new world.

4. Either... or...

I would like to draw some conclusions. The more I study the description of "the last days" in the Bible, the more I am struck by the fact that there will be in the end only two categories of people: the saved and the lost.

You may say, "If you look around the world, you can hardly find anybody who bothers about Jesus." To this I can only reply, "Then there will be many people who will be lost!"

Let me add just a word or two. A word to the lost first of all. My friend Paul Humburg said one day, "I had a dream. It was the Judgement Day. I heard Jesus say to the damned, 'Depart from me, you who are cursed.' (This is written in the Bible.) I saw them go away with their backs bent, frightened, desperate. Then I heard one person say to another, 'Did you notice it?' 'Yes,' answered the other. 'I noticed it. The hand that pushed us away had a hole in it.

It was pierced for us on the cross. But during our lifetime, we never paid attention to it. It's only right that we are now lost.'"

Listen to me carefully. The Lord Jesus died for you. Whether or not you believe in anything is of little importance. Jesus died for you. Come to the Saviour! You may say, "But... I'm a sinner." Jesus came to seek sinners – and we are all sinners. If anyone says that he is good, he's nothing but a liar! The person the farthest from God is the one who thinks he doesn't need a Saviour. He is so far lost that he doesn't even realize it.

And now a word to the saved. In the Bible's description of the world to come, it is said that the new Jerusalem is built upon twelve huge precious stones. Engraved on these precious stones are the names of the twelve apostles, witnesses of the Gospel. I have tried to imagine them. On one stone is the name of Peter, on another the name of John, on another the name of James. On a fourth stone is the name of Matthew. Do you know what Matthew used to be? He was a racketeer, black market specialist, and swindler. One day when he was busy with his shady business, Jesus passed by and told Matthew to follow him. And Levi – that was his name at the time – left everything then and there and followed Jesus. Later he witnessed the death of Jesus. He saw him risen from the dead and watched him return to God's dimension. Finally he witnessed the out-pouring of the Holy Spirit.

His friends said to him some time after, "Matthew, you saw so many things when you were with Jesus. You should write them down." And that is just what he did. That is how the Gospel according to Matthew came into being. This Gospel is found in the Bible and has been the means of helping millions of people to find Jesus.

His new name, Matthew – the name of the rascal whom Jesus saved – will be prominent in the new world.

Such is the power of the grace of Jesus Christ. He uses even the most unlikely people to build his kingdom. This same grace wants to begin a work in you. Don't resist it. Your salvation is at stake – for this life and for eternity!

What's the use of walking with God?

Actually, I could put it another way: Is it worth being a Christian?

By way of introduction, I would like to refer to a sentence which is found at the beginning of the Epistle to the Ephesians: "Praise be to the God and Father of our Lord Jesus Christ, who has blessed us in the heavenly realms with every spiritual blessing in Christ." This Bible verse admirably reminds us of the rich blessings which are available to the Christian through Jesus Christ.

But before entering into the heart of our subject, I have to deal with two preliminary points.

1. Walking with God is no illusion

I want to state this categorically: the Christian life is not a product of the imagination, nor is it the fruit of an illusion. Let me prove this to you.

Ministers working in big cities make all kinds of interesting contacts, as the following conversation I had with a young man not long ago shows. "My friend," I said point-blank, "you could make something great of your life if you surrendered it to God." "Pastor Busch," came the reply, "you'd better come down to earth! God doesn't even exist!" "That's hot news," I exclaimed. "Listen to me carefully," he continued. "Because men in the past felt weak and helpless when confronted with the forces of nature, they concluded that superior forces existed which could help them. They gave these forces different names, such as Allah, God, Jehovah, Buddha, and who knows what. It has since been proven that all this is nothing but the product of the imagination and that heaven, in reality, is empty." These were the kind of remarks the young man made. When he had finished, I replied, "The trouble is, my friend, that you don't know Jesus." "Jesus?" he said. "He's just one of the many founders of a religion!" "That's where you're mistaken. Let me tell you just who Jesus is. It is because I know Jesus that I know God exists. Without Jesus, we would be completely in the dark about God."

Who then is Jesus and how does he reveal God to us?

To help you understand, I will use an illustration. During my life I have passed through many a hard trial. I have, on more than one occasion, been thrown into prison; not for some crime that I had committed, but simply because of my religious convictions. Under Hitler's rule, pastors like myself who worked among the young people were not liked by the authorities. I was therefore thrown into some pretty sinister prisons. The worst one was a huge concrete building. Its partitions were so thin that you could hear others coughing in the cells below, and when a prisoner fell from his bunk on the floor above, you almost jumped out of your skin! I had been locked up in a very narrow space.

One day they brought a new prisoner into the cell next door. He was a prisoner of the Gestapo too. He must have been in the depths of despair, for at night I could hear his stifled sobs coming through the thin wall separating us, as he turned over again and again on his hard bunk. It's awful to listen to a man crying. We were forbidden to lie down during the day-time, so I could hear my next-door neighbour as he paced back and forth in his cell: two-and-a-half steps one way, two-and-a-half steps the other way. He was like an animal in a cage. Sometimes he groaned deeply. And there was I, just two steps away, enjoying the presence of the Lord, my heart at peace! I thought, "You ought to go and see him, and talk to him. After all, you are a minister!" So I rang for the guard. When he arrived, I said to him, "The man next door is desperate. He's going to crack up. Please, let me visit him and talk to him. I am a minister." "Okay," replied the guard. "I'll go and ask for permission." An hour later, he was back with the answer: "Rejected. That sort of thing is not allowed." I never did see the man in the neighbouring cell, even though the distance between us was not more than a hand's breadth.

I never discovered what he looked like, nor how old he was. But I felt the depth of his despair. Sometimes, standing before the thin partition which hid him from my sight, I would think, "If only I could dash that wall to pieces and get to the man!" But not even by hammering with all my strength would I have been able to make the slightest breach in it.

Now God, the Creator of the heavens and the earth, finds himself in a very similar situation to mine in that prison. We humans are imprisoned in this visible, three-dimensional world. God is very near. The Bible says: "You hem me in – behind and before." Which means that the distance separating God from us is no more than a hand's breadth. Nevertheless, between him and us there is a wall, separating two different dimensions. His ears can very clearly hear the cries of human distress. He hears the blasphemies of those who have become embittered, the sobs of lonely people, the lamentations of families in mourning, the sighs of victims of injustice. All this grief gets through to God's heart, as the despair of my fellow-prisoner in the next cell got through to me.

But just think of it: God did what I was unable to do! He smashed the wall which stood between him and us and entered into our world in the person of his Son. God himself came to earth in Jesus Christ – right into the filth and suffering of this old world. Since I have come to know Jesus, I have become certain of the existence of God. I often say that since the coming of Jesus, atheism is only a form of ignorance.

Let me talk to you now about Jesus.

If it were left to me, I would talk about nothing but the life of Jesus at all my meetings. Even then, time would be too short for such a vast and glorious subject.

Jesus was born in Bethlehem. He grew up and became a man. Nothing of his divine glory could be seen in his outward appearance. And yet, people were attracted to him. Instinctively they felt that God's love and grace had come close to them.

At that particular period, the land of Canaan, where Jesus lived in the midst of his people, was occupied by foreign troops, Roman troops. In the city of Capernaum, the Roman garrison was under the command of a centurion. It is worth noting that although the Romans believed in a host of gods, they had no particular god of their own. Now, at Capernaum it happened that one of the centurion's servants, of whom he was very fond, fell sick. His master had several doctors examine him, but they couldn't do a thing for him. He was on the verge of death when the centurion suddenly remembered having heard of a certain Jesus. "Maybe he could help," he thought. "I'm going to try to get hold of him." So this unbeliever, this man raised in paganism, went and found Jesus and said to him, "Lord Jesus, my servant is desperately ill. Would you heal him?" "Of course. I'll go with you," replied Jesus. "But there's no need for you to go out of your way!" objected the centurion. "When I give an order," he went on, "it is executed immediately. You too, all you have to do is to say a word and my servant will be healed!" In other words, this pagan centurion had just declared, "For you, it is possible to do the impossible. You are God in person." Jesus then turned around and said to the crowd following him, "I have not found such great faith even in Israel." It's as if Jesus had said in our twentieth century language, "I have never found faith like this atheist's, not even in the Church." The centurion had understood that God himself had come to us in Jesus.

It is essential that you get to know the life of Jesus. Go and buy yourself a New Testament – please! Read the Gospel of John, then the other Gospels. They are wonderful accounts of the life of Jesus. No magazine in the world contains stories as beautiful as those to be found in the New Testament.

But Jesus, the Son of God, did not come into the world for the sole purpose of healing the centurion's servant and of proving by this healing that God exists. His plan went much farther: in coming to live with man, Jesus came to offer us peace with God.

We are separated from God by the fact that we are in a different dimension. But that is not all. The wall of our sin also separates us from God. Have you ever told a lie? You have? Well, when you lied, you placed a stone between you and God. Have you ever lived a whole day without God, without prayer? You have? That makes another stone. Bad thoughts, adultery, stealing and lying, not to mention the multitude of little things which are just as much violations of the divine law – and, with each transgression, another stone is added. We all, each one of us, have contributed to the building of this wall which separates man from God. God is a holy God. And so, simply pronouncing God's name will inevitably raise the problem of our sin and guilt. It is a problem which must be dealt with.

God takes our sin very seriously. I know of people who secretly think, "God must be really glad that I still believe in him." Good heavens! That's not enough! Far from it! The Devil himself also "believes in God". He certainly is no atheist! The Devil is perfectly aware of the existence of God. Yet, for all that, he is not at peace with God.

We can be at peace with God only when the wall of sin separating us from him has been destroyed. That's why Jesus came – to break down the wall of our guilt. To accomplish this, he had to let himself be nailed to the cross. He knew that someone had to bear the punishment for sin – either mankind or himself. To make it more personal I will say, "either Wilhelm Busch or Jesus". And that is how Jesus, the innocent one, took the place of the guilty one and bore the penalty of my sin – and yours.

Once again I would like to describe the Lord Jesus on the cross. It is the most precious scene in the world to me. Look at him hanging on that cursed tree, the one of whom the Bible speaks in these terms: "The Lord laid on him the iniquity of us all." He bore, as it were, on his own shoulders, all the stones composing the wall of our sin. Thus he did what no other person could do: he took them all away. Read it for yourself in the Bible, particularly in the fifty-third chapter of the book of Isaiah. There on the cross Isaiah's prophecy of a suffering Saviour was fulfilled: "The punishment that brought us peace was upon him, and by his wounds we are healed."

I have a dear friend in Switzerland. We have had some very enjoyable outings together. Of course each time we ate in a restaurant a bill would have to be paid. The problem was, who would pay it? Whose wallet was the fattest? The answer was clear. So I would say to my friend, "Okay, this time I'll let you pay!" But someone had to pay the bill.

It is exactly the same with the debt we owe God as a result of our sins and transgressions. Someone had to pay it. Either you believe that Jesus paid your debt for you, or you will be obliged to pay it yourself some day. That's why, for me, Jesus is of such great importance. I cling to him because he is the one who paid my debt.

But Jesus did not remain in the grave. Death had no power over him. Isn't that wonderful?

Three days after the crucifixion of Jesus, a man could be seen lost in his thoughts. He was wondering: "What should we think about Jesus now? He's dead and gone! I saw for myself how they placed his body in the tomb and rolled a big stone before the opening. Was he, or was he not, the Son of God?" The man's name was Thomas. While he was mulling over his doubts, he saw his friends running towards him, bubbling with joy. "He's alive," they yelled. "Stop looking so glum. He's alive!" "Who's alive?" "Why, Jesus . . . of course." "That's not possible," was Thomas' reply. *"But it is!"* We saw the empty tomb with our own eyes. We can swear to it. And then . . . we met Jesus!" "Has anyone heard of such a thing?" thought Thomas. "Someone rising from the dead? If it were true, then Jesus might really be the Son of God. It would be God's verdict in favour of Jesus."

But Thomas remained sceptical. He continued to think, "I've been fooled so often in my life that now I only believe what I see." Turning to the others, Thomas declared, "Unless I see the nail marks in his hands and put my finger where the nails were, and put my hand into his side, I will not believe it." The disciples tried to persuade him until they were blue in the face, but Thomas kept on repeating, "I don't believe it."

Eight days later, Thomas was with his friends when suddenly Jesus appeared and said, "Peace be with you." Then, turning to Thomas, he said, "Put your finger here; see my hands. Reach

out your hand and put it into my side. Stop doubting and believe."
The poor doubter fell down heavily on his knees and exclaimed,
"My Lord and my God!"

Maybe by now you have understood why I declare that walking
with God is neither an illusion nor the product of the imagination.
God is no vague concept, as people sometimes imagine. "There
must be a God somewhere, but nobody knows exactly what he's
like," they say. No, that is not right. The possibility of walking with
God is a direct result of the Son of God's coming into this world, and
of his death and resurrection for us. That is why we can have clear
and reliable knowledge of God.

Now I come to the second question:

2. What must I do to walk with God?

How many times I've heard this remark: "Pastor Busch, you've got
something we don't have!" I have answered, "Don't talk such
rubbish. You can have it too. Jesus is there for you too." Then
people usually bring up this question: "What must I do to walk with
God?" The Bible gives a very clear answer, in one sentence:
"Believe in the Lord Jesus Christ."

But before trying to persuade you to believe, I must first of all
explain the meaning of the word "believe"; for many people have a
totally wrong idea as to what faith is. If you have a watch, you can
look at it and say, "I know that it is exactly twenty past seven." But if
you don't have one, you have to be content with saying, "I believe it
is twenty past seven." The idea is quite wide-spread that faith is a
sort of vague and uncertain knowledge. However, in this verse of
the Bible – "Believe in the Lord Jesus Christ" – the word "believe"
has quite a different meaning. What does it mean? I am going to try
and make it clear by the following anecdote.

I had just finished a few days of seminars in Oslo, the capital of
Norway. I was scheduled to go home on Saturday morning,
because the following day I had to speak at a big gathering in
Wuppertal. From the moment I set foot in the Oslo airport, things
started going wrong. First they announced that my flight would be
delayed by one hour because of fog. The plane took off at last for
Copenhagen where we were to make a connection. We were
already flying over the Danish capital when the captain suddenly
changed course and headed for Sweden. He explained to us by
way of the public address system that it would be impossible for us
to land in Copenhagen because of the heavy fog covering the area.

For that reason we were en route for Malmö. The last place I wanted to go to was Malmö in Sweden. I had to get to Düsseldorf and from there to Wuppertal where I was scheduled to speak the next day!

In due course we landed at Malmö airport, only to find it swarming with people. Since it was the only airport in the region which was not fogbound, there was a continuous flow of aircraft coming in. The airport facilities at Malmö were modest, and there wasn't a single seat free in the whole place. I had struck up an acquaintance with an Austrian businessman. We were wondering what was going to happen. "For all we know, we may still be standing here tomorrow morning. We'll end up not being able to stand on our feet!" Everyone was grumbling, fuming and groaning as always in such circumstances. Suddenly a voice came over the loud-speaker announcing, "In a few minutes an aircraft will take off southwards. We do not know whether the aircraft will land in Hamburg, Düsseldorf or Frankfurt. Travellers on the way to Germany may proceed to the boarding gate." We didn't know what to do. A woman next to us exclaimed, "You'll never get me on that plane! It's too risky." "Madam," I answered, "no one is forcing you to take this flight. You can very well stay here." Next, my Austrian friend gave his opinion, "A flight in heavy fog is not an ideal solution, especially if they don't know where they are going to land." Just then I saw the pilot of the announced flight passing close by. I was struck by the serious, determined expression on his face. It was clear that he was not taking the situation lightly but was acting responsibly. I shared my impression with my Austrian friend, saying, "That pilot has his head screwed on. We can trust him." Then I added, "Come on, let's get on board." So we got on the plane. From the instant the cabin door was locked we knew our lives were in the hands of this man. But we had confidence in him. I had placed my life into his hands.

This is the meaning of the word "believe": it means "having confidence in someone".

What must I do to walk with God? Believe in the Lord Jesus. In other words: get on board with Jesus! On that occasion, as we were boarding the plane, I got the impression that my Austrian friend would have liked to have one foot on the ground and the other on the plane. But that was impossible! It was a question of either staying behind or putting one's entire life into the hands of the pilot.

It is exactly the same thing where Jesus is concerned. You cannot with one foot live without him and with the other "get on board" with him. It just won't work! Believing in the Lord Jesus Christ, walking with God, demands a total surrender of your life:

> Take my life, and let it be
> Ever only, all for Thee.

On the other hand, who better than the Son of God could we find to trust? No person in the world ever did so much for me as Jesus. He loved me so much he gave his life for me. For you too. No one ever loved us like Jesus. He died for us but he rose again from the dead. So why shouldn't we entrust our lives to the one who triumphed over death? It would be foolish not to.

From the moment we surrender to Jesus, we begin to walk with God.

What about you? Do you want to entrust your life to Jesus, do you want to "get on board" with him, place your life into his hands? If you do, tell him about it, I beg you. He is there, right beside you. He hears you. Tell him: "Lord Jesus, I give up my life to you. Take it."

The day I put an end to my life of unbelief and sin – the day of my conversion – I prayed like this: "Lord Jesus, I now give my life to you. I can't make any promises to improve. You'll have to give me a new heart for that! I've got a really bad character; nevertheless, I come to you just as I am. Lord, make something useful out of my life." It was at that moment I "got on board" with Jesus – with both feet – and entrusted the direction of my life to him.

If we want to advance in our walk with God, what must we do? Time and time again I have repeated that three things are absolutely essential: the study of the Word of God, prayer, and fellowship with other believers.

No one can walk with God if he does not have fellowship with him. That is why you must get hold of a Bible or a New Testament, and set aside fifteen minutes daily for *reading and studying* a portion of it. For the time being, simply leave aside what you don't understand. As you progress in your reading, the text will become clearer and the wonders of God will be unveiled before your eyes. How often my heart overflows with joy at the thought that I belong to this wonderful Saviour and that I have the privilege of proclaiming him to others!

The first requirement for Christian growth is the study of God's Word; the second is *prayer*. Jesus hears you. You don't have to make a big speech. If you are a housewife, it is enough to say, "Lord Jesus, everything is going wrong today. My husband is in a bad mood, the children won't listen to me, it's wash day and I don't have enough money to pay the rent either. Lord Jesus, I bring all these worries to you and lay them at your feet. Help me to be joyful all the same by living close to you. Help me to get through. Thank you, Lord Jesus, because I can wholly trust you."

Do you see what I am trying to get at? We can tell Jesus everything that is on our mind – absolutely everything. You can also make this request: "Lord Jesus, help me to get to know you better and to give myself up more fully to you."

The third requirement for Christian growth is *fellowship with other Christians*, with men and women who, like you, want to walk with God. Someone said to me lately, "I want to believe, but I'm not making any progress." I answered, "What you need is fellowship with Christians." "But," he objected, "I don't get on with those people." "In that case," I retorted, "there's nothing to be done. But if you expect to live with them in heaven some day, it may be a good thing to start practising right now! God can't tailor people just to suit you!"

When I was a young teenager, I knew the director of a bank at Frankfurt. He was an elderly man and would quite frequently talk to me about his youth. When he had passed his "A" levels, his father said to him one day, "Son, here is such-and-such a sum of money. You have my permission to go abroad and visit all the capitals of Europe." What a godsend for a young fellow of eighteen just out of school!

This is the story the old banker told me: "I was deeply aware of how easy it would be for me to fall into sin and shame in those big cities. I was determined to follow Jesus. So I put my New Testament into my suitcase, and every day, wherever I might be, before leaving my hotel room, I had a quiet time. I read my Bible and had a moment of prayer. Then, wherever I was, I tried to locate other Christians. I met Christians in Lisbon, Madrid, London . . . The city where I had most difficulty finding Christians was Paris. I asked left and right whether there were any disciples of Jesus Christ. At long last someone pointed out a certain cobbler, saying, 'That man reads the Bible too.'" Soon the distinguished young man could be seen walking down the steps leading to a cobbler's shop. Once inside the shop, he asked the shoemaker, "Do you know Jesus?" By way of reply, the man's eyes began to shine. So the young man made this suggestion to him: "If you are in agreement, I'll come every morning to pray with you." Having fellowship with other Christians was, for him, of the highest importance.

And now I come to the central question:

3. What's the use of walking with God?

If I wanted to describe all the benefits which come from a life of fellowship with Jesus, I would be here till Doomsday, and even then the subject would not be exhausted.

I will never forget what my father said to me just before he died at the age of fifty-three. These were some of his last words: "Wilhelm, I want you to tell all my friends and acquaintances how happy Jesus made me throughout my life and even now at the hour of my death." When a man is at death's door, he no longer tries to put on a front, he doesn't waste time in small talk. And if, in his agony, he still says he has known true happiness in Jesus, it touches us to the core; believe me. At such a time, no one can help thinking, "What about me? How will I react when my hour comes?"

Early in my ministry, I witnessed an extraordinary scene in a district of the Ruhr Valley. It was about 1925. A large meeting had been organized during which a very scholarly man gave a two-hour speech to prove the non-existence of God. He had made a great show of all his learning. The hall was packed and the atmosphere smoke-filled. Applause broke out in every direction. "Hurrah! There's no God. We can do what we like." When the speaker was seated, the chairman stood up and said, "The debate is open. Those who have a word to say may come up to the platform." No one, of course, had the courage to get up. Everyone was probably thinking, "Who can contradict such a cultivated man?" No doubt there were many people who did not agree with the speaker, but no one seemed to be daring enough to go up to the platform and air his disagreement before a crowd of one thousand persons. Then a woman's voice rose from the back of the hall. It was the voice of an old grandmother, one of those black-bonneted East Prussian women one sees frequently in the Ruhr Valley. The chairman asked her, "Do you want to say something, Grandmother?" "Yes, I'd like to say a few words." "All right," he answered. "Come right up here on the platform, please." To which she replied, "Don't worry! I'm coming!"

The old lady made her way up to the front with a determined step. She got up on to the platform and stood behind the speaker's stand. And this is what she said: "Sir, you have talked to us for two hours about your atheism. Allow me, for five minutes, to say a few words about my faith! I'd like to share with you all that my Lord, my heavenly Father, has done for me. A few years after our marriage, my husband was the victim of an accident in the mines. They brought him home – dead! I found myself suddenly alone with three young children. In those days, there was hardly any social security. I could have despaired at the sight of my husband's lifeless body. But God intervened. He comforted me as no one else could. What people said to me went in one ear and out the other. But the living God knew how to comfort me. I said to him, 'Lord, you'll have to be the father of my children from now on.' (It was moving to hear the way the old woman told her story.) Very often, I would have no idea in the evening where I was going to get the money to feed my children the next day. So I would talk to my God about it. 'Lord, you know all about my misery. Help me, please!'"

Turning towards the speaker, she said, "He has never let me down. No, never! The way was sometimes very dark, but he never once failed me. And God did a whole lot more than that for me. He sent his Son, the Lord Jesus Christ, into this world. He died for me and rose again from the dead for me; and by his blood he has washed all my sins away. I'm an old lady now and soon I shall die. But, you see, God has given me the assurance of eternal life. And I know without a shadow of a doubt that when I close my eyes here below, I'll wake up in heaven. And all that because I belong to Jesus Christ. That is just a short account of what God has done for me. Now I am going to ask you a question. Tell us, Sir, what has your atheism done for you?"

The speaker stood up, patted the old woman on the shoulder, and answered, "Far be it from me to think of undermining this brave grandmother's faith. Religion has its usefulness for older people."

You should have seen the old lady's reaction! Suiting her actions to her words, she exclaimed, "No, no, a thousand times no! Let's stick to facts. I asked you a precise question and I want a precise answer. I told you what my Saviour has done for me. Now it's your turn to tell me what your atheism has done for you!"

There was an embarrassing silence. That grandmother was a shrewd woman.

Today, when the Gospel is under attack from all directions, I too must ask the question: "What profit do you get from your unbelief?" I never get the impression that people have peace of mind or are happier for all their unbelief. No, my friends.

What's the use of walking with God? As for me, I couldn't have coped with life's difficulties if I had not found peace with God through Jesus Christ. There have been times in my life when I thought my heart would break. Only today I learned that a terrible accident happened not far from here which has plunged two families into mourning. If I understand correctly, the children were run over by a car. Accidents happen so quickly. And when they do, suddenly all our certainties vanish into thin air. All we can do is to hold out our hand in the dark and cry, "Is there no one to help me?" Yes, it is when trials come that we appreciate all that Jesus is and does for his own.

When we got married, I said to my wife, "I'd like to have six sons, and all of them will have to learn to play the trumpet!" I had dreams of my own family band. We eventually did have a family of six children: four girls and two boys. But I lost my two sons. God took them from me in horrible circumstances. I can't understand it. As a youth worker, all my life I have had to look after other people's sons, whereas mine...

I remember the day I learned that my second son was dead. I paced to and fro, feeling as if someone had plunged a knife into my heart. People filed in to express their sympathy. But their words didn't speak to my heart, they didn't get through to me. I was a youth worker at the time, and I kept on thinking, "Tonight you have to go to the youth centre and joyously proclaim the Word of God to 150 young people." My heart was bleeding. I went to my room and shut the door. Falling on my knees, I prayed, "Lord Jesus, you are alive. Have mercy on me." Then I took my New Testament, opened it, and read: "Peace I leave with you; my peace I give you. I do not give to you as the world gives. Do not let your hearts be troubled and do not be afraid." I knew that God always keeps his promises. So I persevered in prayer: "Lord Jesus, I don't know why you did this to me, but I beg you, give me your peace. Fill my heart with your peace." And he did!

The day will come when you will need Jesus too, for no one else will be able to comfort you. On that day, when not a single person in the world will be able to do anything for you, you will appreciate knowing Jesus, the one who redeemed you by shedding his blood on the cross, and who rose again from the dead. You will be glad to be able to say to him, "Lord, give me your peace." His peace, like a mighty river, flows into the heart of all those who ask for it.

This is also true of the most difficult moment of our life, the moment of our death. How will you react when your hour comes? No one in the world will be of any help to you then. You will have to let go of the hand of the person you cherish most in the world. How will you get through?

You will have to appear before the living God. Are you going to come before him with all your sins? When we can grasp the strong hand of the Saviour and say to him, "You have redeemed me by your precious blood, you have forgiven all my sins", we can die in peace.

Is it worth being a Christian? Let me list all the benefits I gain from walking with God:

- peace with God;
- joy in my heart;
- love for God and for my neighbour (so that I even love my enemies and all those people who get on my nerves);
- comfort in times of trial (so that each day is bright, even in the midst of suffering);
- the assurance of eternal life;
- the presence of the Holy Spirit;
- forgiveness of my sins;
- patience...

Oh, I could go on for a long, long time!

My heart's desire for each one of you is that you may come to experience all these wonderful things for yourself and thus find true happiness.

Editor's note:

This seminar, held on June 19, 1966, at Sassnitz on the island of Rügen, was Wilhelm Busch's last one. The following day he suddenly died of a heart-attack. Thus, after many years of faithful service, the Lord called his servant to his heavenly reward.

This last sermon was a fitting conclusion to his life and ministry.

Foreign language editions
of this Busch title are available in:

- Bulgarian
- Croatian
- French
- German
- Hungarian
- Italian
- Romanian
- Russian
- Slovakian
- Slovenian

Please address orders or enquiries to:

Brunnen Verlag Basel
Wallstrasse 6
4002 Basel
Switzerland

Phone:	(061) 295 60 00
Fax:	(061) 295 60 69
E-Mail:	info@brunnen-verlag.ch

BRUNNEN
VERLAG BASEL·GIESSEN